Keats: The Myth
of the Hero

Keats: The Myth of the Hero

By Dorothy Van Ghent

Revised and Edited by
Jeffrey Cane Robinson

Princeton University Press
Princeton, New Jersey

Published by Princeton University Press, 41 William Street,
Princeton, New Jersey

In the United Kingdom: Princeton University Press, Guildford, Surrey

Library of Congress Cataloging in Publication Data will be
found on the last printed page of this book

Publication of this book has been aided by the Paul Mellon Fund
of Princeton University Press

This book has been composed in Linotron Sabon and Galliard

Clothbound editions of Princeton University Press books
are printed on acid-free paper, and binding materials are
chosen for strength and durability

Printed in the United States of America by Princeton
University Press, Princeton, New Jersey

To
Roger Van Ghent

Contents

Acknowledgments

I WOULD LIKE to thank the University of Colorado Council on Research and Creative Work for a Faculty Fellowship which aided my progress with the manuscript.

Thanks also go to Colleen Anderson who typed the manuscript through several versions.

Dorothy Van Ghent's study of Keats would never have reached its present published state without the thoughtful and sympathetic criticism of the readers at the Princeton University Press and the enthusiasm and persistence of the Press's editor, Jerry Sherwood. To them I express my gratitude.

Final thanks go, of course, to Roger Van Ghent.

*Keats: The Myth
of the Hero*

Preface by
Jeffrey Cane Robinson

Keats: The Myth of the Hero distills Dorothy Van Ghent's career-long involvement in the works of the young Romantic poet. She died in 1967, however, before her enormous manuscript could be finished. Having been offered (by Professor Aileen Ward) a chance to look at her manuscript on Keats and having met—in early 1980—her son Roger Van Ghent, who showed me through her files* and kindly supplemented them with his own memory, I had to assess first the quality of the work and second the need for a book on Keats which belonged to an earlier era of (largely archetypal and mythic) criticism. As to the quality there was no doubt; she brought to her readings of the poems and to her vision of poetry an extraordinary intensity and power of insight and expression. And it became clear to me that the absence of modern literary theory and criticism was only an apparent lack; for by focusing, as she does, on myth, story, plot, action, suspense, recurring figures and situations, and by immersing herself so completely in these essentials of literary art, Dorothy Van Ghent practiced in many ways what modern theorists often preach. Having decided to accept the fact of the absence of modern critical context, I turned my attention to the shaping of an enormous but fragmentary manuscript into a book.

The manuscript, as I originally reconstructed it, ran to about 550 pages. Much of the material in it consisted of anthropological and mythic-archetypal allusions and associations, echoing the style of writers such as Jane Ellen Harrison, Joseph Campbell, and C. G. Jung, all of whom figured prominently in her pages. My decision to reduce the length of the manu-

---

* He gave me most of the materials directly related to Keats, and they are now in my possession.

script by almost one-third was very hard to make: by choosing to cut out primarily these associations, I was tampering with an essential feature, an atmosphere, of the text. The desire for that original text, however, may be mostly nostalgic, for in fact the vast accumulation of details from world-wide instances of the monomyth tended to hinder the flow of argument or critical "narrative."

In all sections of the manuscript I have cut primarily in the manner just described and wherever I was struck by excessive repetition or by excessive comparison to other Keats poems. Otherwise different parts of the manuscript as I received it required different levels of editorial involvement. Approximately the first half of the manuscript appeared to be approaching final form. The *Hyperion* chapter seemed to be in a much earlier draft (in fact, gave evidence of eventually being two chapters). Here I often followed the suggestions or hints found in marginal notes written by Van Ghent to herself. The chapter on the odes was largely paragraphs and notes in various states of completeness. I removed the section on the "Ode to a Nightingale" (much of the argument here can be found in the 1944 "The Passion of the Groves") altogether and substituted, as an appendix, an essay on that poem which I found intact among her notes and which seems to me very fine. For the rest of this chapter I pieced together and summarized from notes and fragments what I took to be her argument about the odes (I was aided in this by her 1954 essay on Keats). Any section written by me in the odes chapter has been italicized. All chapter titles are Dorothy Van Ghent's. The title of the book—*Keats: The Myth of the Hero*—is mine, since I could not find evidence that she had yet composed one. I have modernized the text of Keats to conform to Jack Stillinger's *The Poems of John Keats*, Cambridge, Mass., 1978.

This book states that Keat's subject is the hero's quest. It is not now popular to speak about poetry of or in the Romantic tradition in terms of heroes and, in particular, the heroes described in the mythological, anthropological, and psychological studies of Frazer, Campbell, and Jung. Indeed, modern criticism tends to apply to this literature a language that mirrors its own contemporary Western middle-class ways of constructing an understanding of its reality, ways that resonate to the academic setting in which most of it appears. On the other hand, one could argue, what could be more typically "academic" and predictable than the application of "archetypes" to literature? It too can find a comfortable location on the contemporary landscape of criticism if only because it is a "method." Yet in reading this manuscript and the scraps of notes that accompanied it, I have been called to reconsider the immense power latent in this method. The power is revealed here largely because the critic clearly believes in the hero's quest as a true way of mapping the step-wise commitment to moments of experience, to the consciousness of life's simultaneous entrapments and freedoms. When I arrived for the first time at the end of my journey through the completed portions of the manuscript, I had only one word to describe what I had experienced: color. Never before had Keats's poetry seemed to me so dyed in the pigments of detail; never before had I felt so embedded in the crisis of the senses in Romantic poetry. Dorothy Van Ghent clearly saw poetry as constitutive of such a crisis, and her method of marking each moment as "critical" is myth.

All criticism of the highest sort is at least implicitly polemical. This is because such criticism knows that literature is forever teasing the borders of what society calls acceptable and legitimate. Most criticism domesticates literature: to paraphrase Louise Bogan, when critics take literature over their door-sills, they should rather let it go by. Throughout her book on Keats Dorothy Van Ghent keeps up a quiet polemic against what she considers the mainstream of Keats criticism and, implicitly, criticism of Romanticism and modernism, a criticism that domesticates and abstracts the unruly subject. I found in her notes on the unfinished "Ode on a Grecian Urn" section irritation at what she called the "trivialization" of the real crisis of that poem by critics who say that is "about art." Similarly she contends that much criticism distances itself reductively from the particular energies of poetry and produces misreadings precisely because it has not entered the circuit of power between the poem and the critic's own un-conscious. This can be, of course, the easiest attack one can make on the academic critic, and I would not dwell on this if Dorothy Van Ghent did not herself take it so seriously. But for her the critic participates in much the same struggle with poetry as the poet with his engagement in the archetype. Each fears the power inherent in his materials. Each fears the con-sequences of being flooded by it, overwhelmed, and therefore each tends to defend against its specific sources of power; the defenses chosen draw one back into the welcoming arms of "society," for part of the fear is that of estrangement from the familiar. The association of power with societal threat appears over and over again in this work as sexuality.

Reading Van Ghent's discussion of the "Ode on a Grecian Urn," I am struck with the uncanny reverberation from the poet's to the critic's experience. The hero encounters in stanza I a fertility rite, full of Dionysian excess, yet poised against this image of sexual energy is the image of an *unravished* bride. He retreats from the Dionysian sensuality to a sense-less world of "*un*heard melodies" which are now assigned greater value than heard ones and which call us to the rarefied realm of imagination and reason. Most critics as well as—momentarily—the hero are quite satisfied to celebrate this precious shift "upward," supposedly, to "spirit." But the poem ends, says Van Ghent, with the hero's temporary defeat: the beauty-truth statement at the conclusion is the meaning of the poem drained of its power; in fact, in its heated concern to pronounce in terms of beauty and truth and to exclude any-thing else as unnecessary knowledge, these last lines exclude that which dominated the hero's attention at the outset, sexual energy. For Van Ghent it is no accident that the statement excludes from its content what the *use* of statement in criticism often excludes. For Keats his hero fails only at this particular effort at knowledge but succeeds at others (such as the "Ode to Psyche"). Will the critic take on the quest of the hero for herself? Van Ghent surely answers "Yes," for in no critic do we feel more the struggle to enter the sacred realm of collective images in order to receive, interpret, and disseminate their power. The book implies a personal struggle that gets elaborated over the poetry of John Keats. We feel this in the wonderful way she has of allowing each image its own autonomous power, such that, for the moment it stands in the foreground of attention, it overpowers its context, does away with the irony that contextual reading often brings to an image. In his Negative Capability letter Keats speculates on Coleridge's failure in literary heroism as a failure to grant the image its potential archetypal power: "Coleridge . . . would let go by a fine isolated verisimilitude caught from the Penetralium of mystery. . . ."

In a rejected introduction Van Ghent discusses her work in terms of Keats's plot of the hero's becoming:

> This book follows the movements of a psychic drama through Keats's major poems. The literary form of such drama is "plot," and it is as plots that the poems are considered here. The question asked of plot is "What is going to happen?" The issue is in suspense, and every immediate moment points forward to something in the future, something unknown that is yet to be born. From the anticipatory point of view of plot, a poem is not "emotion recollected in tranquillity"—a psychic situation that is already in being and is now contemplated as an object in stasis. Rather, it is a psychic situation in the process of being transformed, of "becoming." Thus plot has primacy over other elements of the poem as the essential *creative* element, a generative movement bringing into existence what was not yet in existence—another kind of life.
>
> Keats used the word "Poesy"—formed from *poesis*—to mean this generative movement as the poet experiences it. "Poesy" is not the literary product which the poet makes, but the psychic action involved in the making. It is a very highly charged word in Keats's vocabulary, implying the operation of creative forces not identified with himself but coming as if from outside or beyond himself, while the poet is in a state of "trance" or "dream." Since

Keats was a man of very sturdy and truthful intellect, having—like Coleridge and Wordsworth, and in a sense even more than they—an intense concern with the psychology of the creative act, one cannot discount his observations of this kind as a matter of metaphor. The conception is in the ancient manner of belief, that the poet is possessed by some powerful extra-personal agency, divine or daemonic.

In yet another rejected "Introduction" she emphasizes that to interpret Keats's poems through his biography, to find critical satisfaction or "meaning" in making such connections, misses a truth about his poetry-making instinct, which is to create a "fantasied hero" who "is more likely to be what William Butler Yeats called 'the anti-self' or 'the self I would become.' He is a personification of the potentialities of self, and his mode of being is 'becoming' or transformation. That is why he goes on adventures and takes risks."

It is, of course, difficult to keep separate the biographical poet and the fantasied hero, but then a hero, particularly a modern one, is often heroic in the process of *becoming* a hero. What is exciting about this study of Keats is that it observes the various probings of the biographical poet toward the heroic mode, toward a "life of allegory," a condition simultaneously of representation and agency. As a subject of biography he defines himself by progress and intellect. As a hero he defines himself by an Apollonian serenity that knows its intuition of the universal cyclic images of generation and death. As one becoming heroic he experiences the tearing asunder associated with Dionysus. It is Keats's particular genius, Van Ghent shows, to commit himself over and over again in his poetry to this tearing asunder. This enactment, although it is (in her word) an analogy to the myth of the hero, captures the particular anguish of the Romantic poet, who is conscious of the necessity and the difficulty of casting the withered modern self into the energizing field of myth. But it also suggests the specialness of poetry as a condition of modern life—that if a poet is sometimes a "man speaking to men," he at other

times recognizes that he can tap, through perhaps secret con-
jury, the deepest sources of energy. She would take seriously
Schiller's call for the modern poet's "Greek" education:

> Let some beneficient deity snatch the infant betimes from
> his mother's breast, let it nourish him with the milk of a
> better age and suffer him to grow up to full maturity
> beneath the distant skies of Greece. Then when he has
> become a man, let him return to his century as an alien
> figure; but not in order to gladden it by his appearance,
> rather, terrible like Agamemnon's son, to cleanse it. He
> will indeed take his subject matter from the present age,
> but his form he will borrow from a nobler time—nay,
> from beyond all time, from the absolute unchangeable
> unity of his being.*

Clearly this image of the modern poet demands a heroism, a
risk both of one's enforced isolation from sources of social
power and of the personal consequences of yielding to the
power of the mythic image.

The hero's movement toward myth is largely erotic. He
may discover that his eroticism leads him either towards the
fertilizing, repetitive archetype or to the deadening "neurosis
of the Romantic lover." These two possible goals of eroticism
describe respectively the octave and the sestet of Keats's sonnet
"Bright Star":

> Bright Star, would I were stedfast, as thou art—
>   Not in lone splendour hung aloft the night
> And watching, with eternal lids apart,
>   Like nature's patient, sleepless Eremite,
> The moving waters at their priestlike task
>   Of pure ablution round earth's human shores,
> Or gazing on the new soft-fallen mask
>   Of snow upon the mountains and the moors—
> No—yet still stedfast, still unchangeable,
>   Pillow'd upon my fair love's ripening breast,

---

* Friedrich Schiller, *On the Aesthetic Education of Man*, trans. Reginald
Snell (New York: Frederick Ungar, 1965), 51-52.

To feel for ever its soft fall and swell,
 Awake for ever in a sweet unrest,
Still, still to hear her tender-taken breath,
And so live ever—or else swoon to death.

Van Ghent appears to join the body of readers who deny the quality of the sestet but for very compelling reasons. This desire for permanence and loss of self-consciousness through physical sex cannot bear the burden of the true nature of poetry; the poetic imagination is deadened rather than stimulated; the eroticism has no issue beyond itself. "Bright Star" stands in this sense in striking contrast to the "Ode to Psyche," where the hero fills his incantation with the urgency of something important about to happen, the anticipatory sense of poetry about to spawn countless progeny. Physical sex itself is displaced to Love and Psyche and appears in himself as the poet's urgency to enter the collectivity of universal images.

The lengthy discussion of what Van Ghent calls the "erotic" poems—*The Eve of St. Agnes, Lamia, Isabella,* "La Belle Dame"—points to Keats's fascination with an eroticism that cuts itself off from the archetype and points more generally to his impulse to establish a poetics of desire. The full elaboration of this subject requires of Van Ghent an unusually vivid and precise detailing of the female figures in Keats's poetry. Indeed, no modern work grants as much autonomous existence to Keats's women as does this one (one of the chief virtures of the *Endymion* chapters, a kind of introduction to the entire study, is the careful cataloguing of these figures and the analysis of interrelationships). And by including Keats's letters to Fanny Brawne ("doomed to be one of the cast of characters in his mythical plot") in her section on the erotic narratives, Van Ghent gives this passionate correspondence a place in the literature of the younger Romantics—in particular the literature of passion-love. It is no accident that Keats, in his opening letter (1 July 1819) to Fanny, compares himself to Rousseau's passionate and foredoomed lover St. Preux. In these letters, taking them as a kind of literature, we feel that we have leapt over the poetic generation of Wordsworth and back to Rousseau's, and Goethe's in *The Sorrows of Young Werther*, where heroes are defined by their capacity for submerging themselves in passionate love stimulated by the power of fantasy, "fancy," or as Stendhal called it, "crystallization." It is in this regard significant that Keats's letters to Fanny Brawne are nearly contemporary with Hazlitt's strange epistolary outburst of passion-love, *Liber Amoris*, and Stendhal's eccentric treatise, *De l'Amour* (in her anthology of Continental literature Dorothy Van Ghent places side by side, in a section on love, selections from Keats's letters and from *De l'Amour*). All three "works" are about complete entrapment in fantasy, jealousy, longing, aggression, submission. There is no room for the comforts of imagination, with its contemplative, recollective, and sympathetic qualities.

Van Ghent concludes her study of Keats with chapters on the *Hyperion* poems, because she finds that together they imply a fulfillment of the hero's quest. Yet there are surprises and final questions. To begin with, she discovers that the Apollonian poet who is supposed to result from the struggle between Titans and Olympians already exists and his name is—Hyperion. That is, within the apparent "ripe progress" of history, lies a profoundly repetitive element. Yet Keats himself is unable to write this poem without the domination of his own "male" imagination dedicated to reason and progress. As a result the poems contain some rich contradictions about both the meaning and the nature of the Titans' fall. As she says, "The story of the Titanomachia is Olympianized myth." The Titans are in sorrow, even though they are realized Apollonian, generative beings. The struggle for their domination and that for the Olympians' has taken place without any violence of parent-child battles, the most obvious feature of those myths. The reason is that Keats, rather than trying to create a poem about generations, strife, and progress, is trying to recover a deeper level of archetypal, cyclical generativity. In giving us the hero's quest more or less complete, he, surprisingly, creates an Apollo who, when we recognize the imagery associated with him in the poem, looks strikingly like Dionysus. Perhaps this double epic fragment, with its important confusions and surprises of identity and with its confusion of repetitive and progressive movements, is as close as a modern poet can get to the representation of the archetypal hero.

Surely Dorothy Van Ghent's greatest contribution to Keats and Romantics studies for readers in the 1980s is that she describes for us a "Dionysian" poet, a poet given to "tearings asunder." Keats, like all Romantics taken with the new theories of a Greek golden age, wanted to discover the serene idyllic archaism of Apollo and wanted to perhaps more fervently than most. Yet in his descent into the realm of universal images he encountered his own modern self and seems to have felt the profound separation between the assumptions of enlightenment and those of the archaic. This separation was for him an occasion not so much for mourning as for more strident sacrifice. But stridency characterizes the literature of his period. Much more than the earlier generation of Romantics this new generation, struggling into sharp focus amidst the muddled tyranny of the Regency, brings to life and work an urgency, a desperateness, a sense of crisis.

A MOVING FEATURE of the two boxes and countless folders of material for her study of Keats is the eight or nine introductions Van Ghent either completed or began and abandoned. The energy poured into her prefatory remarks tells us not simply that she was dissatisfied with style or language but that they were part of the struggle that went into this book, and taken together they all form what might be called fragments of a critic's autobiography. The study of Keats held for her the power of a spiritual journey which lasted for her entire professional life, beginning with her dissertation on Keats (1942), continued later with two articles on Keats (1944, 1954), and concluded with the book manuscript left nearly complete at her death in 1967. Her career has the appearance of a journey: a tragic journey of a woman teaching in the humanities in the 1940s and 1950s for very low wages, moving from university to university (nearly a dozen times) across the entire continental United States, teaching, writing, and raising a son all by herself. Even the popular success of *The English Novel: Form and Function* (1953) did not yield financial or professional security. This is the personal context from which to read her exploration of Keats's hero, "a personification of the potentialities of self" and from which to consider the following selected paragraphs from her discarded introductions:

This book is a very personal—and therefore very faulty and hesitant—exploration of the "meaning" of poetry, what it "means" in the most serious sense—that is, what it means for my own profoundly important life (everyone feels his own life to be profoundly important, and it must be so). Perhaps I found in Keats something, or things, that confronted me with a kind of simulacrum of things in myself that I did not yet know. All poetry to which one is strongly attracted seems to have this effect of a *déjà vue*. I have been thinking of this book for many years, for about twenty-three years, and fumbling very blindly and naively with its possibilities. I knew it was something that had to be written, but I did not know exactly what it was to be about, what it was "for," what it "meant." That its fascination held with me for so long a time, even though I was quite ignorant of its "meaning," suggests that Keats's poems were somehow entangled with my own psychic processes, disorders, discontents, fleeting fantasies and promises, "ideals" crippled in the course of life and swallowed by the unconscious because they didn't seem to work in the pressing actualities of existence, were in fact a hindrance and a source of anxiety in meeting economic problems and all those difficulties which make it so doubtful whether one shall sink or swim. Apparently Keats's poems represented buried elements of myself, killed off by the terrible rigors of existence, and insistently hammering for recognition, showing that they were *still there*. I had a notion that there lay in this phenomenon a general description of the "serious meaning" of poetry, not only Keats's.

....

Our literary epoch in America is one mainly of criticism, criticism in all fields and criticism in literature. Criticism, to be expert, rightly hoards up all past experience, to bring it to bear on interpretation of the present. But this hoarding and application have also their menace, the constant intellectual menace of substituting the residues of experience, ideas, for what is going on now, the actualities of the self. It is so much easier and carries so much more authority, to interpret things by ideas that can circulate as a common intellectual coinage, give and take, adjust and readjust, apply logic, diminish, corroborate—than to attempt to find, in the profound equivocations of one's own self, those equivocations that are unlighted by any idea or intellectual conviction, the ground of "criticism." For the self is so far away. It is doused in ideas. How can one find it under that fascinating extravaganza of the intellect, a mouse in the vicar's cupboard, dangerously supporting its family by theft?

Keats's poetry is small in quantity for he did not have much time to write it. He died of tuberculosis when he was twenty-five. It is a very concentrated poetry, in both quality and extent, and therefore affords a feasibly limited opportunity to explore these questions. They are questions that were those of Keats himself, for his poetry is intensely preoccupied with the problems of self and relationship, with what poetry is and what the poet is, with the pleading and inhibiting factors of the mind—appearing as heroes and virgins and snakes and wise old men and goddesses and murderers and trees and birds and statues and wheatfields and the sun and the moon and the stars. These are primitive representations of experience, fortunately still tied to instinct. They show what we have lost historically and are trying to find psychologically, a relatedness within ourselves, on some plane that is not primitive but where we can take our primitive selves into consciousness and sophisticate them to our own precarious adventures with life and death. Keats, to whom death was always near, and who had an exceptional appetite for life and palate for joy, was a schizoid modern like ourselves, suffering the absurd split between ego and self, reason and intuition, that obsesses modern literature, makes our learned teaching impotent, and threatens our existence. Poetry, great poetry, says one thing: "Who are you?" In Keats's poetry, one sees the questions put not as intellectualization but as suffering experience, a long quest and terrible hazards, with doubtful outcome. The appeal of the poetry, the reason we like it, is its secret correspondence and interrogation with the mouse-self in the cupboard: how can we support our families by this cheese and escape the trap?

....

In the following study, the commanding and motivating figures of the poem (figures of action traced by "plot," the characters, including that character or *persona* taken by the poet as an "I," and major images) are assumed to be primary subjective forms; that is, they are the primitive, original, dominating forms of the poet's psychic life. It would not be foolish to speak of them as "divine"— in accordance with ancient intuition as to the nature of those powers that speak through the poet—for their origins are beyond human thought or invention. Aboriginal, untraceably old, ancestral mysteries in the genesis of the human, they simply *are*, as gods are.

....

This book is a very personal—faulty and groping— attempt to find out how poetry is related to life, to my life, to the serious core of anyone's life, where the questions "Who?" "Where?" "How?" "When?" "What?" raise themselves. I don't think that relationship lies in what are called ideas, for the ideas in poetry are only as good as ideas anywhere else. Poetry gives pleasure, but so do good meals and conversation, love and sport and other things; the pleasure of poetry is connected with something more peculiarly personal, an inner question and resolution like the lift and fall of a wave. It is an action in which the reader himself is engaged, even kinetically, his muscles and the nerves that have control over them—in tongue and ear and eye and the other sense organs—responding mimetically to reproduce what is going on in the poem; and if he is so far taken over by the subtle physiological aspects of that mere craft which poets have perfected, what is to be said for his inner person, his mind? and what is to be said for that non-sensuous, psychological "spiritual" factor of poetry which touches the mind? for if it works so intimately on the physical senses, how deeply must that formidable engineering grasp the fragile mind? But *what* does it grasp in the mind, as it grasps the tongue-muscle and the inner ear and directs them to its own conclusions?

It is a matter of the "seriousness" of poetry, that faculty of poetry which is the seriousness of oneself. Oneself is sheer experience, and that is what poetry is too: not ideas or pleasure (edification and delight, as the older critics divided the neat opportunities of reading) but a mimesis of being. The mimesis has to show us something, if it is "great" or "good." It has to show us what we know and do not know, the secret operations of ourselves, going on in this minute.

....

The poetic situation that I have tried to describe corresponds to experience of a much more common and comprehensive kind than that specifically of the poet. The definition of a poem that I have given could be a definition of a novel or of other forms of art—with qualification according to the degree of order achieved. It is also a description of all seriously motivated experience of one's self, that "deep self" of fathomless interior where the ego is merely one other masked and costumed character in a *commedia dell'arte* without script, the improvisations of the soul: an experience "seriously motivated" in so far as the conscious mind makes itself attentive to those improvisations and seeks to translate them into its own hierarchy of knowledge. To observe such an activity in Keats's poetry has been to make clearer to myself the relationship between poetry and life. It has made clearer what is meant by the word "creative," and that sense in which all serious life of the self is creative, not, perhaps, in the making of poems, but in the purposeful activity of making what is unconscious conscious and thus creating a self that knows what it is. Keats's poems, after all, are singularly intensive efforts to do just this.

In reading her studies of Keats from the the dissertation to the present work, we see her gradually discovering how to realize her conviction that (as she said in her Dedication to *The English Novel*) the critical approach to literature is "a search for the principle of form in the work and implicitly . . . a search for form in the self." The dissertation, "Image-Types and Antithetical Structure in the Work of Keats" (University of California, 1942), and all her critical writing assert the enormous power of the image in literature but asserts it not as a New Critic—concerned with ambiguity and complexity within the narrow confines of the poem—but as one who discovers through an image or rather through a set of them a *gestalt* that tells a unique story about the poem that contains it: in the dissertation she called such *gestalten* "imaginal modes" which she would then set "against the background of those psychological traits which are reflected in Keats's letters, and thus to test the validity of the classifications of imagery by their apparent symmetry with recurrent and typical preoccupations in his random daily experience." The procedure (openly following Caroline Spurgeon's study of Shakespeare's imagery) yields, with dissertation-like woodenness, two distinct "imaginal modes," those that suggest "repose" and those that suggest "unrest," the Apollonian and the Dionysian, the "imaginative" and the "rational." The state of repose is the goal for Keats who, however, finds himself in a shifting unrest, a painful identitilessness increased by his application to poetry. To find wholeness in the world around him (in what he saw and created) was to feel the lack of it in himself: ". . . the thesis consisting of all those essentially reposeful images and processes in the expression of which Keats supplied a description of the poetic character as he saw it, and the antithesis consisting of all those essentially analytic and unreposeful conditions which Keats visualized as webbed necessarily in that character, both because it is creative, and because it is merely human, because it must reason and yield to reason like the unimaginative man, must see death and must die" (p. 206). The dialectic between will and representation, self and anti-self she finds in Keats's Apollo and Hyperion (this dialectic being far more important than the historic parent-child relationship). Even in this initial project Dorothy Van Ghent displays her commitment to that irradiating power of the image and to an identification with Keats's (and Keats's heroes') fevered existence in relation to art.

"The Passion of the Groves" (*The Sewanee Review* 52 [1944], 226-46) deepens her discussion of the image of the grove or natural shelter in Keats's poetry (a topic explored in depth by several more recent critics). It is, however, not a matter of merely charting the image but of revealing a central and complicated problem in Keats only hinted at in the dissertation, the problem—noted above—of discovering a relationship to erotic poetry that does not render poetry uncreative of itself. She gropes to find in Keats a kind of oxymoronic ideal of chaste sexuality, seeing in the burial of the nightingale's song in the "next valley glades" a repetition (as preservation of the deathless bird) of the poet's own "burial" ("embalmed darkness") that is the subject-matter of the poem itself. Such repetition or preservation (Keats's refusal to "neglect" the goddess Psyche) becomes in the book the sacramental act of the poet.

The second essay, "Keats's Myth of the Hero" (*Keats-Shelley Journal* 3 [1954], 7-25), is the pivotal study, gathering up the major ideas of the previous two works and, in anticipation of the present book, synthesizing them through the filter of the hero archetype, perceiving all the poems as various experiments with that myth. In many ways it is a skeletal outline of the book, but the addition of the "flesh" of the latter renders her task profound. For by plunging into detail she makes the book itself a kind of journey; each image stands in the magnet-pull of the world collectivity of images, so that each poem at once resides within its own temporal momentum from start to finish and yet releases its connections through larger radii of meaning. Finally, it is through this resonating and elaborated rendering that she becomes a polemical critic attacking others for what she considers thinner, more abstracted readings.

When we admit to the difficulty for modern criticism of both truly understanding and, even more, achieving in one's own writing the "whole-souled" nature of great literary effort, then we are prepared to appreciate this work of extraordinary spiritual and intellectual dedication.

I. Introduction: The Scenario of the Poems

IF ONE WERE to set Keats's poems up as a series of slates or lantern slides, each showing only the visual elements of a "plot," and were to run the sequence through in such a way that repeated episodes converged, one would find a single synoptic action or master plot emerging. The plot is pre-literary; it is psychologically anterior to any of the poems in which it appears. It could even be pantomimed. The individual poems could be looked upon as improvisations of thought, dialogue, and music.

The *dramatis personae* are few and the relationships they may assume with each other are not unlimited. The hero is a gifted young man of a labile, aspiring temperament, torn by conflicting emotions and consumed by ambition. He has a "double" or "anti-self" who is his complete opposite, a serenely powerful being who looks like a statue of Adonis or Apollo. The hero's problem is how to become his double. Three women move through the action. One is a maiden, who may play the part either of sister or bride. The second is a beautiful witch who assumes the mask of the virginal maiden to seduce the hero. The third is a great goddess, associated with vegetation, with the planets of the night sky, and with birth and death. She too may adopt the mask of the maiden. An old man may appear, playing either a benignant or a threatening part. Gods and *numina* inhabit the woods, sea, air, and underworld where the action takes place. A lofty architectural structure representing a castle, palace, or temple may also be used as setting.

The core of the action is a myth. It is about a fertility daemon who dies, descends into a dark seed-place, and is reborn as the son and consort of the queen-goddess of the world. The most ancient myths were simply sets of directions for the annual enactment of fertility and coronation ritual. The part of the nature daemon was played by the king or chief, who in the strictest practical sense *was* the daemon, for on him was projected the collective life of the group and the vitality of the food-area on which the group depended. In analogy with the seasonal cycle of vegetation and the death-birth cycle of animals and men, he had to "die" to be reborn as a young man invested with the group-*mana* of indestructible life. The queen or head-priestess played the part of the earth-goddess from whom all things are born. It was she who gathered up the limbs of her dismembered son and restored him to life. On his return as a youth he married her. It is the liturgy of this story that we shall trace in Keats's poems.

A myth is a collective product, consisting of all its versions. Stanley Edgar Hyman lists the psychological operations in the folk-transmission of myth as:

> splitting, displacement, multiplication, projection, rationalization, secondary elaboration, and interpretation—as well as such more characteristically aesthetic dynamics as Kenneth Burke's principle of "completion" or the fulfillment of expectations, in the work as well as in the audience.[1]

These operations, as he points out, are similar to those Freud found in "dream work." The same processes are found in the different versions Keats gave to his basic plot. The death of the hero is elaborated as a descent under the earth, withdrawal into the forest, the consummation of love ("love-death"), a nightmare of becoming petrified, actual murder, and a convulsive ordeal identical with that of birth. The hero is "split" into two characters, the one ecstatic and anguished, who dies over and over again like the mystery god Dionysos, and his Apollonian double, god of light, harmony, symmetry, and order. The sexual magic, food magic, and death magic associated with the queen-goddess allow her to be multiplied as genial earth-mother, Kore of the fields, muse, virgin bride, sexual sorceress, and veiled goddess of death. Each poem is a "secondary elaboration," at the verbal and conscious level, of the nuclear plot.

In tracing these processes and the archetypal or collective figures they manipulate—the personages of the drama, their ritual behavior—we shall be tracing a history of images, for their permutations in Keats's mind as he matured recapitulate their racial history over millennia. Keats was not aware of this history for he was engaged in making it; the emotional tensions of each poem are those of a discovery of the mind made upon itself. He had encountered the chief images of his plot in classical poetry and mediaeval romances, in the works of ancient scholiasts and mythographers and in those of eighteenth-century antiquarians, in fairy tales and fairy lore. But these representations had already undergone ages of psychological processing. Primitively, they were not representations at all, but, as F. M. Cornford says, "a real fact of human experience, namely the collective consciousness of a group in its emotional and active phase, expressed in the practices of primary sympathetic magic."[2] Long cut adrift from their ritual origins, they had been interpreted as "imaginary" figures. The discovery that Keats's poems constantly make is that they are "real."* They are real psychical powers focusing desire and anxiety on the critical junctures of life—birth, sex, and death—and their reality is guaranteed by their archetypal character. The myths and legends and ritual circumstance that constantly attracted Keats in his reading were those in which his own interior landscape has been culturally crystallized. Where parts were missing, he supplied them.

His nuclear plot naturally takes the form of a quest and discovery, for it is a venture of the mind into its own hidden resources. Like that primary pattern of adventure which Joseph Campbell has found in myths and fairy tales all over the world, and which he calls "monomyth," the quest has three

* Hence his intuitive insistence on the "truth" of imagination: "The Imagination may be compared to Adam's dream—he awoke and found it truth" (22 November 1817). To Benjamin Bailey, in *The Letters of John Keats 1814-1821*, ed. Hyder Rollins, in 2 vols. (Cambridge, Mass.: Harvard U.P., 1958), I, 185. All subsequent quotations from Keats's letters are from this edition.

phases: "separation—initiation—return." This, as he points out, is the formula of *rites de passage*, puberty rites and rites of initiation into priesthood or into magic brotherhoods, when the candidate is segregated from the tribe and put through severe physical ordeals which, if they are not fatal, so closely resemble a "death" that he comes back a changed person, oriented to a totally new set of relationships in the tribal life. This is also the formula of the fertility daemon's disappearance in winter, his "tearing asunder," and his rebirth in the spring. In the vast number of legends Campbell has assembled, the formula is expanded as follows:

> A hero ventures forth from the world of common day into a region of supernatural wonder: fabulous forces are there encountered and a decisive victory is won: the hero comes back from this mysterious adventure with the power to bestow boons on his fellow man.[3]

Under various displacements and projections, the usual pattern in Keats's poems is the separation of the subject-self from the known and rational, its passage over a psychical threshold into a region of dangerous magnetic powers, and its return or attempted return. The return is exceedingly risky and often frustrated. The hero may simply vanish into the dark region of power, as in *Endymion*, or come back as a spectre, as in "La Belle Dame Sans Merci" and the "Ode to a Nightingale." The poet is compelled to improvise version after version of the adventure in order to find a manageable mode of return, by which the hero's "boon," gained from his experience, will be socially recognizable.

II. The Goddess of Many Names:
Endymion

Endymion is a moon-poem. The chief complication of the plot is caused by the moon's appearance in three forms, her planetary form—which is the only one in which Endymion recognizes her—and as two maidens, one golden-haired and one black-haired. In following the plot simply as plot, one has to think of the moon as a separate character from the two maidens, since this is the way Endymion looks upon her. The poem is dominated by women; there are six of them who actively influence the plot, if we include Circe from Glaucus' story. They are the Moon (called variously Dian, Cynthia, Phoebe, and simply Moon), the nameless golden-haired maiden, Endymion's sister Peona, Venus, Circe, and the Indian maid. As for male characters besides the hero, Adonis is encountered in his winter "death" under the earth, and Glaucus, as an old man, accompanies Endymion on his sea-journey.

Since the Moon is the most important female character, she should be considered first. The most lengthy description of her is at the beginning of Book III, and is in two parts, the first part an exordium spoken by the poet, and the second spoken by Endymion from under the sea. The poet addresses her:

> O Moon! the oldest shades 'mong oldest trees
> Feel palpitations when thou lookest in:
> O Moon! old boughs lisp forth a holier din
> The while they feel thine airy fellowship.
> Thou dost bless every where, with silver lip
> Kissing dead things to life. The sleeping kine,
> Couched in thy brightness, dream of fields divine:
> Innumerable mountains rise, and rise,
> Ambitious for the hallowing of thine eyes;

And yet thy benediction passeth not
One obscure hiding-place, one little spot
Where pleasure may be sent: the nested wren
Has thy fair face within its tranquil ken,
And from beneath a sheltering ivy leaf
Takes glimpses of thee; thou art a relief
To the poor patient oyster, where it sleeps
Within its pearly house.—The mighty deeps,
The monstrous sea is thine—the myriad sea!
O Moon! far-spooming Ocean bows to thee,
And Tellus feels his forehead's cumbrous load.

                    (*End.* III.52-71)*

The Moon is the primary symbol of what Endymion is seeking. If the poem is read in terms of *mythos*, or plot, rather than as allegory, she is a good deal more than "the spirit of essential Beauty." She is a very old and venerable goddess, the "oldest trees" are holy to her; she can make dead things live ("kissing dead things to life"); she governs the geodynamic forces and makes mountains "rise and rise"; the beasts and birds and the creatures of the sea are under her governance; the "monstrous sea," the "myriad sea" is hers, and Ocean himself bows his tidal forehead to her, for she controls the tides.

If Keats had virtually "memorized" Lemprière's *Classical Dictionary* as he is said to have done, he knew this goddess' many names from Lemprière's frequently repeated lists: Diana, Proserpine, Hecate, Isis, Cybele, Ceres, Rhea, Ops, Magna Mater, Bona Mater, Bona Dea, and so on. An account of her that he had read in *The Golden Ass* of Apuleius describes her very much as she is described in *Endymion*:

> About the first watch of the night when as I had slept my first sleep, I awaked with sudden fear and saw the moon shining bright as when she is at the full and seeming as though she leaped out of the sea. Then I thought with myself that this was the most secret time, when that God-

---

* All quotations from Keats's poetry are from *The Poems of John Keats*, ed. Jack Stillinger, Cambridge, Mass.: Harvard U.P., 1978.

dess had most puissance and force, considering that all human things be governed by her providence; and that not only all beasts private and tame, wild and savage, be made strong by the governance of her light and godhead, but also things inanimate and without life; and I considered that all bodies in the heavens, the earth, and the seas be by her increasing motions increased, and by her diminishing motions diminished: then as weary of all my cruel fortune and calamity, I found good hope and sovereign remedy, though it were very late, to be delivered from my misery, by invocation and prayer to the excellent beauty of this powerful goddess. Wherefore, shaking off my drowsy sleep I arose with a joyful face, and moved by a great affection to purify myself, I plunged my head seven times into the water of the sea; which number seven is convenable and agreeable to holy and divine things, as the worthy and sage philosopher Pythagoras hath declared. Then very lively and joyfully, though with a weeping countenance, I made this oration to the puissant goddess.

"O blessed Queen of Heaven, whether thou be the Dame Ceres which art the original and motherly source of all fruitful things on the earth, who after the finding of thy daughter Proserpine, through the great joy which thou didst presently conceive, didst utterly abolish the food of them of old time, the acorn, and madest the barren and unfruitful ground of Eleusis to be ploughed and sown, and now givest men a more better and milder food; or whether thou be the celestial Venus, who, at the beginning of the world, didst couple together male and female with an engendered love, and didst so make an eternal propagation of human kind, being now worshipped within the temples of the Isle Paphos; or whether thou be the sister of the God Phoebus, who hast saved so many people by lightening and lessening with thy medicines the pangs of Ephesus; or whether thou be called terrible Proserpine by reason of the deadly howlings which thou yieldest, that hast power with triple face to stop and put away the invasion of hags and ghosts which appear unto men, and to keep them down in the closures of the Earth, which dost wander in sundry groves and art worshipped in diverse manners; thou, which dost illuminate all the cities of the earth by thy feminine light; thou, which nourishest all the seeds of the world by thy damp heat, giving thy changing light according to the wanderings, near or far, of the sun: by whatsoever name or fashion or shape it is lawful to call upon thee, I pray thee to end my great travail and misery and raise up my fallen hopes, and deliver me from the wretched fortune which so long time pursued me."[1]

In this account, she is Isis, Ceres, Venus, the many-breasted Diana of Ephesus, and the "terrible Proserpine" with triple face, or the triple Hecate. She is moon goddess, corn goddess, goddess of love, goddess of childbirth, and goddess of the dead. She governs all things animate and inanimate. Her "divine and venerable face" is "worshipped even of the gods themselves." As her whole figure mounts out of the sea, she is seen to wear the crescent moon on her forehead, with blades of corn sprouting out of it, and serpents from the underworld supporting it. Her clothing is of diverse colors, white, yellow, and red, and she is wrapped in the folds of a dark and fearful cloak—"which troubled my sight and spirit sore."

Keats preserves her threefold character in *Endymion* by having her appear as Moon, as golden-haired maiden, and as the dark-haired Indian maid. As Endymion does not know that these are all the same person, his sense of identity is torn to pieces with guilt for his infidelities ("I have a triple soul!"— "Would I were whole in love!"—"I have no self-passion or identity.") [*End.* IV.95, 472, 476-77]. He thus achieves his main plot-complication and suspense; and by the same means he is able to preserve the ritual form of the ancient mystery initiations, where the candidate for immortality had to go symbolically through all the spheres of nature, earth, water, and air; for his hero is obliged to seek the goddess in all the realms she rules—in Book II, the underworld, in Book III, the sea, and in Book IV, the celestial regions.

But he has used the mythical prototype for still further articulation of his plot. The Great Goddess had not only a son (Thammuz, Attis, Adonis, Dionysos) but at Eleusis she also had a daughter, Kore. Kore and Demeter, her mother, are two gods in one person, but Kore specialized the function of going periodically under the earth and reigning there over the dead. Her typical mode of behavior in a plot is to disappear and be sought for (Northrop Frye points out that the literary ghost of this figure is in Shakespeare's romantic comedies where the heroine disappears for a time). This is what she does in *Endymion*, as the golden-haired maiden, and again in the fourth book, as the dark-haired maiden, when Endymion loses her on their flight through the air. Keats ties up her disappearances with the taboo of chastity, in Diana's role as the chaste goddess, while her procreative role is implied in the love-making underground. As she must conceal the sexual episodes from the other gods, she can make love with Endymion only in secret caves under the earth, from which she disappears, and until the very end of the poem she leaves him in ignorance of who she is or where she goes when she disappears. The Indian maid in the fourth book brings up the taboo again; she is not allowed to make love, though she gives no reason.

> I may not be thy love: I am forbidden—
> ....
> Twice hast thou ask'd whither I went: henceforth
> Ask me no more! I may not utter it,
> Nor may I be thy love.
> (*End*. IV.752-57)

Then she has a significant thought: they might get around the taboo by "dying." Since she is queen of the underworld, this has possibilities:

> we might die;
> We might embrace and die: voluptuous thought!
> Enlarge not to my hunger, or I'm caught
> In trammels of perverse deliciousness.
>
> (*End.* IV.758-61)

There is contained here a typical Romantic conversion of love into death, that is notable in all the sexual sequences of Keats's poems; but it is also implicit in the ambivalent role of the archaic Great Goddess, who ruled over both love and death. However, Endymion and the Indian maid decide to live, but as brother and sister. The chastity taboo is converted at the end of the poem into a more mysterious sublimation, Endymion's "spiritualization" for mystic marriage with the Great Goddess.

The poetic principle of relationship between characters is that of analogy, or resemblance of function. In the second part of the invocation to the Moon in Book III, Endymion, lost under the whelming sea, calls up nostalgic memories of his childhood in the green Eden of Mount Latmos, when the Moon "seemed his sister":

> What is there in thee, Moon! that thou shouldst move
> My heart so potently? When yet a child
> I oft have dried my tears when thou hast smil'd.
> Thou seem'dst my sister: hand in hand we went
> From eve to morn across the firmament.
> No apples would I gather from the tree,
> Till thou hadst cool'd their cheeks deliciously:
> No tumbling water ever spake romance,
> But when my eyes with thine thereon could dance:
> No woods were green enough, no bower divine,
> Until thou liftedst up thine eyelids fine:
> In sowing time ne'er would I dibble take,
> Or drop a seed, till thou wast wide awake; . . .
>
> (*End.* III.142-54)

Endymion's real sister, Peona, is given the benign, maternal characteristics associated here with the Moon and childhood.* She "cradles" him, acts as his "nurse," and guards him from hurt. When she sees him pale and troubled by his dreams, she takes him to her bower in the forest, a "nested" arbour with a "cool bosom":

> Hushing signs she made,
> And breath'd a sister's sorrow to persuade
> A yielding up, a cradling on her care.
> Her eloquence did breathe away the curse:
> She led him, like some midnight spirit nurse
> Of happy changes in emphatic dreams,
> Along a path between two little streams,—
> Guarding his forehead, with her round elbow,
> From low-grown branches, and his footsteps slow
> From stumbling over stumps and hillocks small; . . .
>
> (*End.* I.409-18)

She puts him to sleep on her own bed of flower leaves (in rejected lines she bathes his forehead and gives him an amulet to smell) and sings a lullaby to him:

> 'Twas a lay
> More subtle cadenced, more forest wild
> Than Dryope's lone lulling of her child; . . .
>
> (*End.* I.493-95)

In Book IV, Endymion asks the Indian maid, who is the Moon-maiden herself, to take over the same maternal, sister role. "Be thou my nurse," he says to her (*End.* IV.117). There is a token tasting of the beloved: she weeps and he says, "O let me sip that tear!" (*End.* IV.318). Since she may not be his

---

* In one of Keats's letters to his sister-in-law, Georgiana, he wrote: "The Moon is now shining full and brilliant—she is the same to me in Matter, what you are to me in Spirit—If you were here my dear Sister I could not pronounce the words which I can write to you from a distance; I have a tenderness for you, and an admiration which I feel to be as great and more chaste than I can have for any woman in the world." (*Rollins* I.392)

love because of the taboo of her chastity, he asks her to live with him and Peona and be another sister to him:

> Wilt be content to dwell with her, to share
> This sister's love with me?"
> (*End*. IV.871-72)

She answers that this is an "exalted" arrangement after her own heart, where "white Chastity shall sit,"

> And monitor me nightly to lone slumber.
> With sanest lips I vow me to the number
> Of Dian's sisterhood; . . .
> (*End*. IV.884-86)

There is thus an apparent return, in Book IV, to the situation at the beginning of the poem, the Eden of vegetative innocence. But this is an illusion ("all were dreamers" [*End*. IV.900]) contrived by the Moon. The Indian maid is talking double-talk when she says she will join the chaste sisterhood of Diana, for she is herself the maidenly apparition of Diana, the Great Goddess who has already initiated Endymion in the mysteries of sexuality and the mysteries of death. The leaves in the forest are falling, and there can be no return to the green paradise of the beginning.

In the rest of the invocation to the Moon in Book III, Endymion speaks of her as all the profound and inspiring experiences of nature and art, of the intoxications of love and glory (curiously, the moon is even "the sun" here):

> thou wast the deep glen;
> Thou wast the mountain-top—the sage's pen—
> The poet's harp—the voice of friends—the sun;
> Thou wast the river—thou wast glory won;
> Thou wast my clarion's blast—thou wast my steed—
> My goblet full of wine—my topmost deed:—
> Thou wast the charm of women, lovely Moon!
> O what a wild and harmonized tune
> My spirit struck from all the beautiful!

On some bright essence could I lean, and lull
Myself to immortality: . . .
                    (*End*. III.163-73)

His involvement with the Indian maid is a desperate one, for,
so far as he knows, falling in love with her means giving up
all the great ambitions that have been associated with his
"immortal love," the Moon. He calls her his "executioner,"
who "stolen hast away the wings wherewith I was to top the
heavens" (*End*. IV.109-10). In the mythological relationship
between the Great Goddess and her son-consort or male pro-
tégé, he is supposed to do great deeds. If he is a god—Dio-
nysos, Thammuz, Attis, Adonis—his great deed is to die and
be reborn, bringing back with him from his deathly ordeal
the renewed life-energy of the vine and the corn. If he is a
local hero adopted by her, his heroic actions are such as Jason
performed for Hera, Triptolemos for Demeter, and Perseus,
Herakles, and Theseus for Athens. (Their deeds, too, often
involved going down to the realm of the dead.) As the female
characters in *Endymion* are related to each other by analogy
with the erotic and maternal aspects of the Great Goddess,
Endymion is related to the daemons and heroes who did great
deeds for her and were made immortal by her.

The effect of his mystic marriage with her at the end of the
poem is to bring "health perpetual to shepherds and their
flocks" (*End*. IV.831-32). This magical effect of their mating
is not contained in the traditional story about Endymion and
the Moon, but it is inherent in earlier ritual myths about the
Great Goddess and the fertility daemon, and it is inherent in
Keats's treatment of the love-theme of the poem. An important
passage in Book I, where Endymion justifies to his sister his
quest for an immortal love, deals with love not as a "mere
commingling of passionate breath," but as the cause of the
fructification of the whole earth and the genetic principle of
all its forms, animate and inanimate.* Endymion says that he

---

* The importance Keats attached to this passage is indicated in a letter he
wrote to his publisher: "I assure you that when I wrote it it was a regular
stepping of the Imagination towards a Truth. My having written that Ar-
gument will perhaps be of the greatest service to me of any thing I ever did."
(*Rollins* I.218)

has ever thought that love "might bless the world with benefits unknowingly," and that it produces "more than our searching witnesseth," for

> who, of men, can tell
> That flowers would bloom, or that green fruit would swell
> To melting pulp, that fish would have bright mail,
> The earth its dower of river, wood, and vale,
> The meadows runnels, runnels pebble-stones,
> The seed its harvest, . .

"If human souls did never kiss and greet?" (*End.* I.835-42). The marriage of Endymion with the Moon, that brings perpetual fecundity to man and beast, is a repetition of the archetypal mating of heroes and fertility goddesses by which the fruits of the earth are conceived and brought forth.

Like the ancient agricultural rituals out of which the mystery religions elaborated the myth of the dying and resurrected god, the stages of Endymion's adventure are linked with the calendrical turning-points of the year, the birth and ripening and death of vegetation. This cycle of change appears both in the actual setting of the poem and in the poet's account of his progress in writing. Keats started the poem in mid-April, 1817:

> Now while the early budders are just new,
> And run in mazes of the youngest hue
> About old forests; while the willow trails
> Its delicate amber; . . .
> (*End.* I.41-44)

He says that he hopes to be in the middle of the poem "as the year grows lush in juicy stalks," and to finish it before winter:

> O may no wintry season, bare and hoary,
> See it half finished: but let Autumn bold,
> With universal tinge of sober gold,
> Be all about me when I make an end.
> (*End.* I.54-57)

(He finished it by the end of November.) The poem begins with a spring rite for the goat-god Pan, in which maidens bring baskets of "April's tender younglings" (*End.* I.138) for sacrifice to this patron of the shepherd-people of Mount Latmos. It closes in gathering autumnal imagery, with Endymion lying all day like a corpse in the dying forest, unconsciously enacting the winter death of the fertility daemon:

> Night will strew
> On the damp grass myriads of lingering leaves,
> And with them shall I die; nor much it grieves
> To die, when summer dies on the cold sward.
>
> (*End.* IV.933-36)

SUMMONS AND SEPARATION

In the rites of Pan, a venerable priest leads a procession of worshippers to an altar in a green woodland glade. He pours a libation on the earth and makes an offering of first fruits. Then the young men and maidens dance to the shepherd's pipe. "Fair living forms," they are called,

> not yet dead,
> But in old marbles ever beautiful.

To these immortal creatures, ever living and ever young in the trance of marble, the associated imagery of the spring forest and the generative rites of Pan gives a special fixation or containment. They are contained in the Eden of innocence and simple generation from which Endymion, disturbed by three mysterious summonses, wants to break out. (This view of the marble men and maidens reflects a certain interpretation upon the treatment of the same figures in the "Ode on a Grecian Urn," where the mood is curiously one of nostalgia for innocent esctasy and at the same time one of rejection— "Cold Pastoral!")

The domain of Pan is the forest of Mount Latmos, and the hymn that is sung to him evokes the mystery of the life-cycle of vegetation:

"O thou, whose mightly palace roof doth hang
From jagged trunks, and overshadoweth
Eternal whispers, glooms, the birth, life, death
Of unseen flowers in heavy peacefulness; . . ."
(*End.* I.232-35)

He yielded the food-bounty of nature to farmers and herders
who gave him their first fruits:

O thou, to whom
Broad leaved fig trees even now foredoom
Their ripen'd fruitage;
. . . .
our village leas
Their fairest blossom'd beans and poppied corn;
. . . .
yea, the fresh budding year
All its completions—. . .
(*End.* I.251-60)

He taught the magic spells of agricultural hygiene:

Breather round our farms,
To keep off mildews, and all weather harms:
Strange ministrant of undescribed sounds,
That come a swooning over hollow grounds, . . .
(*End.* I.283-86)

With his wisdom of the life-force, he inspired the priestess of
his oracle at Lykaion:

Dread opener of the mysterious doors
Leading to universal knowledge— . . .
(*End.* I.288-89)

Since the fecundity of the local food-area was identical with
the vital continuity of the tribe, the domain of the goat-god
was protected by sacred curse or *nemesis*, the counterpoise of
his beneficence. As Joseph Campbell interprets the tradition,

The emotion that he instilled in human beings who by
accident adventured into his domain was "panic" fear,

a sudden groundless fright. Any trifling cause then—the break of a twig, the flutter of a leaf—would flood the mind with imagined danger, and in the frantic effort to escape from his own aroused unconscious the victim expired in a flight of dread.[2]

The hymn to Pan ends with an exorcism against this terrifying and overwhelming aspect of the god. In the vegetative Eden of Mount Latmos, the worshippers screen their foreheads and beg him to remain an "unknown":

> Be still a symbol of immensity;
> A firmament reflected in a sea;
> An element filling the space between;
> An unknown—but no more: we humbly screen
> With uplift hands our foreheads, . . .
>   (*End.* I.299-303)

Only Endymion, the prince, has received secret signs urging him to cross the threshold of the dread doors.

The first sign given Endymion, singling him out for adventure beyond the threshold of the known and customary, is the sudden blossoming under his feet of "a magic bed of sacred ditamy, and poppies red" (*End.* I.554-55). (Keats carefully follows Lemprière, who notes that ditamy and poppies were sacred to Diana.) He describes to his sister the experiences that have unnerved him for common intercourse. There came

>   shaping visions all about my sight
> Of colours, wings, and bursts of spangly light;
> ....
> And then I fell asleep. Ah, can I tell
> The enchantment that afterwards befel?
> Yet it was but a dream: yet such a dream
> That never tongue, although it overteem
> With mellow utterance, like a cavern spring,
> Could figure out and to conception bring
> All I beheld and felt.
>   (*End.* I.568-78)

Endymion is well constituted to be the kind of hero whose adventures are those of psychical dissociation, for traditionally his special gift was, as Lemprière says, "to sleep as much as he would; whence came the proverb *Endymionis sommum dormire*, to express a long sleep." It was no accident that Keats chose a hero who dreams all his adventures, for in Keats's psychology of the creative process the poet also has the gift of psychical dissociation, of "inspiration" through dream or trance.

It is not unexpected, then, that in *Endymion* the poet sometimes involuntarily identifies himself with his daemonic hero. The Moon is the patron of both—"Maker of poets" she is called in *I Stood Tip-toe*, and it is suggested at the end of that poem that the mystic birth that took place on the night of the Moon's marriage with Endymion was the birth of a poet. But "Poesy" is, in Keats, not the literary product of an activity but the unique psychical state of the activity itself, involving "separation" of the subject-self from the known and rational, and its inversion into unknown psychical contents. His continual improvisations on his monomythic plot reflect his difficulty in arriving at an objective destiny for his hero, for the hero's destiny is organic with the poet's own.

In Endymion's dream a golden-haired maiden sails down to him and meets him in mid-air. In all the love-passages, Endymion either falls asleep or swoons or "dies," and he does all three here.

> Ah! 'twas too much;
> Methought I fainted at the charmed touch
> ....
> madly did I kiss
> The wooing arms which held me, and did give
> My eyes at once to death: but 'twas to live, . . .
> (*End.* I.636-37, 653-55)

He is "lapp'd and lull'd along the dangerous sky" (*End.* I.646) in the maiden's arms, and they alight in a bower of lime-flowers, whereupon he falls asleep (although he is already asleep): "Why did I dream that sleep o'er-power'd me in the midst of all this heaven?" (*End.* I.672-73). The maiden has disappeared, leaving him to a bitter awakening.

His second sign from the daemonic otherworld is a face seen in a well. The well lies in a deep hollow near the "matron-temple" (*End.* I.862) of Latona and is associated with memories of childhood, when he would sit beside it and "bubble up the water through a reed," and sail toy ships upon it, made of "moulted feathers, touchwood, alder chips, with leaves stuck in them" (*End.* I.880-83). Now, looking down into the water, he sees

> The same bright face I tasted in my sleep,
> Smiling in the clear well.
> (*End.* I.895-96)

The association of the well with memories of childhood and with the "matron-temple" of the mother-goddess Latona corresponds with the maternal and sisterly associations of the Moon, in the invocation to the Moon in Book III—her drying of the child's tears, cooling apples for him to eat, walking hand in hand with him through the green woods and beside tumbling streams (*End.* III. 142-52). For it is the face of the Moon that looks at him from the well, the same face he had "tasted in his sleep." Erotic imagery of the beloved as food and drink recurs in all the love passages.

The third sign from the otherworld comes when he has been discontentedly wandering about in the forest, hurling his lance at random. The lance strikes in the middle of a brook, which he follows until he comes to a cave screened with lush weeds. He thinks that this may be the "grot of Proserpine" through which she ascends and descends. "Oppressed," he hurries in. But Book I is broken off here by another rude awakening. He is not to descend through the cave into the realm of Proserpine, who is the underworld manifestation of the Great Goddess, until Book II.

In Book II, Endymion is again wandering in the forest and comes to a shady spring. He plucks a wild rose, dips its stem in the water; the bud flowers beneath his sight, and in the middle of it is a golden butterfly with strange characters on its wings. He follows its flight and in a deep glen comes to a splashing fountain near the mouth of a cave. The butterfly dips into the water and vanishes, whereupon a nymph arises from the fountain and tells him that it was she who was his guide. In the magic forest of generation, the face seen in the well, the nymph in the fountain, and the wild rose dipped in the spring, all associate a female principal with water. The rose is a vaginal emblem—having the form of the mandala—that is identified in religious art with the Virgin and in love-poetry with the beloved maiden (as in Burns's "My Love Is Like a Red, Red Rose"). In Keats's poems, the rose always inheres in an erotic context. The butterfly is a traditional soul-image, the Greek *psychē* being the name for both butterfly and soul, and was shown in Greek art with the boy Eros tormenting or caressing her. In Keats's "Ode to Psyche," she lies asleep in the arms of Eros. But while the female water is of the earth, the butterfly is of the air, a psychical aspect of generation. In Blake's engraving for his poem "Infant Joy," the butterfly appears as an angel of annunciation, welcoming "holy generation" in the girl with the infant on her lap.

The nymph of the fountain tells Endymion that he must

> wander far
> In other regions, past the scanty bar
> To mortal steps,

before he can be taken "into the gentle bosom of thy love" (*End.* II.123-27). She disappears, and he sits down in despair beside the pool, not knowing what to do and thinking enviously of death, for he has "no depth to strike in" (*End.* II.161). Then a voice from the cavern tells him of a depth to strike in. "Descend," it says,

> Young mountaineer! descend where alleys bend
> Into the sparry hollows of the world!
> Oft hast thou seen bolts of the thunder hurl'd
> As from thy threshold; day by day hast been
> A little lower than the chilly sheen
> Of icy pinnacles, and dipp'dst thine arms

Into the deadening ether that still charms
Their marble being: now, as deep profound
As those are high, descend! He ne'er is crown'd
With immortality, who fears to follow
Where airy voices lead: so through the hollow,
The silent mysteries of earth, descend!
(*End.* II.202-14)

In the sonnet "On Seeing the Elgin Marbles," there are other "pinnacles" that have a "marble being" and a "deadening" atmosphere, like those which the young mountaineer Endymion has often ascended. These are the "steeps of godlike hardship" that are the marble monuments of art. In subliminal imagery, opposites may stand for each other, and Keats's dynamics of descent and ascent are interchangeable modes. As Endymion is told by the voice from the cavern that he must descend to the underworld of death in order to be "crown'd with immortality," so the mountainous steeps of immortal art tell the poet he "must die":

My spirit is too weak—mortality
    Weighs heavily on me like unwilling sleep,
    And each imagined pinnacle and steep
    Of godlike hardship tells me I must die. . . .

The word "die" here has the manifest reference of the "real" death that the poet fears may prevent him from climbing the pinnacles of art. But in terms of the monomythic plot of the poems, it has a latent reference to that "death" which must be undergone in order to win immortality.

The sonnet on the Elgin Marbles ends with a set of cosmic symbols by which the poet, in an "indescribable feud" of feeling, tries to grasp the mystery of the ancient figures:

                                a billowy main—
A sun—a shadow of a magnitude.

The hymn to Pan, in *Endymion*, ends with the same set of symbols:

Be still a symbol of immensity;
A firmament reflected in a sea;

> An element filling the space between;
> An unknown—but no more: . . .
> (End. I.299-302)

The mystery of the "dread opener of the mysterious doors leading to universal knowledge" (*End.* I.288-89) is the same mystery as that of immortal art, whose generic name is "Poesy." In the sonnet "On First Looking into Chapman's Homer," the mystery of poetry is defined by the same symbols—a vast sea, a planet, a mountain peak:

> Then felt I like some watcher of the skies
> When a new planet swims into his ken;
> Or like stout Cortez when with eagle eyes
> He star'd at the Pacific—and all his men
> Look'd at each other with a wild surmise—
> Silent, upon a peak in Darien.

THE UNDERWORLD DESCENT

The lines of the poem show that Endymion, in his descent through the cave down into the labyrinths of the underworld, is not trying to escape something but trying to achieve something by going into the underworld. The nymph in the fountain has told him that he must pass "the scanty bar to mortal steps" if he would find the "gentle bosom of his love." On his dream-flight with the Moon-maiden in Book II, the same idiom is used for the emotional enfranchisement of dream, and takes the form of an aerial ascent rather than of an underearth descent: Endymion says, "I do not think the bars that kept my spirit in are burst" (*End.* II.185-86). In *I Stood Tip-toe*, it is said of the poet who first conceived the story of Endymion,

> Ah! surely he had burst our mortal bars;
> Into some wond'rous region he had gone,
> To search for thee, divine Endymion!
> (I Stood Tip-toe 190-92)

Here the bursting of bars* is, in effect, the liberation of the poet's private consciousness into the collective consciousness of myth, and the direction of such passage may be represented as either "up" or "down." Whether the monomythic hero is Endymion or *Endymion*'s poet, he must cross this psychical threshold in order to go on his quest at all.

When the voice from the cavern commands Endymion to descend into the "sparry hollows of the world" and the "silent mysteries of earth," it is that eventually he may be "crown'd with immortality." Thus the descent is carefully motivated by the narrative. Homer and Virgil (Keats translated the *Aeneid* when he was fifteen and was well aware of this mythical pattern) had their heroes descend to the realm of death, to seek wisdom, and presumably did so by calculated narrative strokes.

The underworld descent is an archetypal quest-image and as such is an ambivalent cluster of associations. There are two main kinds of imagery in this portion of the poem. One is the hard, gleaming, metallic imagery of the labyrinth, with its stony cold and darkness, the fearful vastness of caverns and pits. The other is an imagery of secret underground bowers, luxuriant in vegetation. In one of these bowers Adonis sleeps and Venus descends to him. In another—duplicating the pattern—Endymion sleeps and the golden-haired maiden descends to him. In the classical Freudian terminology, the one type of imagery is that of Thanatos, the other that of Eros. Adonis and Endymion are both sleepers, and sleep is traditionally a simulacrum of death, as it is in Keats's sonnet "To Sleep," where it "embalms" and seals the soul in a "casket":

> O soft embalmer of the still midnight, . . .
> Turn the key deftly in the oiled wards,
> And seal the hushed casket of my soul.

* Cf. the poet's address to the Muse at the beginning of Book IV:

> Great Muse, thou know'st what prison,
> Of flesh and bone, curbs, and confines, and frets
> Our spirit's wings: . . .
> (*End.* IV.20-22)

In the fact that Adonis and Endymion both sleep in the love-bowers, the imagery of Eros is strongly impregnated with that of Thanatos; as, in the placing of the love-bowers in the realm of death, the imagery of Thanatos is strongly impregnated with that of Eros.

There is another love-bower in Book III—Circe's island, described by Glaucus in the story of his past life. There Circe took Glaucus "like a child of suckling time" and "cradled him in roses," but the end of that sensual transport was poisonous intoxication and degeneration leading to death. These three love-bowers with their parallel sets of lovers are a connected series, formed with similar idiom and imagery. In the Venus-Adonis episode, the deathly aspect of the sexual ecstasy is converted to immortality (like Adonis, one has to "die" to become immortal). In the episode in which Endymion and the golden-haired maiden make love in a mossy cave, the deathly aspect is that of a swoon from excess of pleasure. In the Glaucus-Circe episode, the sexual ecstasy becomes a psychic poison, leading to loss of selfhood and dissolution. These are the transformative possibilities implicit in the sexual initiation, with its ambiguous and treacherous association with death. These relationships are represented in the imagery of the settings of the first three books of *Endymion*, indicating the opposite pulls of psychic gravity, toward Eros and "mystic death" and toward Thanatos and "profane death."

A going-down into the bowels of the earth is a figure charged by tradition and dream and language itself with the most powerful associations. For a people who bury their dead the earth-cavern is the grave, but its association with the womb and birth is indicated by the widespread custom of doubling the body into a fetal position. For a food-gathering or agricultural people, the earth is necessarily envisaged as female, "mother earth," because she is the original producer of food. The seed-food is buried and "dies" if it is to come up again. A descent into mother-earth condenses into a single polyvalent figure the burial of the dead, phallic seeding, and the rebirth of life. The consort of the mother-goddess, who is himself the fruits of the earth, dies, couples with her, and is reborn as her son.

The dead, according to Plutarch, were called by the Athenians "Demeter's people." Similarly Cybele, the ancient "Lady of the Wild Things" (at Ephesus, "Artemis of the Wild Things," the Ephesian Diana), with her guardian lions, kept ward over the dead in the tombs of Asia Minor, and "every grave became her sanctuary." Instinctively sensitive to mythological relationships, Keats has Cybele appear to Endymion, in a dusky pit of the underground, drawn by her lions. The description uses with precision details given by Lemprière:

> Forth from a rugged arch, in the dusk below,
> Came mother Cybele! alone—alone—
> In sombre chariot; dark foldings thrown
> About her majesty, and front death-pale,
> With turrets crown'd. Four maned lions hale
> The sluggish wheels; . . .
> ....
> Silent sails
> This shadowy queen athwart, . . .
> (*End.* II.639-48)

In Keats's last major poem, *The Fall of Hyperion, A Dream*, the triple Diana appears in the form of the priestess Moneta, with Cybele's death-pale face and awesome veils, and puts the Dreamer through the ordeal of climbing a vast and nightmare stairway to reach her, then tells him that he has felt "what 'tis to die and live again." The Dreamer's anguished passage through death to life is a later reenactment of the underground ordeal of the dreamer Endymion, and the giant stairway that the dreamer must climb is an architectural counterpart of the labyrinth through which Endymion descends into the earth.

This path is a vein of gold gleaming in the darkness and leading through "a thousand mazes,"

> winding passages, where sameness breeds
> Vexing conceptions of some sudden change; . . .
> (*End.* II.235-36)

It shoots across deep pits and passes under "monstrous roofs" and through "vast antres," lit by the gleam of gems.

> 'Twas far too strange, and wonderful for sadness;
> Sharpening, by degrees, his appetite
> To dive into the deepest. Dark, nor light,
> The region; nor bright, nor sombre wholly,
> But mingled up; a gleaming melancholy;
> A dusky empire and its diadems;
> One faint eternal eventide of gems.
> (*End.* II.219-25)

"Oft turning his veil'd eye down sidelong aisles," he "began to thread all courts and passages" (*End.* II.263-71), until, weary,

> he sat down before the maw
> Of a wide outlet, fathomless and dim,
> To wild uncertainty and shadows grim.
> (*End.* II.271-73)

When Endymion, exhausted, sits down to "wild uncertainty and shadows grim" before the "maw" of an abyss, he tries to regain his former consciousness of self:

> how crude and sore
> The journey homeward to habitual self!
> (*End.* II.275-76)

He cannot, of course, return now to "habitual self," for that is what the labyrinth is designed to undermine. The landmarks have been removed:

> He cannot see the heavens, nor the flow
> Of rivers, . . .
> ....
> nor felt, nor prest
> Cool grass, nor tasted the fresh slumberous air; . . .
> (*End.* II.285-90)

"Thick films and shadows" (*End.* II.323) float before his eyes, and he is grasped by "the deadly feel of solitude" (*End.* II.284).

He prays to Diana to deliver him from "this rapacious deep" (*End.* II.332). He is now in the realm of the Infernal Diana, goddess of death. Endymion has reached the nadir of his quest, the most perilous moment of initiation, where personality can either be overwhelmed or receive a completely new and positive orientation. His prayer to Diana brings strange signs of a redirection of his path.

The Garden of Adonis

Flowers bloom through the marble floor—"a long whispering birth enchanted grew." "Sleepy music," "noiseless" music, leads him to the bower where Adonis is sleeping.

> After a thousand mazes overgone,
> At last, with sudden step, he came upon
> A chamber, myrtle wall'd, embowered high,
> Full of light, incense, tender minstrelsy, . . .
> (*End.* II.387-90)

In Spenser's Garden of Adonis, the boughs bear "laughing blossoms" and "with fresh colours decke the wanton pryme"; but the vegetation with which Keats adorns his underground bower consists of sumptuous vines that have a somewhat funerary character—for the god is still "dead":

> round him grew
> All tendrils green, of every bloom and hue,
> Together intertwin'd and trammel'd fresh:
> The vine of glossy sprout; the ivy mesh,
> Shading its Ethiop berries; and woodbine,
> Of velvet leaves and bugle-blooms divine;
> Convolvulus in streaked vases flush;
> The creeper, mellowing for an autumn blush;
> And virgin's bower, trailing airily; . . .
> (*End.* II.409-17)

"Safe in the privacy of this still region all his winter-sleep" (*End.* II.479-80), Adonis lies on a silken couch, with cupids hovering about him, one touching a lyre, others shaking "odorous dew" from willow-branches on his hair and scattering violet petals on his eyes. They whisper to Endymion that the presence of a stranger here "might seen unholy," and that it is a sign of great favor when some high donor "presents immortal bowers to mortal sense" (*End*. II.435-38). They bring him exquisite foods to eat, to prepare his senses for the epiphany of Venus. Her dove-drawn car appears; there is a cry of voices:

> Arise! awake! Clear summer has forth walk'd. . . .
> ....
> Once more sweet life begin!
> (*End*. II.502-6)

and Adonis opens his eyes to "Queen Venus leaning downward open arm'd" (*End*. II.526).

Northrop Frye says that, in general, the Garden of Adonis is a "natural point of epiphany," representing sexual fulfillment. Like Eden, it is "place of seed, into which everything subject to the cyclical order of nature enters at death and proceeds from at birth."[3] Spenser's Garden of Adonis contains the chief traits of the archetypal cluster—the secrecy and luxuriance of this seed-place of all the world, where Venus enjoys her lover, and the strange deathly eternalness of the god who both dies and lives:

> There wont fayre Venus often to enjoy
> Her deare Adonis ioyous company,
> And reape sweet pleasure of the wanton boy;
> There yet, some say, in secret he does ly, . .
> By her hid from the world,
> ....
>   for he may not
> For euer die
> ....
> All be he subiect to mortalitie,
> Yet is eterne in mutabilitie
> ....
> For him the Father of all formes they call;
> Therefore needs mote he liue, that liuing giues to all.[4]

According to Lemprière's account, when Adonis was tusked by the boar and died of his wound, Venus pleaded with Jupiter for his life, but Proserpine also demanded her due. The decision was that he spend the winter in the underworld, and be restored to life in the summer. Keats's version is that when Venus wept over his corpse,

> the tremulous shower
> Heal'd up the wound, and, with a balmy power,
> Medicined death to a lengthened drowsiness:
> The which she fills with visions, and doth dress
> In all this quiet luxury; . . .
> *(End.* II.482-86)

The myth of the sharing of Adonis by Proserpine and Venus indicates the archaic analogy of the two goddesses—analogy that is actually identity, in one ambivalent goddess-figure. The question as to whether Keats had any information about the underworld Aphrodite does not have particular relevance here, though his reading contained abundant suggestion of the ambivalence of the Great Goddess. He has Cybele appear to Endymion in the abyss immediately after the Adonis episode. And the fact remains that he places Venus, goddess of sexual generation, in the underworld of the dead, where she would have to be since her lover, the fertility daemon Adonis, is dead there.

The Immortal Statue-Double

Like Endymion, Adonis is a young boar-hunter, a long sleeper, and the lover of an other-world being, but he has already achieved immortality, as Endymion has not. He has an "Apollonian" figure ("an Apollonian curve of neck and shoulder") and is posed or "stationed" as a reclining statue. We shall consider here the potency of the image of "marble men" in Keats, who appear in the sonnet on the Elgin Marbles, the "Ode on a Grecian Urn," *Hyperion* (where they are expanded to giants), and as the image-base of Keats's metaphors whenever his heroes are "deified."

Adonis is tenderly girlish in appearance, like the sculptured

Hermaphrodite who sleeps with head on arm like a fallen flower, and like the statues Hadrian commissioned for Antinous, which commingle the sexes in the manner that was traditional for young divinities.

> In midst of all, there lay a sleeping youth
> Of fondest beauty; fonder, in fair sooth,
> Than sighs could fathom, or contentment reach:
> And coverlids gold-tinted like the peach,
> Or ripe October's faded marigolds,
> Fell sleek about him in a thousand folds—
> Not hiding up an Apollonian curve
> Of neck and shoulder, nor the tenting swerve
> Of knee from knee, nor ankles pointing light;
> But rather, giving them to the filled sight
> Officiously. Sideway his face repos'd
> On one white arm, and tenderly unclos'd,
> By tenderest pressure, a faint damask mouth. . . .
>   (*End.* II.393-405)

The aesthetic formula for the interpretation of the sculptured Adonis, Apollo, and Bacchus, had been established by Winckelmann and popularized by dozens of lecturers and writers on Greek statuary—including, in Keat's period, Fuseli and Flaxman (Fuseli was Winckelmann's English translator, and both men lectured on sculpture for the Royal Academy), and Hazlitt, whom Keats looked upon as his "mentor." According to the aesthetic tradition, the statues of these gods were given an effeminate beauty because they were to represent eternal youth, or that phase of adolescence where the traits of the two sexes appear to be mixed. The position of the head resting against the arm ("sideway his face repos'd on one white arm") was interpreted by the academicians as signifying both eternal reposefulness and the softness of the effeminate character. As Winckelmann says:

> This was the manner in which the ancient artists sought to express . . . partly repose, and partly a soft, effeminate character. This is its signification . . . in different statues of Apollo and Bacchus. . . .[5]

As for the draperies which fall "in a thousand folds" about Adonis, the academicians gave exhaustive attention to the way the folds of draperies were arranged on the ancient figures so as to expose rather than hide the forms of the limbs. The draperies on the sleeping god do not "hide up" the Apollonian curve of his neck and shoulder, "nor the tenting swerve of knee from knee," but rather, "give them to the filled sight officiously." The sculptural attributes of Keats's Adonis do not necessarily suggest that he had a particular model, or models, in mind, but the details he uses were common in the aesthetic tradition and certainly common in the intellectual atmosphere of Leigh Hunt's house, Haydon's studio, which was filled with casts of the Elgin Marbles, and Hazlitt's lecture room.

Stephen Larrabee, in his *English Bards and Grecian Marbles*, commenting on this and other sculptural figures in Keats's poetry, says, "One discovers that he presented all his sculptural figures as though they possessed lives of their own."[6] The metaphor of statues as "breathing stones" was a commonplace of poetry, from Thomson and Akenside up through Wordsworth, as it was a commonplace of art criticism. Hazlitt, for instance, says of the Elgin Marbles that it is "as if the very marble were a flexible substance, and contained the various springs of life and motion within itself."[7]

> This is the great and master-excellence of the Elgin Marbles, that they do not seem to be the outer surface of a hard and immovable block of marble, but to be actuated by an internal machinery, and composed of the same soft and flexible materials as the human body.[8]

In the history of the use of images to represent human or divine beings, this aesthetic attitude is a very late one. Older and more continuous is the symbolical use of images, which merges—at some indefinite perimeter in the psychology of images—with their magical use. It is this quasi-magical idea of the statue as a living being that is contained in Keats's images of "marble men," rather than the specifically aesthetic attitude of his contemporaries. It is a type of response to the sculptured image that is psychologically as well as historically archaic, and it is profoundly consonant with the collective, subliminal "reality" of his monomythic plot. The Apollonian marble man is alive with the life called "immortality," the kind of life that the hero will have after he has passed his initiation.

The idea of immortality is that of death as a living state. Adonis, for instance, though he is undergoing his winter death as a statue, is still alive, for he is going to be "reborn" in a few minutes when Venus comes. In Venus' mourning over the corpse of Adonis Keats says that her tears had a "balmy power" that healed up the wound and "medicined death to a length-ened drowsiness" (*End.* II.483-84). The "balmy" effect of Venus' tears is to "embalm" Adonis with their "medicine." An embalmed person is a statue of the person.

Apollonian homeostasis is the polar opposite of the "dread-ful siege of contraries," the conflict of pain and pleasure, the severed consciousness and sense of loss of "identity," and the "burning forehead and parching tongue" of Keats's heroes. His heroes have the labile Dionysian temperament and con-stantly suffer subjective "tearings asunder." Therefore they seek metamorphosis or rebirth into their opposite, the Apol-lonian and immortal marble man. The figure of Adonis in *Endymion* is the hero's "double" in a special sense: he is that double Yeats called the "anti-self," the self one would become.

THE FOOD OF LIFE

When Venus comes to awaken Adonis in the garden, she takes Endymion under her protection, because she has pitied him in the hours when she had to wait through "the endless sleep of this new-born Adon' " (*End.* II.554). The intercession of Venus rescues him from the deadly grasp of Thanatos and the "Terrible Mother." He is now to be initiated in Eros, the life-principle. He is prepared by food for this initiation, for food is the primary need of life. The luxuriant plant-life in the garden is the vegetational abundance of the earth that provides food, which enters and becomes the living body. The union of Venus with her "new-born" lover is the ritual magic that makes the earth provident.

Endymion is given wine, the traditional god-intoxicant, juicy pears, manna, cream "sweeter than that nurse Amalthea skimm'd for the boy Jupiter," and plums "ready to melt between an infant's gums" (*End.* II.441-51). In high barbaric coronation ritual and in the ritual of the mystery religions, the initiate received infantine food suitable for one newly born, but here it is Adonis who is "new-born," while Endymion receives the infantine food. Nurse Amalthea, who suckled the hidden babe Jupiter, was, according to Lemprière, a goat, and her horn became the horn of plenty, the cornucopia—emblem of the maternal and inexhaustible food at the source of life. In *The Fall of Hyperion*, the Dreamer has a similar meal of "summer fruits" (grapes are the only fruit specifically mentioned—for the food of the vine is the Dionysian and Orphic food of rebirth) and other unnamed "pure kinds" in "more plenty than the fabled horn thrice emptied could pour forth" (*Fall of Hyp.* 29-36). The fabled horn is the cornucopia or *rhython*, the enormous cup out of which deified heroes drink in hero-feasts depicted on Greek vases, with the great laden vine bending over it. The food etherealizes Endymion's senses ("his every sense had grown ethereal for pleasure") and makes him "feel immortal" (*End.* II.671-72, 636). Similarly the Dreamer in *The Fall* is energized by the divine food so that he is able to climb the stairway of rebirth. Food as sacrament is incorporation of divine substance, "communion" in the most literal sense, as the food becomes part of the body of the participant.

THE CAVE OF LOVE

"Feeling immortal" after his banquet in the garden, Endymion continues on his path through the underworld, where, in another garden in a secret cave of the abyss, he is to reenact in elaborate ritual detail the divine union he has just witnessed. He follows a diamond balustrade that "spirals through ruggedest loopholes," stretching over voids and enormous chasms where subterranean streams and a thousand fountains foam,* "so that he could dash the waters with his spear" (*End.* II.597-605). The diamond path suddenly ends "abrupt in middle air." The phrase is repeated as his anxiety increases: "He was indeed wayworn; abrupt, in middle air, his way was lost" (*End.* II. 652-56).

If, in the symbolism of the unconscious, the unconscious itself is represented by the image of dark, unknown depths, as it is said to be, then Endymion has to plunge to most extraordinary depths of the unconscious to meet his goddess:

> Without one impious word, himself he flings,
> Committed to the darkness and the gloom:
> Down, down, uncertain to what pleasant doom,
> Swift as a fathoming plummet down he fell
> Through unknown things; . . .
> (*End.* II.659-63)

That he must go to such depths to find, in a dream, the image of his love, is in keeping with what Venus has told him of the need for extreme secrecy in this affair: she had said that "of all things 'tis kept secretest," and " 'Tis a concealment needful in extreme" (*End.* II.572-76). In all the love sequences in Keats's poems there is the same need for intense secrecy. It is a need that Keats observed, to an extreme, in his own love affair.

When Endymion nears the bottom of his plunge into the depths, he breaths the exhalations of asphodel—the flower that grows in the Elysian fields (for this is still the region ruled by Proserpine). He lands in a terrain of dim passages and little caves "wreath'd so thick with leaves and mosses, that they seem'd large honey-combs of green." The place where he finds himself is "a jasmine bower, all bestrewn with golden moss." As in the other garden winged cupids hovered in the air and shook down dewy petals on Adonis' eyes, here, above En-

---

* The exiguous diamond path over a void "half seen through deepest gloom," where a vast deluge roars, is like the "sword bridge" of Chrétien's *Le chevalier de la charrette.* Also in the realm of death, Lancelot has to walk over a foaming gulf on the edge of a sword.

dymion's head "flew a delight half-graspable" and a "dewy luxury was in his eyes." He calls on his unknown love, wherever she may be, to come to him, but knowing that because of his human powerlessness "this cannot be," he decides to go to sleep and dream about her:

> O let me then by some sweet dreaming flee
> To her entrancements: hither, sleep, awhile!
> Hither most gentle sleep!
> ....
> And at that moment felt endued
> With power to dream deliciously; . . .
> (*End*. II.703-08)

Immediately she is in his arms.

They weep in their love-joy and caress with sobs (*End*. II.732-36). "O bliss! O pain! " she cries, and "Woe! woe! is grief contain'd in the very deeps of pleasure?" (*End*. II.773, 823-24). (The line rejected here was "There is a grief contain'd in the very shrine of pleasure." The "sovran shrine" of Keats's veiled and awesome goddess Melancholy, in the "Ode on Melancholy," was traditionally that of Volupia, pleasure.) Endymion swoons away, and the goddess says that she will die too:

> Revive, dear youth, or I shall faint and die;
> Revive, or these soft hours will hurry by
> In tranced dulness; speak, and let that spell
> Affright this lethargy!
> (*End*. II.766-69)

This deathlike spell is a simulacrum of Adonis' mystic death in the other garden.

The sexual idiom of the lovers is that of child with nurse: "O he had swoon'd drunken from pleasure's nipple" (*End*. II.868-69). The infantine food-motif is a linguistic extension of the infant-food Endymion took in the Garden of Adonis. He "tastes" her: "Now I have tasted her sweet soul to the core" (*End*. II.904)—as he had earlier "tasted in his sleep" the face of the Moon-maiden seen in the well. He "sips" her "essence":

> O known Unknown! from whom my being sips
> Such darling essence, wherefore may I not
> Be ever in these arms?
>   (*End.* II.739-41)

To be "ever in her arms" would be to eat forever of the inexhaustible food of the life-source.

She tells him that the obstacle to their love, the reason it must take place in such secrecy, is the taboo of her chastity. Previously she "was as vague as solitary dove, nor knew that nests were built" (*End.* II.805-6). But soon they will have "an immortality of passion" (*End.* II.808). She describes what they will do when he has won immortality:

>   we will shade
> Ourselves whole summers by a river glade;
> And I will tell thee stories of the sky,
> And breathe thee whispers of its minstrelsy. . . .
> Lispings empyrean will I sometime teach
> Thine honied tongue—lute-breathings, which I gasp
> To have thee understand, . . .
>   (*End.* II.810-13, 819-21)

In other words, by his mystic marriage with her, Endymion will not only become immortal but will also become an immortal *poet*, and in her heavenly capacity she will be his Muse, teaching him cosmic poetry. That he will learn in "lispings" will be consonant with his being, like Adonis, "new-born" as a god. The suggestion at the end of *I Stood Tip-toe* that there was "a poet born" of the marriage of Endymion and the Moon is to be carried out in the transformation of Endymion himself into a poet, a transformation following the model of the fertility daemon's marriage with the mother-goddess and rebirth as her son—only his "boon" of fertility to the earth will now be that of immortal poetry.

In her simplest late classical character, Diana was a virgin-goddess. Her divine virginity makes it necessary that the love-making in this episode be handled as a mystery, a sacred thing, forbidden and holy: it must occur in the most secret part of the underworld and in Endymion's sleep, the psychical underworld. Whether by design or not (archetypal situations have their own unconscious organization and design), the golden-haired maiden is here the Kore who takes over the mother-goddess's breeding function in the seed-place of the earth. In late mythology Kore was Demeter's daughter, but she was not originally so; the mother-goddess had a son rather than a daughter. Kore is simply the maiden form of the mother.

The shy, maidenly character of the Moon's Kore-form appears in Endymion's first dream of her, in Book I:

> She took an airy range,
> And then, towards me, like a very maid,
> Came blushing, waning, willing, and afraid, . . .
> *(End.* I.633-35)

and in her own description of herself before she fell in love:

> I was as vague as solitary dove,
> Nor knew that nests were built.

This is her appropriate character as virgin-goddess. Psychologically, it is also the pure, chaste and maidenly image of ideal love (appearing throughout Keats's poetry): it is Madeline of *The Eve of St. Agnes* and Isabella of *The Pot of Basil*, and it is that maiden-image to which the invocation to Love, at the beginning of Book II, is addressed:

> Juliet leaning
> Amid her window-flowers,—sighing,—weaning
> Tenderly her fancy from its maiden snow, . .
>
> ....
>
> the silver flow
> Of Hero's tears, the swoon of Imogen,
> Fair Pastorella in the bandit's den, . . .
> *(End.* II.27-32)

It is the image Keats speaks of in a letter of July, 1818, as his schoolboy idea of "a fair woman as a pure goddess"—a letter confessing the "gordian complication" of his feeling about women:

> I am certain I have not a right feeling towards Women—at this moment I am striving to be just to them but I cannot—Is it because they fall so far beneath my Boyish imagination? When I was a Schoolboy I thought a fair Woman a pure Goddess, my mind was a soft nest in which some one of them slept, though she knew it not—I have no right to expect more of their reality. I thought them etherial above Men—I find them perhaps equal—great by comparison is very small. . . . (*Rollins* I.341)

But the fact is that Endymion's virgin goddess is not chaste at all: she initiates him in sex. Psychologically, therefore, there is every reason why this initiation should occur in the most profound depths of the mythological underworld and the underworld of the psyche. The love-making is distinctly a Mystery: a world different from the "real" world has to be entered before it can occur, a world that is secret, sacred, and taboo. The mechanism is sleep: the sleep of Endymion is the means to sexual initiation through the maiden, ever virgin, of ideal love.

THE FOOD OF LOVE

The infantine food taken by Endymion in the Garden of Adonis and the breast-feeding imagery of the erotic sequence are part of a more general pattern of food-and-love imagery in the poems, where the lovers take food or a banquet is prepared for them. The whole constellation also involves those passages where some special food or drink is taken in connection with a visionary experience that has the character of religious mystery, and where there is an epiphany of the Great Goddess.

As to the connection of sex and food, Freud speaks of the common transposition of the "sexual representation-complex" to the "eating-complex." In his letters as well as his poetry, Keats's descriptions of food and drink are notably luxurious, and in one letter he whimsically suggests the folk superstition that certain foods effect pregnancy:

> Talking of Pleasure, this moment I was writing with one hand, and with the other holding to my Mouth a Nectarine—good god how fine. It went down soft pulpy, slushy, oozy—all its delicious embonpoint melted down my throat like a large beatified Strawberry. I shall certainly breed. (*Rollins* II.179)

In the love-episode between Endymion and the Moon-maiden, where, through the imagery of drinking from the body of the beloved, the erotic motif is condensed with that of maternal nourishment, this idiom reflects the ritual tendency of the monomythic plot, over which reigns the Great Goddess who is the giver of all life and who appears here in her form of mother-as-maid or Kore.

THE "LOVE-DEATH"

The identification of bliss and pain in the Moon-maiden's cry "O bliss! O pain!" and "Woe! woe! is grief contain'd in the very deeps of pleasure?" and the representation of the sexual embrace as a kind of "death"—as in Endymion's first dream, when the maiden's "charmed touch" makes him faint and give himself "at once to death," and his later "tranced dullness" in her arms, that makes her think he is dead—are a constellation that is continuous in Keats's poetry and a common Romantic phenomenon. When Mme de Warens first offered Rousseau her favors, he saw the hour approach with "more pain than pleasure." Instead of being intoxicated with rapture, as he felt he ought to be, "A certain unconquerable feeling of melancholy poisoned its charm; I felt as if I had been guilty of incest." Similarly with the beautiful Zulietta, who could not have exercised the same maternal spell as did Mme de Warens:

> I entered the room of a courtesan as if it had been the sanctuary of love and beauty; in her person I thought I

beheld its divinity. . . . Suddenly, my legs trembled under me; and, feeling ready to faint, I sat down and cried like a child.

With Mme d'Houdetot, who was in love with Saint-Lambert at the time, he shared "delightful tears" (like the "joyous tears" and "soft caressing sobs" of Endymion and the Moon-maiden): "We were both intoxicated with love; she for her lover, I for her. Our sighs, our delightful tears mingled together." And on a moonlit night under the acacias: "What intoxicating tears I shed upon her knees!" He speaks of "the agitation, the shivering, the palpitation, the convulsive movements, the faintness of heart, which I felt continually." As he approaches her, he becomes dizzy from thoughts of her kiss and nearly faints.

In *The Sorrows of Young Werther*, Werther speaks of his "unsteady and uncertain heart" in terms of that "siege of contraries" with which Keats was so constantly concerned. "Need I confess this to you," Werther writes his friend, "who have so often endured the anguish of witnessing my sudden transitions from sorrow to immoderate joy, and from sweet melancholy to violent passions?" With his mistress, Charlotte, he goes through the same palpitations and swoonings as Rousseau and Endymion:

> When I have spent several hours in her company, till I feel completely absorbed by her figure, her grace, the divine expression of her thoughts, my mind becomes gradually excited to the highest excess, my sight grows dim, my hearing confused, my breathing oppressed as if by the hand of a murderer, and my beating heart seeks to obtain relief for my aching senses. I am sometimes unconscious whether I really exist.

Werther's hysteria (a condition which Rousseau, speaking of his own emotional lability, called "the ailment of happy people") leads him to suicide, actually a "love-death," for he shoots himself with Charlotte's pistol. There is a need for an "obstacle" or "obstruction" between the lovers of romance, such as the adulterous situation of Tristan and Isolde, which is further complicated by Tristan's fealty to the king. The obstacle or taboo coincides, as a narrative device for complication, with the mystique of love as pain.

The obstacle in Endymion's and the Moon-maiden's love is that she is goddess of chastity. Since she is also, as the Diana *triformis*, the Great Goddess of life and death, her chastity taboo is implicitly bound up with the more awful taboo of her maternal mystery. In the final book of the poem, the "obstruction—the taboo on love—becomes the main motif of the book. Again and again Endymion and the Indian maid come together and are mysteriously separated or find that it is impossible for them to make love. "Ah, bitter strife!" she says, "I may not be thy love: I am forbidden—"(*End*. IV.751-52). The lovers must "burst the mortal bars" to fulfill their love. In romantic love, says Denis de Rougemont in *Love in the Western World*:

> Eros is complete Desire, luminous Aspiration, the primitive religious soaring carried to its loftiest pitch, to the extreme exigency of purity which is also the extreme exigency of Unity. But absolute Unity must be the negation of the present human being in his suffering multiplicity. The supreme soaring of desire ends in non-desire. The erotic process introduces into life an element foreign to the diastole and systole of sexual attraction—a desire that never relapses, that nothing can satisfy, that even rejects and flees the temptation to obtain its fulfillment in the world, because its demand is to embrace no less than the All. It is infinite transcendence . . . without return.[9]

In *Endymion*, this ultimate form of love-death or mystic death, which is necessary for Endymion's "immortality of passion," is represented at the end of the poem by a total disappearance of the lovers—as it is, in *The Eve of St. Agnes*, by the lovers' vanishing into a "faery" night.

The whole constellation of transcendent desire is contained in the "Bright Star" sonnet, the longing for an "unchangeable" state in the love-union and the equation of that state with death. Here also, in the "bright star" itself, is the luminous divinity of the night (like the Moon in *Endymion*), watching, "with eternal lids apart," the seas at their ritual task of purifying the human earth:

> Brighr star, would I were stedfast as thou art—
>   Not in lone splendor hung aloft the night,
> And watching, with eternal lids apart,
>   Like nature's patient, sleepless eremite,
> The moving waters at their priestlike task
>   Of pure ablution round earth's human shores,
> Or gazing on the new soft-fallen mask
>   Of snow upon the mountains and the moors;
> No—yet still stedfast, still unchangeable,
>   Pillow'd upon my fair love's ripening breast,
> To feel for ever its soft swell and fall,
>   Awake for ever in a sweet unrest,
> Still, still to hear her tender-taken breath,
> And so live ever—or else swoon to death.

In the original version of the sonnet, the last lines are:

> To hear, to feel her tender-taken breath,
>   Half-passionless, and so swoon on to death.

Here the "unchangeable" love-union becomes, through sheer unchangeableness, its own negation—a "half-passionless" state that merges into the swoon of death, as Endymion in his love-ecstasies goes to sleep or swoons into the condition of the immortal Adonis in his death-sleep in the Garden.

THE OTHER GARDEN

There is another garden of love in *Endymion*, another sexual enchantress, and another form of love-death. These Glaucus tells about when he recounts his past life in Book III. Glaucus had been a daring young man like Endymion, who wanted to be a god, and who, like Endymion, made a "plunge for life or death." He fell in love with a water nymph, who fled from him in shyness. To obtain an enchantment for her love-favors, he consulted Circe on her island, and fell into the sexual snare of that "arbitrary queen of sense." After living with her for some time in luxurious sensuality, he witnessed her exercising her rites of black magic over a zoo of hideous animals who had once been men. Her vengeance was horrible: she killed Scylla, the water nymph, and sentenced Glaucus to a thousand years of decrepit old age, whereupon he should die. This episode forms one of the sequence of love-garden episodes in the poem, and the very close correspondence of its imagery to that of the others suggests that it be treated as a variation of the one motif.

In later poems, this malignant version of the love-bower and the love-death tends to become dominant, and it is significant that it occurs as early as *Endymion*, though it is displaced here from Endymion's personal story onto that of another character, Glaucus; one might say of this psychological mechanism what Denis de Rougemont says of myth as such:

> A myth is needed to express the dark and unmentionable fact that passion is linked with death, and involves the destruction of any one yielding himself up to it with all his strength.[10]

Glaucus' story is that he swam to Circe's isle, and just when he lifted his head above water to look at it, he was thrown into a death-resembling swoon, like Adonis and Endymion. The island

> seem'd to whirl around me, and a swoon
> Left me dead-drifting to that fatal power.
> *(End.* III.416-17)

He finds himself in a bower, where the imagery of seduction is like that of the other love-gardens—rich vegetation and a voice singing to a lyre:

> When I awoke, 'twas in a twilight bower;
> Just when the light of morn, with hum of bees,
> Stole through its verdurous matting of fresh trees.

How sweet, and sweeter! for I heard a lyre,
And over it a sighing voice expire.
It ceased—I caught light footsteps; and anon
The fairest face that morn e'er look'd upon
Push'd through a screen of roses. Starry Jove!
With tears, and smiles, and honey-words she wove
A net whose thraldom was more bliss than all
The range of flower'd Elysium.
                    (*End.* III.418-28)

This is the "young witch" in Erich Neumann's description of
the negative "mysteries of intoxication" that are part of the
lesser mysteries of the Great Goddess. Psychologically, this
seductive figure causes very dangerous confusion in Keats's
poetry because she wears the appearance of the ideal love-
maiden ("the fairest face that morn e'er look'd upon") and
hence it is easy to get into her toils. But she has a "net": she
ensnares, captivates, "enthralls." This idiom, of being en-
snared and made a "thrall," invests all episodes of this kind
in the poems, as in the cry of the pale kings and princes in
the ballad:

> They cried, La belle dame sans merci
> Hath thee in thrall!

The experience of Glaucus takes precisely the same idiom
as that of the other love-sequences: this is why the experience
is so baffling and treacherous—its expression, its love-lan-
guage, is the same as that of the benign Eros. Circe weeps
over Glaucus, thinking him dead, just as Venus wept over the
dead Adonis when she "medicined" his death with her tears:

>   Why, I have shed
> An urn of tears, as though thou wert cold dead;
> And now I find thee living, I will pour
> From these devoted eyes their silver store, . . .
>   (*End.* III.431-34)

As Venus' tears had a "balmy power," so Circe "shed balmy
consciousness within that bower." The love-pain is sung by

birds, "warbling for very joy mellifluous sorrow" (*End.* III.466, 471). The relationship of Glaucus and Circe, like that of Endymion and the Moon-maiden, takes the form of suckling child with nurse, with the sensual idiom of "tasting." He "tastes a long love dream" (*End.* II.440):

> She took me like a child of suckling time,
> And cradled me in roses. Thus condemn'd,
> The current of my former life was stemm'd,
> And to this arbitrary queen of sense
> I bow'd a tranced vassal: . . .
> (*End.* III.456-60)

But—like the knight-at-arms, in "La Belle Dame Sans Merci," who has a horrid vision of the "pale kings and princes" who have been thus hypnotized and have lost their former selves—so Glaucus, wandering in the forest, sees Circe at her sadistic rites in her stew of animals who had once been men:

> And all around her shapes, wizard and brute,
> Laughing, and wailing, groveling, serpenting,
> Shewing tooth, tusk, and venom-bag, and sting!
> O such deformities!
> (*End.* III.500-3)

"Fierce, wan and tyrannizing was the lady's look," as Circe feeds her swine (*End.* III.506-7). The fodder she has for them seems strangely unsuitable—she empties before them a basket full of "clusters of grapes"—but the grape has always a special role in Keats's fantasies of intoxication. The treachery of intoxication by the grape is that it can make men into gods or beasts. Circe then performs a black magic parody of one of the erotic rites that take place in the other bowers. Whereas the benign form of the rite is that a "dewy luxury" is shaken over the eyes of the lover, from a flower or a willow branch, Circe takes a branch of mistletoe, smears it with poison from "a black dull-gurgling phial," and "whisk'd against their eyes the sooty oil." (Venus uses "medicine," Circe narcotics and poison.) Then the whole herd writhes together into a huge phantom snake and goes "through the dismal air like one huge Python" (*End.* III.514-30). When she discovers that Glaucus has seen all this, she takes her vengeance on him by turning him into a dying old man, "gaunt, wither'd, sapless, feeble, cramp'd, and lame." "Poison'd was my spirit," he says (*End.* III.638, 602).

The identification of the female love-object with the repulsive and the malignant occurs, says Joseph Campbell, "when it suddenly dawns on us, or is forced to our attention, that everything we think or do is necessarily tainted with the odor of the flesh." Then,

> not uncommonly, there is experienced a moment of revulsion: life, the acts of life, the organs of life, woman in particular as the great symbol of life, becomes intolerable. . . .

When this "Oedipus-Hamlet revulsion" besets the soul, "no longer can the hero rest in innocence with the goddess of the flesh; for she is become the queen of sin."[11] When Keats was reading Burton's *Anatomy of Melancholy*, he wrote in the margin opposite a description of the objects of love:

> Here is the old plague spot: the pestilence, the raw scrofula. I mean that there is nothing disgraces me in my own eyes so much as being one of a race of eyes, nose and mouth beings in a planet called the earth who all from Plato to Wesley have always mingled goatish, winnyish, lustful love with the abstract adoration of the deity. I don't understand Greek—is the Love of God and the Love of women expressed by the same word in Greek? I hope my little mind is wrong—if not I could—Has Plato separated these loves?

And on the next page, pursuing Burton's argument, he writes: "Hm! I see how they endeavour to divide—but there appears to be a horrid relationship."

Luckily, Endymion escapes the enchantment of a "goatish, winnyish, lustful love"—the experience of woman as prostitute—though the poet who wrote his story found a place for the fantasy in the poem. The displacement of the "young witch" into Glaucus' story provides a psychological means of exorcism: she can be seen, objectively, as *somebody else's incubus*. But in *Lamia* and "La Belle Dame" the hero does not escape; he succumbs to the power of the witch.

III. The Old Man and
the Taboo Maiden: Endymion

ENDYMION FOLLOWS two divine streams, two water spirits
that are in love with each other, that gush out from springs
in a lofty grotto, shoot up in fountains, and chase each other
breathlessly. They lead him from under the earth into the sea.

> He turn'd—there was a whelming sound—he stept,
> There was a cooler light;
> ....
> He saw the giant sea above his head.
> (*End.* II.1018-23)

In the Latmian forest of Book I, the vegetation was nourished
by abundant earth-water, and Endymion's various calls and
signs from the daemonic world were associated with streams,
wells, and fountains. All along his path under the earth in
Book II there have been vast subterranean rivers falling in
profound cataracts. In fairy tales, a well is often the gate to
the underworld; but the rising, erupting nature of springs and
fountains is associated with creative movement rather than
with "containing." Man is reborn of water and the spirit, and
Endymion is released from the earth-womb by this energetic
and spirited element.

The exordium of Book III is the hymn to the Moon, pro-
nounced partly by the poet and then continued by Endymion
himself, apropos of glances of moonlight that come down to
him at the bottom of the sea. But the opening lines of the
exordium are an impatient outburst against worshippers of
false gods that have not "one tinge of sanctuary splendour."
The real Powers are those who

> keep religious state,
> In water, fiery realm, and airy bourne.
> (*End.* III.30-31)

Among these is the earth-mother, "our own Ceres," while the "gentlier-mightiest" of them all is the Moon. These mighty Powers correspond with the primal divisions of the cosmos—earth, water, air, and fire. Endymion's quest is a journey of exploration through the same primal realms, and the cosmic "Poesy" that he will learn from the Moon at the end of his quest will be the mysterious *physis* of all things. This fulfillment is prophesied to the youth who will "consummate all" by a magic scroll which he receives from the old sea-god Glaucus on his sea-journey:

> If he utterly
> Scans all the depths of magic, and expounds
> The meanings of all motions, shapes and sounds;
> If he explores all forms and substances
> Straight homeward to their symbol-essences;
> He shall not die.
>
> (*End.* III.696-701)

Naturally he shall not die if he does this (though he has had to "die," enter into the earth-grave like the fertility daemon, in order to carry on his explorations), because by actually *entering into* all the primal "forms and substances" in the course of his journey he has identified his own nature with their eternal *physis*—which, Thales said, is "alive and full of gods and daemons."

The famous opening lines of *Endymion*, about the "things of beauty" that are a "joy for ever," are a review of the same elemental types or archetypes that it is the poet's and the hero's mission to explore:

> A thing of beauty is a joy for ever:
> Its loveliness increases; it will never
> Pass into nothingness; but still will keep
> A bower quiet for us, and a sleep
> Full of sweet dreams, and health, and quiet breathing.
> ....
> Such the sun, the moon,
> Trees old, and young sprouting a shady boon
> For simple sheep; and such are daffodils

With the green world they live in; and clear rills
That for themselves a cooling covert make
'Gainst the hot season; the mid forest brake,
Rich with a sprinkling of fair musk-rose blooms:
And such too is the grandeur of the dooms
We have imagined for the mighty dead;
All lovely tales that we have heard or read:
An endless fountain of immortal drink,
Pouring unto us from the heaven's brink.

   Nor do we merely feel these essences
For one short hour; no, even as the trees
That whisper round a temple become soon
Dear as the temple's self, so does the moon,
The passion poesy, glories infinite,
Haunt us till they become a cheering light
Unto our souls, and bound to us so fast,
That, whether there be shine, or gloom o'ercast,
They always must be with us, or we die.
(End. I.1-33)

Among the major species of "things of beauty" mentioned here are the planet-fire, the "green world" of the earth, and the earth-water. It is quite literally true that these always must be with us or we die. The other things of beauty are "lovely tales" like that of Endymion—the myths that are archetypes of human desire and endeavor—and the destinies of ancestral heroes ("the dooms we have imagined for the mighty dead") that are those myths themselves, and again the moon, and "the passion poesy." The passion poesy is that energy which sends the talismanic poet to explore earth, water, air, and fire, a psychical energy that corresponds with their *physis* and that leads him to repeat, in his adventure through them, the sacral acts of the ancestral heroes of myth who went on the same adventure.

THE SEA-JOURNEY

The hymn to the Moon in Book III shifts its address slightly for a few verses and becomes an address to Love:

O love! how potent hast thou been to teach
Strange journeyings!
....
Thou leddest Orpheus through the gleams of death . . .
(*End.* III.92-98)

The Great Goddess retains her identity either as Moon or
Love; it was she, as Eurydice—another Proserpine—who led
Orpheus "through the gleams of death" (the "gleams" repeat
the imagery of the vein of gold, the "gleaming melancholy,"
that led Endymion through the "dusky empire"). And now it
is Love who sends "a moon-beam to the deep, deep water-
world to find Endymion." But the Moon is the one who sends
moon-beams. He "felt the charm to breathlessness," and nat-
urally he "tastes" it, laying his head on a pillow of sea-weed
"to taste the gentle moon" (*End.* 101-10).

Then he takes up his "fated way" again and fares past vast
heaps of oceanic debris, aeons of geological deposits, behe-
moth carcasses, buried civilizations,

                                    mouldering scrolls,
    Writ in the tongue of heaven, by those souls
    Who first were on the earth; and sculptures rude
    In ponderous stone,

made in the time of "ancient Nox" (*End.* III.129-33). Here
Keats follows the typical anthropological surmises of his pe-
riod, followed also by Blake, Wordsworth, and Shelley: the
earliest sculptures, monuments, and inscriptions were forms
of a primordial symbolism "writ in the tongue of heaven"
and communicated to early man. From among the "mould-
ering scrolls" in these sea-deposits came that scroll Endymion
is to receive later, telling him to "explore all forms and sub-
stances." The debris of civilizations he is exploring right now
at the bottom of the sea is one of the records of those "symbol-
essences" that are the object of his quest.

An access of anxiety now comes over him as he thinks of
the golden-haired Unknown with whom he has just made love
in the cave. He has been guilty of infidelity to his first love,

70

the Moon, who had been like a sister to him in boyhood, taught him the times of the calendar ("In sowing time ne'er would I dibble take, or drop a seed, till thou must wide awake"), and enlightened his youthful mind to love and art ("Thou wast . . . the sage's pen—the poet's harp . . . the charm of women, lovely Moon!"). But then his "strange love" came and the Moon began to fade from his thoughts: "She came, and thou didst fade. . . ." But he corrects himself, for the two goddesses are confused: the Moon did not fade entirely—"no, thy starry sway has been an under-passion to this hour." He feels her "orby power" coming fresh upon him and gets into a state of further mental Disorder as to where his allegiance really lies. He begs the Moon to "keep back her influence" and prays the unknown goddess to forgive him for thinking of anyone but her. Then immediately, with another guilty turn, he asks pardon of the Moon for his unfaithfulness (*End.* III.153-87).

While he is in this confusion of soul an old man suddenly appears:

> He saw far in the concave green of the sea
> An old man sitting calm and peacefully.
> Upon a weeded rock this old man sat,
> And his white hair was awful, and a mat
> Of weeds were cold beneath his cold thin feet;
> And, ample as the largest winding-sheet,
> A cloak of blue wrapp'd up his aged bones,
> O'erwrought with symbols. . . .
> (*End.* III.191-98)

The old man has a "pearly wand" and in his lap a book. In awed voice he hails Endymion: "thou are the man!"—"I shall be young again, be young! . . . with new-born life!" Endymion starts back from this apparition in dismay and horror, thinking that the old man wants to kill him, tear him "piece-meal with a bony saw" and feed him to the fish. But he pulls himself together with a strenuous effort, swearing, "By Pan, I care not for this old mysterious man!" He walks up to him defiantly. But the old man begins to weep and Endymion is moved to pity for him, starts weeping himself, a "penitent shower," and kneels down before him for forgiveness.

Glaucus lifts Endymion up and tells him he has "a very brother's yearning" for him. Endymion, he says, has been "commission'd to this fated spot for great enfranchisement" because he has loved "an unknown power." And then the old sea-god tells his story: "I was a fisher once. . . ." He gave the poor folk of the sea-country their "daily boon of fish," and in gratitude for his bounty they would strew flowers on the "sterile beach." But, like Endymion, he began to feel "distemper'd longings: to desire the utmost privilege" from the sea, and so he "plung'd for life or death" as Endymion plunged into the underworld. Glaucus tells about his unhappy love for the shy water-nymph Scylla, and Circe's vengeful enchantment which turned him into an old man, destined to die after a thousand years despite his semi-divinity.

He shows Endymion his mystic "book" and wand. The scroll contains a prophecy that a youth will come, "by heavenly power lov'd and led," who will "consummate all"—if he "explores all forms and substances," which is what Endymion has been doing on his quest through the elements. Glaucus says that they are "twin brothers in this destiny," and they make a brotherhood pact. Then he directs Endymion in the performance of some magic actions: Endymion must wind a thread to a "clue," like Theseus, read some mysterious symbols on a shell, and break the magic wand on a lyre that is conveniently placed on a pedestal near at hand. Finally he has to strew some minced leaves over Glaucus and over the drowned lovers whom Glaucus has been carrying for the past thousand years to a submarine necropolis, where they lie arranged like statues on sarcophagi, their "ranges of white feet . . . in silent rows." They all come to life, Glaucus becomes a young man, and they follow "the new born god" to a "mighty consummation" in Neptune's palace. Keats's commentators usually give a humanitarian significance to this episode. There is no reason why the episode should be interpreted this way, for the archetypal cluster is ambiguous enough to include the idea; but its significance is thinned down by equating it with a univocal allegory. Though Endymion does a "good work" by bringing the lovers to life, there is no particular indication that he does so through a humanitarian motive: he is "missioned" to be a fertility hero, and the magic scroll tells him that if he does not "consummate all" both he and the old man will be destroyed.

In the terms used by Joseph Campbell, the episode would be one of "father atonement." Glaucus is first an uncouth and terrifying apparition, with his "awful" white hair and his "cold thin feet" wrapped in a winding-sheet, and Endymion is defiantly ready to kill him or be killed by him. But then the old man weeps so pitifully that the youth asks his forgiveness, whereupon they embrace each other as twin brothers in a common destiny. Glaucus gives Endymion his book and wand, a wand which he himself had received from "an old man's hand" that came out of the sea. The succession of the wand is a sort of father-to-son succession, and it comes appropriately at a moment when Endymion has been in a state of baffling confusion over his love-object, whether she be mother or maid. The wand is emblem of his phallic manhood, and fittingly he receives it from a father-figure. The motif is archetypal, rather than merely a "neurotic" symptom as reductive criticism would have it. In *The Eve of St. Agnes*, the old man dies when the lovers consummate their love. In *Lamia*, he forces his way into the "purple-lined palace of sweet sin," and succeeds in separating the lovers, by showing Lycius that his mistress is nothing but a snake-woman. Finally, however, in Keat's last major poem, *The Fall of Hyperion*, the motif of father-atonement is carried out by the Dreamer when he finds safety beneath the huge image of the father-god Saturn. There the Dreamer is allowed to witness a father-son succession, as the myth of the fall of Saturn unrolls before his eyes. In this poem the young hero who takes the "old man's" place is Apollo, the immortal poet.

Book III ends in triumphant recognition of the hero who has shown his stature by restoring multitudes of dead people to life and making Glaucus and himself immortal; he is recognized in a great processional celebration. The whole multitude of resuscitated lovers, led by the "new born god" Glaucus, goes to Neptune's palace where the sea-gods—including Endymion's patroness, Venus, in her character as Venus Anadiomene, "the ooz-born Goddess"—have assembled. The magnificent submarine palace has the blue sea for its vaulted roof:

> as the blue
> Doth vault the waters, so the waters drew
> Their doming curtains, high, magnificent, . . .
> (*End.* III.868-70)

At the four points of the compass, four sunsets blaze forth "a gold-green zenith 'bove the Sea-God's head." The floor is "of lucid depth" like a lake but nevertheless it is made of "breath-air"—

> This palace floor breath-air,—but for the amaze
> Of deep-seen wonders motionless,—and blaze
> Of the dome pomp, reflected in extremes,
> Globing a golden sphere.
> (*End.* III.884-87)

In this cosmic setting Endymion's triumph is celebrated by fountains of nectar and "plunder'd vines, teeming exhaustless" that keep putting out new growths of grapes to replenish the shells that are used as cups by the guests for the god-intoxicating drink that pours from the inexhaustible life-source. Everybody makes love, the magic of fertility, in a riot of vegetation—pulling down "fresh foliage and coverture" and striving "who should be smother'd deepest in fresh crush of leaves"— while winged Love sprinkles from his pinions "on all the multitude a nectarous dew."

"Giddy Endymion," "there far strayed from mortality," has his usual reaction to love-making: he cries, "O I shall die!" and in the same moment he feels his immortal wings: "I die . . . I feel my wing—. . . ." The Nereids crowd around him and try "to usher back his spirit into life," but he has fallen dead asleep. So, like nursing maenads, they take him in "their cradling arms," to convey him "towards a crystal bower far away." Meanwhile to his "inward senses," he sees his triumph "written in star-light on the dark above," the primordial dark that bears all light, in an imagery of the mother-dove hatching her eggs:

> Dearest Endymion! my entire love! . . .
> 'tis done—
> Immortal bliss for me too hast thou won.
> Arise then! for the hen-dove shall not hatch
> Her ready eggs, before I'll kissing snatch
> Thee into endless heaven. Awake! awake!
> (*End.* III.1023-27)

This grand festival, ending in a duplication of the waking of Adonis, is the *anagnorisis* of the poem, the recognition of the triumphant hero. Book IV is a strange aftermath of despair, lost identities, and a general atmosphere of confusion and sadness. It deepens and complicates the psychological aspect of the poem, but it also suggests that Keats, as a modern poet, had great difficulty in finding an adequate dramatic figure for the final monomythic phase—the hero's return with his boon won from the depths.

THE "OBSTRUCTION"

Waking up in the forest of Mount Latmos, Endymion hears deep in the woods the lamentations of an Indian maid. She is another Kore-form of the Great Goddess, associated now, like "Artemis of the Wild Things," with the forest. But to Endymion, ignorant of the disguises of his love, she is simply an Indian maid.

Standard interpretations of the Indian maid have her representing human love, as the final and highest aspect of "the parable of the poetic soul in man seeking communion with the spirit of essential Beauty in the world." But as a representative of the highest form of love, namely human love, she is a very tricky woman. When Endymion first sees her she is lying "with all her limbs on tremble," "sweet as a muskrose upon new-made hay," moaning that she wants to be loved:

Is no one near to help me? . . .
....
No hand to toy with mine? No lips so sweet
That I may worship them? No eyelids meet
To twinkle on my bosom?
(End. IV.44-48)

Endymion naturally falls in love with her on the spot, and wants to "sip her tears." But when it comes right down to it, she will have nothing to do with him, she "may not be his love," she is forbidden, though she will not tell him why. She will live with him only in chastity, as his sister. To read this episode in terms of a moral allegory of Endymion's perfection through love of a real woman is to read it with curious disregard of the Indian maid's personality, which is not a very pleasant one, humanly speaking.

The fourth Book is really balanced on the motif of separation, division, the "obstruction" or "obstacle" of which Denis de Rougemont speaks. The lovers want something other than fulfillment in "earthy love" and their separations have a specious air. First they fall asleep on horseback and the Indian maid fades away while Endymion continues to sleep on in a cave. Then, when they meet again, she puts up an arbitrary and nameless taboo against love—though her limbs have been all "on tremble" before. The motif of obstruction is the only one dramatically feasible here, for the vegetation of the autumn forest is dying and, as vegetation daemon and fertility hero, Endymion's "kingdom's at its death": "and just it is," he says, "that I should die with it."

Fertility myth has an essential repetitiveness rather than progressiveness of episode, for the fertility hero has nothing to do but die and be reborn, die and be reborn, over and over again. In Endymion's release by the generating waters from the underworld of death, at the end of Book II, he has already had a rebirth. In Book III he won rebirth for thousands of dead people, and there he had his processional recognition and epiphany. The starlit writing on the sky told him that his mission was done, and that he is to awake now to new-born life like Adonis. If the monomythic return is to be carried out, he must go back to the forest of Mount Latmos where he started, but here it is not spring but fall, going into winter. It is time for him to die again.

When a hero is *under* the earth (buried), his rebirth can be dramatically accomplished by having him come out. When he is under the sea, again a dramatic figure of *anodos* is easy to arrange—he has only to come to the surface. But when he is on *top* of the earth and another rebirth or *anodos* figure is required, there is nothing to do with him but have him go into the air—which has no "top" to come out of, so he vanishes. Vanishing is not a very satisfactory dramatic conclusion, and the ending of *Endymion* is not a very satisfying one: one is left with no dramatic image of what this final apotheosis may be like. As to an allegory of moral progress in Book IV (which it would be quite natural for Keats to have intended), the essentially cyclical career of the fertility hero and the sad, confused uneasy tone of the fourth book do not support it.

Combined with the obstruction of the Indian maid's unnamed taboo, Endymion's own sense of being divided within himself by his three loves, of having no "identity," formulates the psychological impasse at which he has arrived. "He surely cannot now thirst for another love," the poet comments. Endymion wonders why he has been led "through the dark earth, and through the wondrous sea" only to fall in love again, and his sense of guilt makes him wish he were dead. "I have a triple soul!" he cries: "would I were whole in love!"

> What is this soul then? Whence
> Came it? It does not seem my own, and I
> Have no self-passion or identity.
> Some fearful end must be: where, where is it?
> By Nemesis, I see my spirit flit
> Alone about the dark— . . .
> (*End.* IV.475-80)

What identity is Keats defines in the notable "vale of soul-making" passage in the letters. He speaks of how souls acquire identities, "till each one is personally itself," "having identity given them—so as ever to possess a bliss peculiar to each one's individual existence." Poets—in another famous passage of the letters—have no identity:

> As to the poetical Character itself . . . it is not itself—it has no self—it is every thing and nothing—It has no character. . . . A Poet is the most unpoetical of any thing in existence; because he has no Identity—he is continually in for—and filling some other Body—The Sun, the Moon, the Sea and Men and Women who are creatures of impulse are poetical and have about them an unchangeable attribute—the poet has none; no identity. . . . (*Rollins* I.386-87)

In saying that the poet is "continually in for and filling some other body," he was saying what Rimbaud was to say later: *Je est un autre*. Maritain's comment on this is:

> In saying "*Je est un autre*," Rimbaud laid himself open to a kind of transmutation of his own being invaded and inhabited by all things, by the mysterious powers wandering in the world, by the *anima mundi*.[1]

Endymion, as a dramatic analogy of the fertility daemon, has the vocation of being *un autre*, of being "in for and filling some other body," for that is the moving principle of the fertility daemon's career—to be *in* the vine, to be *in* the corn, not as a separable spirit but as the vine itself, the corn itself. As hero of a mythical quest, he goes *into* the earth, the water, the air, and at the end of the quest he is to unite with the planetary fire.

But it is psychologically uncomfortable not to have an identity. One is a "fever of himself," like the Dreamer in *The Fall*, who confuses categories, mixes up pain and pleasure, suffers Dionysian tearings-asunder, deaths and rebirths. "Ever to possess a bliss peculiar to one's individual existence," to have "an unchangeable attribute," hero and poet seek their "anti-self," the Apollonian ideal of homeostasis or identity, not the Dionysian palingenesia, but the athanasia of the Olympians. But the difficulty in the last Book of *Endymion* is in finding a suitable dramatic and psychological figure for the transformation of the Dionysian into the Olympian, the poet into Apollo, Endymion into an "identity."

Another "death" is considered. The Indian maid has it on her mind:

> there's not a sound,
> Melodious howsoever, can confound
> The heavens and earth in one to such a death
> As doth the voice of love: . . .
> *(End.* IV.79-82)

Endymion, feeling that this earthly love has cut off his chances of the heroic achievement he has always dreamed of in his dreams under the moon—she has stolen "the wings wherewith I was to top the heavens," she is his "executioner"—asks her to be his "nurse" while he "dies":

> Be thou my nurse; and let me understand
> How dying I shall kiss that lily hand
> *(End.* IV.117-18)

Her tears have given him "a thirst to meet oblivion." He asks for "music dying," and she sings him her graceful Sorrow Song, which is about the deaths and rebirths in nature, the dying of maidens so that roses may bloom:

> O Sorrow,
> Why dost borrow
> The natural hue of health, from vermeil lips?—
> To give maiden blushes
> To the white rose bushes?
> Or is't thy dewy hand the daisy tips?
> *(End.* IV.146-51)

The song ends with a congeries of images of confused family relationships. The Sorrow to whom the maiden's song is addressed has been her nursing "babe"—"Like an own babe I nurse thee on my breast"—and also her mother, brother, playmate, and wooer:

> Thou art her mother,
> And her brother,
> Her playmate, and her wooer in the shade.
> *(End.* IV.288-90)

This family confusion is precisely the difficulty between the Indian maid and Endymion. The Great Goddess is not exogamous. She is mother, nurse, sister, playmate, and lover—as Endymion is babe, brother, and "wooer in the shade."

The evocation of a love-death continues. Endymion asks the maid to murder him by halves:

> Do gently murder half my soul, and I
> Shall feel the other half so utterly!
> *(End.* IV.309-10)

But then two horses spring out of the earth, "two steeds jet-black, each with large dark blue wings upon his back," and carry them into the air. The poet gets mixed up with Endymion here, for as Endymion flies away on the winged horse the poet gets giddy on the same flight:

> Muse of my native land, am I inspir'd?
> This is the giddy air, and I must spread
> Wide pinions to keep here; . . .
> *(End.* IV.354-56)

Then the god Sleep comes drifting by, on his way to the Moon's wedding. Under this influence Endymion and the Indian maid go to sleep on their horses:

> And on those pinions, level in mid air,
> Endymion sleepeth and the lady fair.
> Slowly they sail, slowly as icy isle
> Upon a calm sea drifting: and meanwhile
> The mornful wanderer dreams; Behold! he walks
> On heaven's pavement; brotherly he talks
> To divine powers: . . .
> *(End.* IV.403-9)

There follows a literary vision of what would happen to a

deified hero. Endymion sees Juno's peacocks pecking, tries Apollo's bow, asks about the golden apples, tries Athena's shield and Jove's thunderbolt; Hebe brings him something to drink, the four Seasons and the Hours perform a morris dance; Endymion sees a bugle and asks whose it is, is told it is Dian's, and suddenly sees the crescented goddess before him in his dream. This elaborate, self-conscious, and undreamlike dream is in a different psychological mode from the archetypal mode of Endymion's dreaming so far; it belongs to effete mythological convention and reflects the crippledness, confusion, and obscurity of Endymion's "fated way" at this point. What is needed is a way *out*, an *anodos*, and the poem seems to weave about rather helplessly trying to find what it should be. Endymion is dropped right back on his horse, in "perplexity," with the Indian maid for "bed-fellow." But she is asleep, and he groans, "Is there nought for me, upon the bourne of bliss, but misery?"

He drives the horses toward the galaxy of constellations, thinking of himself as Icarus,* "who died for soaring too audacious." The moon appears, the moon disappears; he turns to the Indian maid and she too is disappearing. He tried to kiss her hand "and, horror! kiss'd his own." Endymion's libido, at the moment, is in (as Freud would say) the narcissistic condition. His "object-libido," the Indian maid, has withdrawn, and he kisses his own hand instead of kissing hers.

THE SLEEP-HEALING

At this moment, with the Indian maid's disappearance, when the obstruction between Endymion and his love has become an absolute impasse, he does a very natural thing for a man in a situation of extreme anxiety and frustration: he goes to sleep in a dark cave (being already asleep on a horse that is

---

* In *Sleep and Poetry*, the same identification is made between the poet and Icarus: "let the hot sun melt my Dedalian wings, and drive me down convuls'd and headlong!" Here the poet is viewing his quest for "Poesy" with the desperation of Endymion in his quest for union with the Moon—a union that is a projection of the subliminal psychical state called "Poesy."

flying through the air). Since the whole poem *Endymion* is concerned with rebirth, a motif that is over-determined again and again in a great variety of ways in the poem, it is natural and to be expected that the Cave of Quietude where the hero sleeps should be associated with rebirth symbolism. But it should be noted that, at the level of poetic discourse, rebirth symbolism is not the same thing as regressive or pathological symbolism of retreat to the womb.

The passage involves a specific rebirth figure—that of the second birth of Dionysos. It is said that whoever enters the Cave of Quietude first takes a cool draught from an "urn," a drink that is richer than anything drunk by Semele in "her maternal longing." A few lines later, the "spirit-home" of the cave is said to be "pregnant" to "save" Endymion in its depths. Semele was the mother of Dionysos, and the analogy is thus drawn between the strange double birth of Dionysos, and the pregnancy of the cave which saves Endymion. When Semele was seven months pregnant with Dionysos, Jupiter appeared to her in thunder and lightning and she had a miscarriage from fright; whereupon the father-god snatched up the babe and put it in his own thigh, and carried it—saved it—to the natural term of pregnancy. (This is typical Olympian and patriarchal myth, revising more ancient cult-myth to fit a new orthodoxy: the mother has nothing to do with the birth of her own child—a biology that is legally proved in the *Eumenides*, as well as in *Tristram Shandy*.) The myth of the double birth of Dionysos rationalizes what had always been true of the rites of his cult, which were rites not of birth but of rebirth. In the passage on the Cave of Quietude, the cave is called a "spirit-home," for Endymion is to be "spiritualized" here for mystic marriage with the Great Goddess. Spirit-birth, or birth in the spirit, is rebirth. Semele was mother of Dionysos in the flesh, Jupiter in the spirit.

The description is as follows:

> There lies a den,
> Beyond the seeming confines of the space
> Made for the soul to wander in and trace

Its own existence, of remotest glooms.
Dark regions are around it, where the tombs
Of buried griefs the spirit sees, . . .
. . . .
                       the man is yet to come
Who hath not journeyed in this native hell.
But few have ever felt how calm and well
Sleep may be had in that deep den of all
. . . .
                            Enter none
Who strive therefore: on the sudden it is won.
Just when the sufferer begins to burn,
Then it is free to him; and from an urn,
Still fed by melting ice, he takes a draught—
Young Semele such richness never quaft
In her maternal longing! Happy gloom!
Dark Paradise! where pale becomes the bloom
Of health by due; where silence dreariest
Is most articulate; where hopes infest;
Where those eyes are the brightest far that keep
Their lids shut longest in a dreamless sleep.
O happy spirit-home! O wondrous soul!
Pregnant with such a den to save the whole
In thine own depth. Hail, gentle Carian!
For, never since thy griefs and woes began,
Hast thou felt so content: a grievous feud
Hath led thee to this Cave of Quietude.
               (*End.* IV.512-48)

As to the deathly associations of the cave, it is said to be
located beyond the proper confines of the space where the
soul ordinarily "traces its existence"—which would seem to
suggest that it is located beyond existence itself, but this other
kind of "space" could be that of sleep as well as of death.
Nevertheless the imagery of dark regions, glooms, tombs, an
urn, and so on, is death-imagery. The earth-cave is tomb as
well as womb, and a cave may be a grave as well as a womb-
symbol; in those cave-burials where the corpse is doubled up

in the position of a foetus, it is both. In going to sleep, Endymion is certainly under a compulsion to repeat what he has been doing from the beginning of the poem, namely, sleeping: but then, his mythical character is that of a sleeper. He is also obeying the "pleasure principle," for the cave is a "Happy gloom! Dark Paradise!" and he is happy to get rid of his "grievous feud" for a little while: "never since thy griefs and woes began, Hast thou felt so content." Ritualistically considered, the sleep in the Cave of Quietude, like the six-day sleep of Gilgamesh, is both a sleep-healing and a sleep of initiation: that is, a gathering of psychical powers for the vital transformation of the sleeper.

THE MARRIAGE OF THE HERO AND THE MOON

The "moonlight Emperor," Endymion, has still to come into his empire. The necessary remaining rite is a "Mystic Marriage," with the goddess whose absolute majesty has been veiled all this time. Large preparations for the marriage have been made. While Endymion was sleeping in the Cave of Quietude, all the constellations were gathering for the wedding: Hesperus, Aquarius, Castor and Pollux, the Lion, the Bear, the Centaur, Andromeda—cosmic imagery which Jung says is always a sign of the overwhelmingly psychic presence of an archetype. But the obstruction is still working on Endymion's fate, and his cosmic dream-horse has disappointingly dropped him back on the earth. "His first touch of the earth went nigh to kill," and he feels that he has

> clung
> To nothing, lov'd a nothing, nothing seen
> Or felt but a great dream!
> (*End.* IV.636-38)

He makes plans of despair for a forest retreat for himself and the Indian maid:

Under the brow

Of some steep mossy hill, where ivy dun
Would hide us up, although spring leaves were none;

....

Dusk for our loves, . . .

....

The mountaineer

Thus strove by fancies vain and crude to clear
His briar'd path to some tranquillity.
(*End.* IV.670-76, 721-23)

The poem had started in spring, with the offering of April first fruits in the festival of Pan; it ends in autumn, the season of the death of the vegetation daemon. Endymion prepares to die, while night strews "myriads of lingering leaves" on the grass. "Nor much it grieves to die," he says, "when summer dies on the cold sward." He lies all day in the forest, "and so remain'd as he a corpse had been." He is unconscious, in his despair, that this "death" is a sacrifice made to guarantee perpetual renewal of life—

whence will befal,

As say these sages, health perpetual
To shepherds and their flocks; . . .
(*End.* IV.830-32)

But suddenly the Indian maid's black hair becomes golden, her eyes blue, and she tells him that

'twas fit that from this mortal state

Thou shouldst, my love, by some unlook'd for change
Be spiritualiz'd.
(*End.* IV.991-93)

This unlooked for change was apparently accomplished in the Cave of Quietude, the Chamber of New Birth. All that remains to be done is to have the wedding, which has been so long in preparation. A Mystic Marriage was a traditional part of fertility mysteries.

In the ritual organization of Endymion, the mystic marriage has been given every preparation for coming at the end of the poem. But it is November, the leaves are falling, and Keats has filled up his quota of a thousand lines for the book. He finishes it off quickly with three or four more lines, by having Endymion and the golden-haired Kore vanish, after which

> Peona went
> Home through the gloomy wood in wonderment.
> (*End*. IV.1002-03)

All the ambiguities of the poem are collected together here at this final point, where the sacred marriage and the sacred birth should occur in a dramatic figure. But Keats leaves it a blank. In the Great Pyramid, a veil hangs before the throne in the throne-room where the Osirian apotheosis is accomplished. Keats's Great Goddess is a veiled majesty—veiled Cybele in the labyrinthine abyss of the second book, "veil'd Melancholy" in her "sovran shrine" in the "Ode on Melancholy," veiled Ops in *Hyperion*, and the veiled priestess of Cybele, Moneta, in *The Fall of Hyperion*. As for a dramatic figure of the birth of the new-born god, Endymion has already gone into and issued from the Cave of Quietude, but he has not yet been seen in an image of metamorphosis which would show how he looked in his divine form. The tomb in the Osirian mysteries, behind the veiled throne, was an open tomb— it was empty.

But the whole of Book IV is under an atmosphere of sadness and confused lack of issue. According to Heinrich Zimmer, this sadness is appropriate to the last act of the story of the monomythic hero. He says:

> The representations that have come down to us in Celtic fairy tale and Arthurian romance disclose features deriving from the primitive matriarchal civilization that flourished throughout western France and in the British Isles in pre-Celtic times. Among the multitudinous females of the ageless lineage of motherhood, descending age by age from the primordial great-great-grandmother of the mat-

rilineal clan, the knight, the manly youth, the boy hero (*puer aeternus*), being wearied of his long adventure, discovers at last his rest. Higher he has come—to this hidden sanctuary of the fountainhead—for a solution of the riddle of life and death. And here he shall win the long-desired and withheld reply. His oracle shall be maternal womanhood, the unspoken intuitive wisdom of the life force which, by its living presence, shall make intelligible to him the mystery of its own repeated rebirth through the transient generations.

The realm, however, as described in the romances, is not precisely one of happiness. It is a region of a certain bliss, but destitute of action and adventure, a world of the departed, a sort of exile, beyond struggle and strife. . . .

That dim domain has been for millenniums the holy goal of all the great questing heroes, from Gilgamesh to Faust, for it is the repository of the spiritual treasure of the mystic wisdom of rebirth. The keys that unlock the tabernacle of life unending are to be discovered there, and the boon of immortality itself. But the hero discovers then that he is bound (as all mankind is bound) to the maternal principle of Mother Earth, Mother Life, bound to the ever-revolving wheel of life-through-death; and he becomes enwrapped therewith in the heroic melancholy that was known to all the valiant seekers of yore who descended into the abyss of the domain beyond. Gawain is such a hero. Gawain is shrouded in the composed sadness of Gilgamesh and Aeneas.[2]

This is the sadness, also, of the last book of *Endymion*.

IV. The Ravished Bride

THE MARBLE URN in Keats's "Ode on a Grecian Urn" is addressed as "Thou still unravish'd bride." The relief carvings on the urn depict a fertility orgy, with young men and maidens in erotic pursuit of each other through the forest. But the curious thing about this traditional orgiastic rite of spring is that there is no ravishing. The lovers can "never, never" kiss, never, never get any closer to each other, because they are transfixed in marble. The maidens, like the urn itself, are "still unravished brides." In the five poems we shall consider in this chapter, the brides all lose their virginity. In one of the poems (*The Eve*), the hero and his ravished bride simply vanish into the night, like Endymion and the moon-maiden. The other four show an increasingly somber and violent picture of what happens when the ideal love-maiden allows herself to be loved. In *Isabella* the hero is killed by her brothers as a direct consequence of the lovers' mating. In *Lamia* he dies from shock on finding, by the light of reason, that she is actually a daemon from the underworld, whose real form is a snake. In "La Belle Dame," she is shown to be a wholesale murderess of men, and after the seduction the hero is turned into a specter. At the end of this sequence we shall consider Keats's love-affair with Fanny Brawne and the role she played as "ravished bride." From what is known of Fanny, she seems to have been a chaste, pure-minded girl, but Keats insisted, with the obsessiveness of overwhelming fantasy, that she was a loose flirt, unchaste, promiscuous. As sexual love-object, she was doomed to be one of the cast of characters in his mythical plot, and with complete consistency he accused her, when he was dying, of being his murderess.

Scholars have pointed out various specific literary "sources" for the poems in this series, but the one significant point about the sources is a point that is never made: namely, that each of them is itself a reworking of earlier and yet earlier sources—

anonymous traditional tales of ritual origin. The images (of character, setting, action) to which Keats was consistently attracted in his reading were of the kind Jung calls "primordial." Our method is to observe the functions of these images in the poems under the dynamic organization of plot or *mythos* and in two main interlocking modes of significance: their mode as energetic psychical entities, images that arise spontaneously to focus the great crises of life in an order of drama; and their mode as historical and protohistorical responses to the same crises, for this latter method of observation shows their collective role and thus the multiple magnitudes of reality they embrace.

THE MAIDEN IN THE LABYRINTH:
The Eve of St. Agnes

In *The Eve of St. Agnes*, the hero enters a dangerous castle where the love-maiden is immured, finds his way by tortuous passages to the secret, inner chamber where she sleeps, and there consummates a mystic marriage with her under the enchantments of a holy night. This glowing ritual of love and youth takes place in mid-winter, during freezing cold and icy storm. An old man and old woman die the same night, decrepit, abandoned, frozen to death. The poem suggests no moral reason why they should die, for they are "good" characters: old Angela has guided the hero through the labyrinth and helped him carry off his bride-theft, and the old man has had nothing to do with the plot at all, but has been saying his prayers all night.

This apparently gratuitous sacrifice of the old people is poetically sustained by more than aesthetic, textural contrast. The aesthetic contrast itself—of cold age with warm youth, death with love, "winter" with "spring"—suggests the ancient season ritual by which the plot takes its form: the supplantation of the old year by the new year, the killing of winter by spring.

Keats's poem builds its chief effects out of magical enterprise and supernatural associations, so that criticism—sensitive to moral cohesiveness—is not alerted at all to the moral outrage in the fact that a good old man and woman die in brutal cold and neglect while a youth deflowers a virgin, getting into her bed while she is asleep.

Actually, there is nothing supernatural in what happens. The girl innocently carries out the formula of St. Agnes' Eve, which allows a maiden to see her future husband in a dream. Madeline has fasted all day and kept her mind on her lover, so that it is quite likely that she will dream about him. Meanwhile Porphyro manages to enter the castle, avoiding a fight with her "hyena" kinsmen; the old crone takes him to the girl's room, he gets in bed with her, and she wakes up to see what she has been dreaming about. Nevertheless, by the subtle and elaborate use of magical suggestion, the union of the lovers seems an occult event, taking place in the realm of the daemonic. In the underlying myth, this is where it really does take place; and in that daemonic realm the death of the old people is not gratuitous but necessary. What disenables criticism of this event is not only Keats's craft in manipulating "faery" detail, but the strong unconscious intuition of the reader that the ritual plot is traditional and inevitable.

As if to shore up the daemonism with religious sanction, the poem has a Christian vestibule, so to speak, in the three opening stanzas. Here the old beadsman, a "holy man," performs his penance on the saint's night, in the chapel of the castle. This also is a ritual of the casting out of evil. The old man tells his rosary, saying his prayers to the Virgin's picture, and then among

> Rough ashes sat he for his soul's reprieve,
> And all night kept awake, for sinners's sake to
> grieve. . . .
>
> (*Eve* III)

He is surrounded by the dead in attitudes of prayer, purgatorially emprisoned by freezing iron and stone:

> The sculptur'd dead, on each side, seem to freeze,
> Emprison'd in black, purgatorial rails:

> Knights, ladies, praying in dumb orat'ries,
> He passeth by; and his weak spirit fails
> To think how they may ache in icy hoods and mails.
>   (*Eve* II)

Old age, death, and winter cold are identified in the associative imagery:

> St. Agnes' Eve—Ah, bitter chill it was!
> ....
>   —already had his deathbell rung;
> The joys of all his life were said and sung:
> His was harsh penance on St. Agnes' Eve: ...
>   (*Eve* I)

The poem does not mention the old man once again until the very last lines, where his and old Angela's death rounds out the warm and rosy ritual of young love:

>   Angela the old
>   Died palsy-twitch'd, with meagre face deform;
>   The Beadsman, after thousand aves told,
>   For aye unsought for slept among his ashes cold.
>   (*Eve* XLII)

The *pathos* and *sparagmos* of the mythical action are split off or displaced onto the minor characters. Keats wrote about "the faery power of unreflecting love" in *The Eve*, where love is consummated under specifically magical agency, and where death is displaced upon the old people instead of cutting down the poet before he has fulfilled his daemonic role as the living grain of the poetic ripening.

The "peerless bride" whom the hero is to win is consistently thought of as more than mortal, an angelic being, having—through St. Agnes—direct correspondence with heaven. In the mythical mode of *Endymion*, the bride is really a goddess, but in the romance mode of *The Eve* the word "seems" does the same work of characterizing her as a heavenly spirit. Immediately after the old Beadsman has been left at his prayers of penance, the associative imagery begins to build its cunning suggestions of angelism, and the "sculptur'd dead" freezing in the chapel are replaced by angel-caryatids holding up cornices in the great halls where dancing and revelry are going on:

> The carved angels, ever eager-eyed,
> Star'd, where upon their heads the cornice rests,
> With hair blown back, and wings put cross-wise on
> their breasts.
> (*Eve* IV)

Amidst the throng of dancers, Madeline is bemused in her fantasy, under "wing'd St. Agnes' saintly care," thinking of the love-magic she is to perform as soon as the "hallow'd hour" approaches. Hidden outside the doors of the castle, which he is forbidden to enter, Porphyro dreams of how he may gaze at her and "worship." Madeline retires to her chamber, "all akin to the spirits of the air," holding a silver taper like "a mission'd spirit." The casements of her chamber are of stained glass like those of a chapel, emblazoned with "twilight saints," and she kneels there to pray, hands folded over the silver cross on her breast, aureoled like an angel in the moonlit glow of the stained glass: "she knelt, so pure a thing, so free from mortal taint."

> Full on this casement shone the wintry moon,
> And threw warm gules on Madeline's fair breast,
> As down she knelt for heaven's grace and boon;
> Rose-bloom fell on her hands, together prest,
> And on her silver cross soft amethyst,
> And on her hair a glory, like a saint:
> She seem'd a splendid angel, newly drest,
> Save wings, for heaven: . . .
> (*Eve* XXV)

Sleeping, she is compared to the closed book of the Mass in a country of the pagan: "clasp'd like a missal where swart Paynims pray." Her chamber is paradise where she is a "seraph fair"; she is Porphyro's heaven and he her eremite; she is his silver shrine and he is a "famish'd pilgrim" there, "sav'd by miracle." In the *mythos* of romantic love that dominates the poem, all of this exalted religious idiom tends to make of Madeline, not just a mortal virgin, but an incarnation of the Virgin herself, "fair woman as pure goddess"—although the miracle by which she saves Porphyro is to allow him to take her virginity.

The monomythic motif of combat with kin for possession of the bride appears indirectly in the poem as stratagem. The obstacle to the lovers' union, which forms the plot-complication, is that there is a blood-feud between their families—as between the Montagues and Capulets in *Romeo and Juliet*. For Porphyro, the castle holds

> barbarian hordes,
> Hyena foemen, and hot-blooded lords,
> Whose very dogs would execrations howl
> Against his lineage: . . .
> (*Eve* X)

There is "old lord Maurice" and "dwarfish Hildebrand," who have cursed the hero, his house and his land. To carry off his bride-theft, he has to do it despite enemies "more fang'd than wolves and bears" and "dragons all around, at glaring watch"— a suggestion of the "dragon-battle" of monomyth. But the hero-test of combat is turned into a test of strategy: Porphyro has the wit to blandish the old crone Angela into guiding him secretly to his love's chamber. Angela plays the part of the magic "helper" of fairy tale, despised and apparently feeble— she is "a poor, weak, palsy-stricken, churchyard thing," with "agues in her brain." But in the mythical background, she corresponds with the old "nurse" of the fertility mummings, who brings up the daemonic child and helps find him a bride. She calls Porphyro "my child," and he looks at her like an "urchin":

> Feebly she laugheth in the languid moon,
> While Porphyro upon her face doth look,
> Like puzzled urchin on an aged crone
> Who keepeth clos'd a wond'rous riddle-book.
> (*Eve* XV)

In the mythical quest-model, as described by Joseph Camp-bell, the hero passes a "threshold" and enters into "a region of supernatural wonder: fabulous forces are there encountered and a decisive victory is won. . . ."[1] In *The Eve*, the field of daemonic forces is the castle itself, whose threshold the hero must cross. At first he is hiding outside it, "beside the portal doors, buttress'd from moonlight." Then he "ventures in." Old Angela, with her ancient wisdom of the occult, tells him in a shocked whisper that to bring off this venture he must be lord of all the daemonic powers:

> Thou must hold water in a witch's sieve,
> And be liege-lord of all the Elves and Fays,
> To venture so. . . .
> *(Eve* XIV)

The motif of the magic castle, palace, or temple, with a super-natural female at the heart of it, is a constant one from Keats's earliest to his most mature poetry. The danger at the threshold, the physical seclusion and secrecy, the occultism and sense of moral taboo surrounding the woman, are carried out in the architectural image.

In the castle there are passages through "little doors," other hall doors heard opening and shutting at a distance, and "many a dusky gallery" where the old woman leads Porphyro, her "aged eyes aghast from fright of dim espial"—and the castle image also serves for his own beating heart, which is "Love's fev'rous citadel."

> He follow'd through a lowly arched way,
> Brushing the cobwebs with his lofty plume,
> And as she mutter'd "Well-a—well-a-day!"
> He found him in a little moonlight room,
> Pale, lattic'd, chill, and silent as a tomb.
> "Now tell me where is Madeline," said he,
> "O tell me, Angela, by the holy loom
> Which none but secret sisterhood may see,
> When they St. Agnes' wool are weaving piously."
> *(Eve* XII)

In the little tomb-like room with the old witch, Porphyro's swearing by the loom which the "secret sisterhood" weaves carries a suggestion of the loom woven by the ancient Fates, fabulously ugly, secretive old women who brought men through birth, life, and death—a sisterhood of which Angela herself appears to be one. She hides Porphyro in a closet opening into Madeline's chamber where he can spy on the girl while she undresses.

The passage through the castle-maze corresponds with ancient labyrinth ritual of initiation, presided over by a priestess of the Great Goddess (who was the original of the triple Fates) and leading to a radical reorientation of personality and a mysterious revelation at the center. In *The Eve of St. Agnes*, the hero's passage through the castle-maze to reach the maiden at its center is a pattern that follows the grooves of this deep-laid background, but it also follows grooves of the mind, where the love-maiden is taboo and must be approached tortuously, and, at a still deeper psychological level, where the sexual penetration is itself a dangerous entrance into a labyrinth.

The sleeping castle with the maiden asleep at its center, to be awakened by the hero, is a parallel of the story of Sleeping Beauty. Joseph Campbell says of the legendary sleeping castle that it "is that ultimate abyss to which the descending consciousness submerges in dream."[2] But the castle-labyrinth-maiden configuration is more specific than this and suggests more than a generalized symbol of the unconscious. In the Circe episode and the Indian maid episode of *Endymion*, and in *Lamia* and "La Belle Dame" (each with its palace, "grot," or castle), as well as in Keats's love-letters and poems to Fanny Brawne, the female who involves the hero in love is an enchantress who ensnares and entrammels him, cuts off wings of his freedom, makes him her thrall, her captured and emprisoned slave. She is a net and a trap. In their purely kinetic aspect, the maze-figure and the figure of entrammelment are the same, though in different poetic contexts they may have opposite emotional associations—the castle-maze in *The Eve* and the labyrinth in *Endymion* leading to transcendent erotic consummation, while entrammelment in the other poems leads to the lover's death or the death of his masculine ambition. The ambiguous maze-image is thus a kinetic or architectural counterpart of the ambiguous sexual taboo with which all the "brides" of the poems are invested (translated poetically as the taboo of their supernatural or angelic character); for taboo or *mana* is essentially ambiguous, both sacred and dreadful, holy and menacing; and in the sublimation of the seraphic maiden of *The Eve* there is psychologically implicit the dreadfulness of the daemonic brides of *Lamia* and "La Belle Dame."

The ambivalence of archetypal imagery, the way in which such an image can be transplanted from inside to outside, from male to female, and the reverse of these movements, is illustrated in the detail of Keats's poetic idiom. Porphyro's heart is a "fev'rous citadel" while he enters the citadel that holds the maiden. The thought of his sexual stratagem comes to him "like a full-blown rose," flushing his brow and making "purple riot" in his heart, whereas it is the rose of the maiden that he is going to deflower. Madeline is his "silver shrine"; Endymion's goddess has an actual shrine at the end of a labyrinthine passage—a little mimic temple, as Madeline's chamber is a little mimic chapel. Endymion's thoughts of his mistress wander about "the labyrinth in his soul of love," while he himself is wandering in a "thousand mazes" searching for his love. Lamia's lover wants to "trammel up and snare" her in his soul and "labyrinth her there," but it is he who is tangled in her mesh, labyrinthed in her "palace of sweet sin." Images of this kind are like nuclei that can pass from one cluster of associations into different—even opposite—clusters of association. Hence the impossibility of attaching univocal symbolic meaning to them.

The inner chamber of the castle, where Madeline sleeps her charmed sleep under the spells of St. Agnes, is an architectural variation of the paradisal seed-place so frequent in Keats's poetry. This point of epiphany for the consummation of love is, in its natural form, associated with vegetation, for the sacramental aspect of love-making is direct communion with the body of nature. In *Isabella*, the lovers meet in a "bower of hyacinth and musk," a place secret and apart from the world; Endymion and his goddess make love in a cave of golden moss and under-earth plants; the fertility god Adonis waits for Venus to come to him in a vine-embraced garden. The carved decor of Madeline's chamber is of fruits and flowers and grasses. But the imagery of all Keats's love-bowers is subtly modulated to context, and here the mediaevalistic and religious idiom of the poem gives to the little room glowing stained-glass coloring, like a chapel.

> A casement high and triple-arch'd there was,
> All garlanded with carven imag'ries
> Of fruits, and flowers, and bunches of knot-grass,
> And diamonded with panes of quaint device,
> Innumerable of stains and splendid dyes,
> As are the tiger-moth's deep-damask'd wings;
> And in the midst, 'mong thousand heraldries,
> And twilight saints, and dim emblazonings,
> A shielded scutcheon blush'd with blood of queens
> and kings.
>
> (*Eve* XXV)

In its architectural mode, the chamber is analogous to the image of the secret garden where natural desire enjoys itself without conflict—Baudelaire's "*innocent paradis, plein de plaisirs furtifs,*" where "*tout n'est qu'ordre et beauté, luxe, calme, et volupté.*"

The high religious character of the act that is to be performed is reflected in Porphyro's sacred fear as he enters "this paradise," where the maiden of the virginal rose sleeps "as though a rose should shut, and be a bud again." As the threshold of a castle must be crossed for the hero to enter the field of daemonic force, so the ritual sleep of Madeline affords another and psychical limen of the adventure, beyond which lies the mysterious abyss of instinct, alive in the unconscious. It is here that Joseph Campbell's comment on the legendary sleeping castle applies: "that ultimate abyss to which the descending consciousness submerges in dream." In Keats's later poetry the initiatory sleep of dream-vision reappears regularly as an image of the mind's crossing a boundary into an unknown place of revelation. In *Endymion* Adonis sleeps and

Venus enters his dream; Endymion himself has to fall asleep to obtain voluptuary fulfillment and "win an immortality of passion." But here it is the maiden who sleeps and the lover who must pass the boundary of her dream and enter it. In *Isabella* the lover also comes to the girl in a dream, but Lorenzo is the slain lover, the autumn lover, the dying year, buried under fallen leaves—he has had his springtime with the May Queen. Porphyro is the new lover, the waking year, who must break through the wintry, icy spell of sleep in which his mistress lies:

> 'twas a midnight charm
> Impossible to melt as iced stream: . . .
> (*Eve* XXXII)

To break the charm of the winter night where she lies under "enchantment cold," he has to perform a sacramental act of food-magic. Food-magic and love-magic are inseparable in the re-awakening of life. This primitive cluster of associations has profound authority in the mind, for human fertility is confirmed by love and vital continuity is confirmed by food. In language, the symbols of eating and making love are interchangeable. Keats's erotic sequences, as well as those having the character of religious revelation, inevitably involve *participation mystique* through food.

The old witch Angela has stored food in the closet where Porphyro was hiding, and now he prepares a splendid banquet, for Madeline has been fasting all day and she will probably be hungry when she wakes up.

> And still she slept an azure-lidded sleep,
> In blanched linen, smooth, and lavender'd,
> While he from forth the closet brought a heap
> Of candied apple, quince, and plum, and gourd;
> With jellies soother than the creamy curd,
> And lucent syrops, tinct with cinnamon;
> Manna and dates, in argosy transferr'd
> From Fez; and spiced dainties, every one
> From silken Samarcand to cedar'd Lebanon.
> (*Eve* XXX)

These foods have an *Arabian Nights* flavor, suitable to the gorgeousness of the poem's decor, but they also formally duplicate the feast prepared for Endymion in the Garden of Adonis to adjust his senses for the epiphany of the love-goddess. In the feast set out by Porphyro there are plums, the "creamy curd" of jellies, and manna—whereas Endymion is given plums fit for an infant's gums, cream skimmed by the nurse Amalthea, and manna from Syrian trees. Manna is a mystery food. The Belle Dame will also feed the knight-at-arms "manna-dew" when she puts him under her love-enchantment. Keats's poems and letters to Fanny Brawne are full of the same idiom: she is his "feast" and his "sacramental cake."

In *The Eve of St. Agnes*, the banquet that Porphyro prepares is not eaten. The lovers make love instead. The food is necessary though it does not need to be eaten, for it is an offering to the fertility powers,* to put the young lovers into community with daemonic forces of instinct that are the human analogue of the powers fertilizing the food-producing earth.

Food and sexual fulfillment are the sole and prime requirements that instinct places upon the outside world, the one sustaining the body, the other sustaining the race. Between them they create all human reality. Their symbols—along with the symbols of death—are the ultimate and controlling archetypes.

In ritual drama the sacramental taking or presentation of food, or the planting of seed-food, leads immediately to the call of resurrection, like the cry of voices that awakens Adonis, lord of life, from his sleep, immediately after the sacramental feast in *Endymion*:

> Come! come!
> Arise! awake! Clear summer has forth walk'd . . .
> ....
> Once more sweet life begin!
> (*End.* II.501-06)

---

* In a canceled line, the viands are called a "sacrifice."

So, also, in *The Eve of St. Agnes*, after Porphyro has prepared the feast in "lustrous salvers," he cries to his love to awake from her winter-bound sleep:

> These delicates he heap'd with glowing hand
> On golden dishes and in baskets bright
> Of wreathed silver: sumptuous they stand
> In the retired quiet of the night,
> Filling the chilly room with perfume light.—
> "And now, my love, my seraph fair, awake!"
>
> (*Eve* XXXI)

Looked upon as an element in the action of a love-story about a youth's obtaining his bride despite the furious hostility of her kinsfolk, the extensive formal description of Porphyro's setting the table with luxurious foods that are not to be eaten is, like the death of old Angela and the beadsman, a plot throw-away, a useless element not integral to plot-complication. But the reader does not feel this way, and his sense of justification for the uneaten banquet is like his sense of justification for the old people's deaths. It is more than a feeling for brilliant textural decor; it is an instinctive sense of the relationship of food and love—as, with the death of the old people, it is a sense of the symbolic relationship of warm youth and love and wintry age and death. The sacral character of the food is indicated by its not being eaten—however hungry Madeline may be after her fast. It is for presentation only, as a symbolic mode of contact with fertility powers, a mode of invoking them for the bridal union that is to take place. Porphyro's test as hero in a fertility drama has not been the usual monomythic test of combat but is the test of his skill and efficacy in carrying out the magical food-ritual so that the sexual initiation will be successful—for, after all, the maiden is a sheltered virgin and she may be traumatized by finding her lover actually in her bed. What would be otherwise a mean and brutal trick, a ruthless defloration, is converted by the strength and authority of the mythical substrate and the sacramental approach of the lover, into a high religious act, the resurrection of life from its wintry sleep. At Porphyro's

call to his love to awake, she opens her eyes and sees in reality
what she has been dreaming about:

> Her eyes were open, but she still beheld,
> Now wide awake, the vision of her sleep: . . .
> (*Eve* XXXIV)

In the famous passage in his letters about "Negative Ca-
pability" Keats says:

> It struck me, what quality went to form a Man of Achieve-
> ment especially in Literature & which Shakespeare pos-
> sessed so enormously—I mean *Negative Capability*, that
> is when man is capable of being in uncertainties, Mys-
> teries, doubts, without any irritable reaching after fact &
> reason—Coleridge, for instance, would let go by a fine
> isolated verisimilitude caught from the Penetralium of
> mystery, from being incapable of remaining content with
> half knowledge. (*Rollins* I.193-94)

The phrase "a fine isolated verisimilitude caught from the
Penetralium of mystery" is an expert definition of what we
call an archetype—an image or "verisimilitude" rising out of
the mysterious penetralia of the primary unconscious process
where human responses to the conditions of life are first shaped.
It is through these penetralia that Porphyro goes when he fol-
lows his old guide through the castle labyrinth, to waken the
dream-maiden of young love "asleep in lap of legends old."

The next movement of the poem is the "mystic marriage."
When Madeline opens her eyes, Porphyro is kneeling beside
the bed "pale as smooth-sculptured stone." She weeps a little
from the shock of seeing him, and then his stillness and pallor
make her think that he is dead or dying:

> How chang'd thou art! how pallid, chill, and drear!
> Give me that voice again, my Porphyro,
> Those looks immortal, those complainings dear!
> Oh leave me not in this eternal woe,
> For if thou diest, my love, I know not where to go.
> (*Eve* XXXV)

This is one of Keats's usual variations on death-in-love or "love-death," as when Endymion swoons from love and the Moon-maiden implores him not to die or she will die too—

> Revive, dear youth, or I shall faint and die;
> Revive, or these soft hours will hurry by
> In tranced dullness; speak, and let that spell
> Affright this lethargy!
> (*End.* II.766-69)

But then Porphyro regains his "looks immortal" and rises up "beyond a mortal man impassion'd," throbbing like a star.* This imagery of transfiguration—statue, star, and "immortal" appearance—corresponds with Endymion's immortalization by mystic marriage with his goddess. Porphyro "melts" into Madeline's dream—which is to say, he gets into her bed (Keats insisted on his literal meaning here). The idiom is similar to Endymion's when he says to the Moon-maiden, "O let me melt into thee" (*End.* II.107). The sexual union—called a "miracle"—is accomplished under the usual Keatsian flower-figure (or "defloration" figure) of a blending of rose and violet:

> Beyond a mortal man impassion'd far
> At these voluptuous accents, he arose,
> Ethereal, flush'd, and like a throbbing star
> Seen mid the sapphire heaven's deep repose;
> Into her dream he melted, as the rose
> Blendeth its odour with the violet, . . .
> (*Eve* XXXVI)

The image-base in this passage—the configuration of "throbbing star," dreaming maiden, and the lovers' embrace on the borderline of sleep—is the same as that of the "Bright Star" sonnet. Whereas the star "seen mid the sapphire heaven's deep repose" is a metaphor here for Porphyro, in the sonnet the "stedfast" star is external, "in lone splendour hung aloft the night," while the lover lies "unchangeable" upon his

---

* Stanley Edgar Hyman has suggested that this type of imagery, here and in *Endymion*, is "erection imagery."

"fair love's ripening breast." Kenneth Burke, speaking of the ambiguity of the " 'transcendent' sexual consummation" or love-death in the sonnet—

> Still, still to hear her tender-taken breath,
> And so live ever—or else swoon to death—

says that the final line may be read as "naming states not simply alternative but also synonymous":[3] living forever in the love-embrace and swooning to death in it are the same thing. This ambiguity may be read also in the last episode of *The Eve*, where the lovers disappear into the night immediately after their union, just as Endymion and the Moon-maiden disappear at the moment of their mystic marriage.

In fairy tales of a similar kind, like that of Sleeping Beauty, the hero, after passing his "tests," penetrating the labyrinth, and obtaining the bride, issues to become the reigning king, awakening the land to fertility and prosperity. This is the monomythic phase of "return" of which Campbell speaks.[4] But Keats makes a radical change in the ending of the fairy-tale model, by having the lovers disappear forever in the dream-region of daemonic power. There is an authentic historical and cultural sense in the fact that "these lovers fled away, ages long ago," for Porphyro and Madeline belong to ritual and romance, and they fled away with the death of myth. But there is also a psychological dimension to their disappearance at the moment of the love-union. The night into which they vanish forever is a deeper and darker magnitude of their dream-embrace in the deathly enchanted sleep which is the dominant magical motif of the poem.

As the lovers glide away "like phantoms," the faery storm from across the moors sends cold draughts through the dark hallways of the castle; the arras

> Flutter'd in the besieging wind's uproar;
> And the long carpets rose along the gusty floor.
>
> They glide, like phantoms, into the wide hall;
> Like phantoms, to the iron porch, they glide; . . .

....

> And they are gone: aye, ages long ago
> These lovers fled away into the storm.
> (*Eve* XL, XLI, XLII)

One visualizes them floating forever in that storm, like the lovers in the sonnet "As Hermes once. . . ." This sonnet is on a real dream that Keats had, and of which he wrote in a letter,

> The dream was one of the most delightful enjoyments I ever had in my life—I floated about the whirlwind atmosphere as it is described with a beautiful figure to whose lips mine were joined it seem'd for an age . . . o that I could dream it every night. (*Rollins* II.91)

Strangely, this dream Keats found so enjoyable is of the lovers Paolo and Francesca in the fifth canto of Dante's *Inferno*, the doomed pair who are carried in eternal embrace on the sad whirlwind to the daemonic underworld. The dreamer is himself the lover, who escapes from "the dragon-world" with "all its hundred eyes"—as the lovers in *The Eve* escape from "sleeping dragons all around, at glaring watch." As Porphyro and Madeline flee away into a faery storm, the dreamer goes to

> that second circle of sad hell,
> Where in the gust, the whirlwind, and the flaw
> Of rain and hail-stones, lovers need not tell
> Their sorrows. Pale were the sweet lips I saw,
> Pale were the lips I kiss'd, and fair the form
> I floated with, about that melancholy storm.
> ("As Hermes once . . .")

In dreams, pallor is the signature of death. Whereas the love-union in this and the "Bright Star" sonnet, in *Endymion* and *The Eve of St. Agnes*, is a deathly transcendence without return, in the other poems in this sequence it is actual murder.

THE HEAD-BURIAL: *Isabella, or The Pot of Basil*

As *Endymion* begins with the rites of spring, develops while "the year grows lush in juicy stalks," and ends with the hero lying like a corpse in the autumn woods, so this poem follows the seasonal course of vegetation. Isabella and Lorenzo fall in love in May:

> A whole long month of May in this sad plight
> Made their cheeks paler by the break of June: . . .
> (*Is*. III)

Their union is consummated in mid-summer:

> Great bliss was with them, and great happiness
> Grew, like a lusty flower in June's caress.
> (*Is*. IX)

The metaphors of their love-talk follow the calendrical issues of the turning year:

> "Love! thou art leading me from wintry cold,
> Lady! thou leadest me to summer clime, . . .
> (*Is*. IX)

It is in autumn that Isabella finds her lover's corpse in the forest, under falling leaves, and plants it to nourish the basil.

The obstacle to their love—the reason the bride must be stolen and the union carried out in the most intense secrecy—is that Lorenzo is a poor employee of Isabella's rich merchant brothers. These "ledger-men," these "money-bags," have been scheming to marry off their sister to "some high noble and his olive trees," and they are furious when they see that she has fallen in love with a "servant of their trade designs." The taboo on the maiden runs through all these poems in one way or another, paralleling the chastity taboo of the Moon-maiden in *Endymion*. In the other poems, an architectural structure of some sinister or forbidding kind articulates the taboo on the maiden with a taboo on the place where she lives. In *Isabella* the architectural imagery of the city mansion is fairly slight—an incidental mention of doors, Isabella's chamber and her couch, her chamber-window, her "morning-step upon the stair," Lorenzo leaning over a balustrade at sunrise, the court-yard from which he and the brothers ride out into the forest where the murder is committed, Isabella's face looking from

an "in-door lattice"—but sufficient to give a well-defined sense
of the grand Florentine villa where the maiden is kept under
guard. This mansion is open only by sufferance to a poor clerk
like Lorenzo. The counting-house and storerooms where he
works are no doubt on the ground floor, around the courtyard,
but he eats at the same table with the masters and sleeps under
the same roof, so that the young people see each other often
enough for love-sickness to pale their cheeks. When they suc-
cumb to love, they have to meet in profound secrecy, corre-
spondent to the secrecy of the love-unions in *The Eve of St.
Agnes* and *Lamia*, the isolation of the Belle Dame's "grot,"
the love-cave in *Endymion*, and the Garden of Adonis, where
a mortal may not enter except by supernatural selection, which
is always a dangerous favor.

Isabella is only a mortal maiden living in the mercantile
environment of Renaissance Florence, but she is imagined by
her lover as an "Otherworld Bride," and the effect of their
mating is to bring about an actual invasion of the daemonic
into the bourgeois villa. Her investment with supernatural
mana is carried out by a sinuous act of identifications between
the object of sexual love and an object of religious worship,
identifications provided by the very verbal forms of the ro-
mantic imagination: her erotic desirability and her superior
social station that removes her so awfully from her lover's
reach make her appear to him as a divine being like the Moon-
maiden of *Endymion*, a "seraph" like Madeline of *The Eve*.
She is

> A Seraph chosen from the bright abyss
>   To be my spouse: . . .
>   (*Is.* XL)

Lorenzo is "fever'd" by his "high conceit of such a bride,"
made physically sick by the awfulness of his love for "one
mark'd out to be a Noble's bride." He thinks of making love
to her in sacramental terms: "I cannot live another night and
not my passion shrive." "Shriving" is the sacrament of confes-
sion and absolution, used here as a metaphor for sexual union.

In a rejected line, she offers to clip a lock of her hair for him: " 'Then should I be,' said he, 'full deified.' " Rejected lines have somewhat the same significance as dream-associations that are rejected by the waking consciousness. Lorenzo's idea of being "deified" is consonant with the submerged mythical core of the plot, where, like Endymion, the lover becomes immortal by union with his "immortal love." The same controlling idiom appears in *The Eve* when Porphyro, "beyond a mortal man impassion'd far," rises up with "looks immortal" from his statue-like swoon.

Isabella is another fictional type of that "schoolboy idea" Keats said he had of women as "ethereal above men," an idea* which he knew to be a part of the "gordian complication" of his feelings about women and which disastrously infected his relationship with Fanny Brawne. The treachery of the image of the love-maiden as "pure goddess" is that the breaking of the sexual taboo can convert her instantly into the "young witch," harlot and murderess. Modulating toward this sinister shift, where the love-goddess is also death-goddess, is that form of the mythical plot where the lover is killed in combat for the divine maiden. Death is already implicit in the verbal forms of Lorenzo's wooing: "I cannot live another night and not my passion shrive"—"believe how near my soul is to its doom." This is conventional diction for the romantically impassioned lover, but it has a psychological dimension beyond formality since the lover's doom is real.

Their mating takes the traditional metaphor of flower-imagery, the sexual rose that is always love's emblem in Keats:

> Parting they seem'd to tread upon the air,
> Twin roses by the zephyr blown apart
> Only to meet again more close, and share
> The inward fragrance of each other's heart.
>
> (*Is.* X)

---

* The idea is reflected again in a letter congratulating Reynolds on his marriage but speaking of his own erotic impulses as dead and blank except when he longs for "the lips of Juliet." (*Rollins* I.325)

Lorenzo must, of course, "taste" the blossoms of love's summer:

> And I must taste the blossoms that unfold
> In its ripe warmth this gracious morning time.
>
> (*Is.* IX)

The erotic flower-imagery broadens out into an image of the secret floral bower where they meet, adorned and scented with vegetation in traditional ritual manner like the Garden of Adonis:

> All close they met again, before the dusk
> Had taken from the stars its pleasant veil,
>
> ....
>
> Close in a bower of hyacinth and musk,
> Unknown of any, free from whispering tale.
>
> (*Is.* XI)

Though the poem as a whole assumes a realistic convention of space—a merchants' villa in Florence—the lovers' bower is undefined in place. It is deliberately uncertain that they make love in Isabella's chamber, for she is watched closely by her brothers, and the "bower of hyacinth and musk" is "unknown of any." The place of the "mystic marriage" is necessarily set apart from ordinary living-space, concealed by a veil of dusk, perfumed with the foliage of desire. The musky hyacinthine bower is another model image of the seed-bed of nature, set apart in secrecy from the world for the magical act of fruitfulness. Later the vegetational symbolism, associated with the seasonal cycle, death and renewal, becomes more clearly defined when the hero is killed and buried in the forest, then replanted to make the basil grow.

As in *Endymion*, the erotic relationship is described as that of mother with child. Isabella's cheek

> Fell thin as a young mother's, who doth seek
> By every lull to cool her infant's pain: . . .
>
> (*Is.* V)

The effect of love on Lorenzo is to bring him "to the meekness of a child." Tasting or drinking of the beloved is an inevitable part of this construct: "I will drink her tears," he says. To sing him "one latest lullaby," she puts his moldy glove between her breasts—"those dainties made to still an infant's cries." She hurries from chapel to nurse the pot of basil, "as swift as bird on wing to breast its eggs again," and sits by it "patient as a hen-bird." No doubt private unconscious elements enter into this type of erotic configuration, as they enter into every strongly motivated psychical structure. But poetic language demands a public or communicable set of symbols. However genuine a role personal psychological factors may play in *Isabella*, they are "reintegrated" in a traditional symbolic structure, a collective representation rather than a private one. As in Attic drama and Celtic legend, the passions involved in tales of the monomythic type are frequently of a domestic kind, reflecting obscurely or transparently the limited family relationship of the ritual actors. Keats's typical conversion of the idiom of his lovers to the idiom of mother and child unconsciously reproduces a primary or "pre-existing" symbol of human dependency, the double relationship of the fertility bride, source of life, to her son and lover.

The fight for the prize female also invokes kinship relations or surrogates for them. The classical typological enemy is the "old man," but the old man's role may devolve upon a brother, whence the father-son battles and brother-battles of monomyth. It is a "brother's bloody knife" that kills Lorenzo. Infuriated with jealousy when they become aware that the low-born intruder has stolen the love of their sister, Isabella's brothers fix on a way to make him "atone" for his "crime":

> And many a jealous conference had they,
>   And many times they bit their lips alone,
> Before they fix'd upon a surest way
>   To make the youngster for his crime atone;
> And at last, these men of cruel clay
>   Cut Mercy with a sharp knife to the bone;
> For they resolved in some forest dim
> To kill Lorenzo, and there bury him.
>   (*Is.* XXII)

In the mythical substrate it is a foregone conclusion that the hero must die, and a powerful verbal condensation makes Lorenzo already "their murder'd man" when the three of them ride out of the city:

> So the two brothers and their murder'd man
>   Rode past fair Florence, to where Arno's steam
> Gurgles through straiten'd banks. . .
>   They pass'd the water
> Into a forest quiet for the slaughter.
>   (*Is.* XXVII)

The ritual nature of the killing is suggested by Lorenzo's lack of resistance: under the dark pine roof, in a sodden turfed dell, "without any word, from stabs he fell."

The next movement of the poem is the mourning of Isabella and her search for her slain lover. The season is the fall of the year, time of the death of the fertility daemon:

> In the mid days of autumn, on their eves
>   The breath of Winter comes from far away,
> And the sick west continually bereaves
>   Of some gold tinge, and plays a roundelay
> Of death among the bushes and the leaves, . . .
>   (*Is.* XXXII)

In ballad-like lines of pastoral imagery, Lorenzo, appearing as a revenant in the girl's dream, describes where he is buried:

>   Isabel, my sweet!
> Red whortle-berries droop above my head,
> And a large flint-stone weighs upon my feet;
>   Around me beeches and high chestnuts shed
> Their leaves and prickly nuts; a sheep-fold bleat
>   Comes from beyond the river to my bed: . . .
>   (*Is.* XXXVIII)

Isabella takes with her an "aged nurse" to help her dig up the corpse—the old nurse who (like Angela in *The Eve*) is one of the traditional cast of characters in folk versions of the fertility daemon's biography.

When the full morning came, she had devised
 How she might secret to the forest hie;
How she might find the clay, so dearly prized,
 And sing to it one latest lullaby;
How her short absence might be unsurmised,
 While she the inmost of the dream would try.
Resolv'd, she took with her an aged nurse,
And went into that dismal forest-hearse.
                              (*Is.* XLIII)

Several stanzas are given to the business of digging up the body. Critics have frequently spoken of these stanzas as "morbid," and laid their quality to an excessive, if perhaps temporary, morbidity in Keats's imagination. But in the mythical substructure, the exhumation of the fertility daemon is the most important event of his career, for on it depends the rebirth of vegetation; to dwell on the fearful details of his episode is consistent with its importance. When Isabella finds the grave and starts digging with her knife,

Soon she turn'd up a soiled glove, whereon
 Her silk had play'd in purple phantasies,
She kiss'd it with a lip more chill than stone,
 And put it in her bosom, where it dries
And freezes utterly unto the bone
 Those dainties made to still an infant's cries:
Then 'gan she work again; nor stay'd her care,
But to throw back at times her veiling hair.

That old nurse stood beside her wondering,
 Until her heart felt pity to the core
At sight of such a dismal labouring,
 And so she kneeled, with her locks all hoar,
And put her lean hands to the horrid thing:
 Three hours they labour'd at this travail sore;
At last they felt the kernel of the grave, . . .
                              (*Is.* XLVII, XLVIII)

The metaphors of this passage—the imagery of mother with infant, the old nurse's aid to Isabella in her "labouring" and "travail"—intuitively reproduce the central mythical symbolism of rebirth from death, as the phrase "the kernel of the grave" glances—with the ancient insight contained in the commonplaces of our language—at the seeding function of the dead daemon of vegetation.

Then comes the gruesome cutting off of the head, which Isabella performs. This is the *sparagmos*, the traditional dismemberment or "tearing asunder" of the fertility hero. In her widowed fantasties, Isabella had brooded over the sexual embraces of her lover:

> She weeps alone for pleasures not to be;
> Sorely she wept until the night came on,
> And then, instead of love, O misery!
> She brooded o'er the luxury alone: . . .
>
> (*Is.* XXX)

In cutting off the head and bringing it home, embalming it with certain essences from precious flowers (so that afterwards the basil smells more "balmy" than other basil), and carefully dressing its hair and painting the eyelashes, she is resurrecting in living form the manhood of her lover—as the greatest care of Isis was to find the dismembered phallus of Osiris.

> In anxious secrecy they took it home,
> And then the prize was all for Isabel:
> She calm'd its wild hair with a golden comb,
> And all around each eye's sepulchral cell
> Pointed each fringed lash; . . .
>
> Then in a silken scarf,—sweet with the dews
> Of precious flowers pluck'd in Araby,
> And divine liquids come with odorous ooze
> Through the cold serpent-pipe refreshfully,—
> She wrapp'd it up; and for its tomb did choose
> A garden-pot, wherein she laid it by,
> And cover'd it with mould, and o'er it set
> Sweet basil, which her tears kept ever wet.
>
> (*Is.* LI, LII)

Here at last Lorenzo "drinks her tears," which he had wanted to do in the beginning.

The basil flourishes with supernatural abundance, "as by magic touch," but then the forced growth of the pot of basil comes to a sudden end. The brothers steal the pot to examine it, and find the mouldered head, "guerdon of their murder." Like the officiants in Babylonian ritual who enacted the transference of evil to a *pharmakos* and then, having touched a sacred thing, had to flee away into the desert and were forbidden to return for an extended time, Isabella's brothers

> left Florence in a moment's space,
> Never to turn again.—Away they went,
> With blood upon their heads, to banishment.
>
> (*Is.* LX)

THE SNAKE-GODDESS: *Lamia*

The principal character in Lamia is a snake who, in the form of a beautiful woman, seduces an earnest young philosophy student of Corinth. She takes him to an invisible palace she has raised by magic in the city and keeps him in seclusion there, teaching him luxurious pleasures—for she has a "sciential brain" and is "of love deep learned to the red heart's core." Eventually the youth grows restless for public life and insists on exhibiting his bride at a ceremonial marriage banquet. Much against her will, she has her magic servants prepare the palace for the fête and Lycius goes into the city to invite the wedding guests. On the night of the banquet an uninvited guest appears—his old philosophy teacher, Apollonius. The old man sees through the serpent-woman's disguise and changes her back into her snake form, whereupon she vanishes and the young bridegroom dies from shock. In this story the monomythic pattern appears again, with the hero crossing a "threshold" into a field of daemonic forces— the palace with the supernatural female at its center. The motif of "bride-theft" is reversed: in *Isabella* and *The Eve*, the hero steals the bride, but here the bride steals the hero and keeps him shut up. Separated from the world, he undergoes sexual initiation. He attempts to return to the common social life, but the return is frustrated by psychological combat with the old man who is his spiritual father. As in those versions of fertility ritual where Winter kills Spring, the old man wins. The love-goddess is revealed as goddess of death, and the hero dies as sacrificial victim.

It is as if, in the manner of a director of Commedia dell' Arte, Keats had handed his standard scenario to his characters and allowed them to improvise an ironic parody of it. The parodistic tone is felt also in the versification, a fast-moving heroic couplet modeled on Dryden's, with deft Alexandrine changes and ironically balanced phrasing of a worldly kind, as in the description of the woodland nymph at the beginning,

> At whose white feet the languid Tritons poured
> Pearls, while on land they wither'd and adored. . . .
> *(Lamia* I.15-16)

and of Lamia's strategy of seduction,

> So threw the goddess off, and won his heart
> More pleasantly by playing woman's part, . . .
> *(Lamia* I.336-37)

and the cynical, aphoristic commentary on love at the start of Part II,

> Love in a hut, with water and a crust,
> Is—Love, forgive us!—cinders, ashes, dust;
> Love in a palace is perhaps at last
> More grievous torment than a hermit's fast: . . .
> *(Lamia* II.1-4)

Keats seems to have written the poem with the approbation of the reviewers and the reading public in mind. His two published books had failed badly. He had a poor opinion of *Isabella*—it was "weak-sided" and "too smokeable," there was "too much inexperience of life, and simplicity of knowledge in it"—and he felt that the same objection could be made to *The Eve of St. Agnes*. "I intend to use more finesse with the Public," he said. "It is possible to write fine things which cannot be laugh'd at in any way. . . . There is no objection of this kind to *Lamia*" (*Rollins* II.174). He made it the title-poem of his new book. His publishers had forced him, despite his furious opposition, to delete the stanzas in *The Eve* which had shown Porphyro acting "all the acts of a bona fide husband" in Madeline's bed, because these would "render the poem unfit for ladies." In *Lamia* the lovely sensual woman who initiates the hero in sex is shown to be vile and brutish, a snake, thus satisfying moral judgment, while the slick neo-classical versification was of a kind to appeal to popular literary taste. But the public that Keats brings into his poem is treated contemptuously and hostilely. The citizens of Corinth who are guests at the wedding banquet are a vulgar herd, a "gossip rout," gluttons who get drunk and talk so loudly they drown the music (in a holograph line, one of them "makes his shiny mouth a napkin for his thumb"). The invasion of the crowd into the lovers' bower is disagreeable and destructive:

> The day appear'd, and all the gossip rout.
> O senseless Lycius! Madman! wherefore flout
> The silent-blessing fate, warm cloister'd hours,
> And show to common eyes these secret bowers?
> (*Lamia* II.146-49)

The whole handling of the tale is exceedingly ambiguous, with a shifting of attitude and emotional focus. It seems morally appropriate that the old philosopher, the rational man, should prevent his pupil from falling under the sensual enchantment of the snake; yet Lamia's desire to live and love like a woman is presented sympathetically, and since the old man's interference with the marriage issues only in death, one is left in uncertainty as to which is the more unnatural and wickedly illusionary—the disguise of the snake as a woman or the old man's conceit of rationality.

The poem starts with an introductory episode that takes place in a forest on the island of Crete. Here the god Hermes, seeking for an elusive nymph of the woods with whom he is in love, encounters a snake of dazzling colors and with a woman's mouth in her serpent's head, who says that she was once a woman. It is she who has made the nymph invisible by her magic, and she makes a bargain with the god: if he will change her back to her former shape, by touching her with his Caducean wand, she will return the nymph to visibility. The bargain is performed, the shy nymph appears, and Hermes goes off with her into the forest:

> Into the green-recessed woods they flew;
> Nor grew they pale, as mortal lovers do.
> (*Lamia* I.144-45)

This episode—which does not appear in the legend of the lamia Keats appropriated from Burton's *Anatomy of Melancholy*—provides a structural contrast with the treatment of love in the main part of the poem, a contrast of love in the forest with love in a palace. The palace in Corinth is an illusionary edifice. Until the destructive night of the marriage banquet it is invisible to any eyes but those of the lovers. On that night Lamia does some more architectural magic to it so that it appears to be "mimicking a glade" of forest trees with branches interlocking over the aisles. The sense of mimicry, forgery, disguise is present throughout the poem, from the snake's disguise as a woman to the disguise of the palace as a forest glade. But the disguise is ineffective, for the lovers do grow pale and their love ends in frightful *sparagmos*, while the lovers who fled away into the forest—the sacred forest of symbolic vegetation—presumably achieved, like Endymion, an "immortality" of passion," for

> Real are the dreams of Gods, and smoothly pass
> Their pleasures in a long immortal dream.
> (*Lamia* I.127-28)

The sensual dream of the lovers in the palace is a false dream when placed under the scrutiny of rational truth in the person of the old philosopher, who sees through the sensual illusion and condemns it to death. In this parody of erotic initiation, dream and truth, instinct and reason, have no point of contact. In confrontation, one must destroy the other.

The *sparagmos* at the end of the poem, when Lamia is changed back hideously into a snake, has a duplicate form at the beginning, when she goes through the violent process of changing from a snake into a woman. As a serpent she had been gorgeous; clearly no ordinary snake, she seemed "some demon's mistress, or the demon's self."

> She was a gordian shape of dazzling hue,
> Vermilion-spotted, golden, green, and blue;
> Striped like a zebra, freckled like a pard,
> Eyed like a peacock, and all crimson barr'd; . . .
>
> (*Lamia* I.47-50)

Her metamorphosis, after Hermes has touched her with his "serpent rod," is painful and ugly:

> Her mouth foam'd, and the grass, therewith besprent,
> Wither'd at dew so sweet and virulent;
> Her eyes in torture fix'd, and anguish drear,
> Hot, glaz'd, and wide, with lid-lashes all sear,
> Flash'd phospher and sharp sparks, . . .
> The colours all inflam'd throughout her train,
> She writh'd about, convuls'd with scarlet pain: . . .
>
> (*Lamia* I.148-54)

Her form is dissolved in volcanic heat and "nothing but pain and ugliness were left." Keats is competing here with the virtuosoship of Ovid and Lucan in describing metamorphoses, but more especially with Dante's elaborate description of the conversion of damned souls into serpents. Dante's damned souls who changed violently from men into snakes and snakes into men were murderers, who had violated human form in life and were thus violated in death; but Keats's poem gives no such moral witness against Lamia, as to why violation of bodily form should be associated with her.

In the context of the poem, female sexuality is her one attribute. This, as in the mythology of the lamiae from which Burton's story derived, is the only explicit association the poem offers to account for her treatment as a dehumanized, bestial creature. Robert Graves says that the lamiae of Greece— beautiful women who seduced, enervated, and sucked the blood of travelers—"were in Aristophanes's day regarded as emissaries of the Triple Goddess Hecate." He assumes that they "had been the orgiastic priestesses of the Libyan Snake-goddess Lamia."⁵ But Keats makes his own precise correlation by setting the opening episode in Crete, the home of the Minoan mother-goddess, goddess *par excellence* of the Aegean world, who, under whatever name she appeared, was accompanied by snakes.

It is inconsistent that Lamia should have powerful enough magic to make the nymph with whom Hermes is in love invisible and then make her visible—which Hermes, though a god, cannot do himself—and yet that she has not the magic to manage her own metamorphosis from snake to woman. From being the original snake-goddess, all-powerful divine matriarch with snakes as associates, she has become culturally confined to the snake-form and is ignominiously reduced to begging help from one of her sons, the "heroized" snake Hermes. Having recovered her woman's body, she will be put back in her degraded place by the old philosopher Apollonius, who naturally disapproves of her cohabitation with his intellectual foster-son Lycius, whose austere studies she has interrupted. On his own grounds of late Greek legend, Apollonius is patriarch of a rational and masculine orthodoxy that was continually threatened by the cult of the Great Goddess. To degrade her into one of her snakes was a way of degrading her worship and along with it the feminine, generative life-principle she represented. The historical pattern reflected in the antagonism of the philosopher for the snake is reenforced psychologically by the correspondence of the old man's interfering and condemnatory role with that of the father in the "Oedipus complex." He exposes the sensual allure of the female as a bestial, paralyzing force from the underground of the id. It is this dehumanization of sensuality, with its overwhelming attraction, that is the pivot of Keats's poem.

When Hermes has done his magic on Lamia and her metamorphosis into a woman is complete, she vanishes and reappears in a valley near Corinth where she knows Lycius will pass on his way to the city. She is now "a maid more beautiful than ever twisted braid," "a virgin purest lipp'd." She is that "fair woman as pure goddess" who haunted Keats's imagination and who, even in her benign forms in *Endymion*, was called enchantress and executioner. Before her transformation she had a "Circean head," and she is to play the part now of Circe—but confusedly, for Circe's intentions were explicitly evil, as represented in *Endymion*. She practiced the black magic of changing the human form into that of a beast, and in a final ecstasy of evil, transformed all the beasts in her sty of old lovers into one huge writhing snake. But Lamia wants only to love as a woman, and it is the black art of the old philosopher's headstrong rationalism that conceives her as bestial and changes her into a beast. This obscurity of emotional attitude is examined in the letter Keats wrote to Bailey about the "gordian complication" of his feelings toward women:

> I am certain I have not a right feeling towards Women.
> . . . When among Men I have no evil thoughts, no malice,
> no spleen. . . . When I am among Women I have evil
> thoughts, malice, spleen. . . . You must be charitable and
> put all this perversity to my being disappointed since
> Boyhood. Yet with such feelings I am happier alone among
> Crowds of men, by myself or with a friend or two. . . .
> I must absolutely get over this—but how? The only way
> is to find the root of evil, and so cure it "with backward
> mutters of dissevering Power"—that is a difficult thing;
> for an obstinate Prejudice can seldom be produced but
> from a gordian complication of feelings, which must take
> time to unravell and care to keep unravelled. I could say
> a good deal more about this but I will leave it in hopes
> of better and more worthy dispositions—and also content
> that I am wronging no one, for after all I do think better
> of Womankind than to suppose they care whether Mister
> John Keats five feet high likes them or not. (*Rollins*
> I.341-42)

Those of Keats's poems that have an erotic content are them-
selves "backward mutters of dissevering power" on this gor-
dian complication, exorcisms, adjurations, conjurings, or—to
use the psychological term—projections of it. In *Lamia* he
further elaborates the conjuring act by having the old philos-
opher and father-figure perform "backward mutters of dis-
severing power" on the "gordian shape" of the snake-woman.

The student Lycius walks bemusedly toward Corinth, se-
rene, abstracted, and Olympian, "like a young Jove with calm
uneager face," his mind occupied with Plato's pure Ideas:

> His phantasy was lost, where reason fades,
> In the calm'd twilight of Platonic shades.
>   (*Lamia* I.235-36)

This rational purity is immediately convulsed and over-
whelmed in his meeting with the emissary of the fertility god-
dess. The specious moral of the consequences could be put in
lines of Baudelaire, who also suffered the incommensurable-
ness of the life of the mind and the life of the body: "*Ah! ne
jamais sortir des Nombres et des Êtres*," or the expression of
hatred for the mobility of the sensual and mortal which he
puts in the lips of that great white abstraction *La Beauté*—
"*Je hais le mouvement qui déplace les lignes.*"

Lamia tells Lycius that she fell in love with him on the night
of "the Adonian feast" in the temple of Venus. (The temple
of Aphrodite in the notoriously licentious city of Corinth was
famous for its sacred prostitutes.) Lycius falls in love the min-
ute she speaks, and the idiom is, as usual, that of drinking
and tasting: he "drinks her beauty up," and Lamia speaks of
her sensual "tastes" and "thirsts" that can be appeased only
in a palace. Like Endymion, he swoons into a death-like trance
from the pain of love, then "from death awoke into amaze,"
and keeps dying and coming to life while the goddess feeds
him from her lips, meanwhile "tangling him in her mesh."
"As he from one trance was wakening into another," the
"cruel lady"

> Put her new lips to his, and gave afresh
> The life she had so tangled in her mesh: . . .
> (*Lamia* I.294-95)

In a blind daze he walks with her into Corinth. As they enter the city they pass old Apollonius—

> With curl'd gray beard, sharp eyes, and smooth bald crown,
> Slow-stepp'd, and robed in philosophic gown: . . .
> (*Lamia* I.364-65)

Trembling with apprehension, Lamia asks, "Who is that old man?" and Lycius says that he is "my trusty guide and good instructor," and muffles his face in fear of being seen with the woman. This phase of his life is to be passed in secrecy and separation, "shut from the world."

The love-deaths and resurrections continue in the "purple-lined palace of sweet sin" in Corinth. Trapped in the palace, Lycius learns from Lamia perverse pleasures. As he is kept so by his "paramour," his masculine ambition is lost as his intercourse with men is forsworn. This situation is implicit in the treatment of the erotic theme in *Endymion*, although in that poem it is idealized whereas in *Lamia* it has become sinister. "So delicious is the unsating food" of love, Endymion tells his sister,

> That men, who might have tower'd in the van
> Of all the congregated world . . .
> ....
> Have been content to let occasion die,
> Whilst they did sleep in love's elysium.
> And, truly, I would rather be struck dumb,
> Than speak against this ardent listlessness: . . .
> (*End.* I.816-25)

But here "love's elysium," where the hero is separated from "all the congregated world," is a prison paradise. His trouble is that he cannot think:

> he mused beyond her, knowing well
> That but a moment's thought is passion's passing bell—
> (*Lamia* II.38-39)

and she asks him apprehensively, "Why do you think?" Thinking and love are in ruinous opposition. Entanglement or entrammelment is the dominant kinetic figure for love in both poems. Endymion, speaking of the hierarchal degrees in happiness, says,

> But there are
> Richer entanglements, enthralments far
> More self-destroying,

of which the "chief intensity" is love (*End*. I.797-801). In the Indian Maid sequence, the thought of dying in love takes the figure of a net or trammel:

> We might embrace and die: voluptuous thought!
> Enlarge not to my hunger, or I'm caught
> In trammels of perverse deliciousness.
> (*End*. IV.759-61)

Lycius, while he is trammeled and snared in the vulval labyrinth of the purple-lined palace, uses the same idiom, in a curious psychological inversion of his own situation. When Lamia asks him, "Why do you think?" he evasively tells her that he is thinking

> How to entangle, trammel up and snare
> Your soul in mine, and labyrinth you there. . . .
> (*Lamia* II.52-53)

The self-destroying effect of love, idealized in *Endymion*, is subtly changed in *Lamia* to a destructive threat to the freedom of the male consciousness and personality. "Net and noose," Erich Neumann says, "are typical weapons of the Feminine's terrible power to bind and fetter, and the knot is a dire instrument of the enchantress."[6] Eventually, in *Otho*, "the entrapp'd, the caged" lover, "fast-limed in a cursed snare—the

122

white limbs of a wanton," will turn her own instrument against her, trammel up, snare, and murder her in the love-palace.

The Eros of Lamia's palace is a harpy-like creature:

> there, nightly, with terrific glare,
> Love, jealous grown of so complete a pair,
> Hover'd and buzz'd his wings, with fearful roar,
> Above the lintel of their chamber door,
> And down the passage cast a glow upon the floor.
> (*Lamia* II.11-15)

The poem is about a double-cross—the disguise of the snake-woman as a "virgin purest lipp'd"—and its idiom and moral attitudes are of a double-crossing kind, disguising obscure subliminal material in the cynical, parodistic vein and the specious lucidity of the quick rhymes. The lovers are not so complete a pair that Love could be jealous of them; this is a fanciful rationalization of the ruinousness of sexual love that is implicit in the legend. The harpy that glares above the lovers' chamber door is another projection of the monster-female.

In *Mon coeur mis à nu*, Baudelaire says, "The more a man cultivates the arts, the less he fornicates. A more and more apparent cleavage occurs between the spirit and the brute." Woman is the opposite of the fastidious aesthete and ascetic:

> Therefore she should inspire horror. Woman is hungry and she wants to eat, thirsty and she wants to drink. She is in rut and she wants to be possessed. Woman is *natural*, that is to say, abominable.

In Keats's letters and poems to Fanny Brawne, he speaks continuously of his art and his mental freedom as threatened by her. In *Lamia* it is the hero's philosophical studies, his rational intellect, that are menaced by the woman. The woman, being natural, is conceived of as being unnatural—monster, incubus, snake. Burton's legend of the snake-woman offered the poet the opportunity to have his hero shift responsibility for this subliminal fear and antagonism onto the old philosopher and snake-killer Apollonius, the fatherly embodiment of the independent male intellect.

The snake, more than any other animal form, is able to embody this threat to consciousness, because it comes from "underground" and as a collective representation it exercises enormous compulsive power of the unconscious. The mythology of the lamiae, Burton's retelling of the story of the snake-woman, and Keats's elaboration of it, are all reenactments of the attraction and menace of archaic forces, in both the historical and the psychological plane, and of conscious resistance to them. By yielding to the lure of the snake-goddess, Lycius puts himself under the peril of an *abaissement du niveau mental,* by which the conscious mind apparently extinguishes itself.

Lycius resists the snake-woman's understandable desire for secrecy, isolation, invisibility, by insisting on inviting the public into those secret bowers. He wants to show off his bride, parade her in a bridal car. But the ending is equivocal, for it is the hero's "return to the world"—the rational and social order—that brings death, while the moral sympathy of the poem is with the miserable lovely woman who

> set herself, high-thoughted, how to dress
> The misery in fit magnificence
>
> (*Lamia* II.115-16)

for her own destruction. The wedding banquet, the transformation of the palace into a leafy setting, and the death of the hero are not in the legend as told by Burton, but they are integral to the ritual structure of Keats's poems. Burton's tale is an anecdote only. Keats gives it aesthetic "completion" by adapting it to the monomythic form. But he inverts the import of the form. This is the manner of parody. In a story cited by Jessie Weston, the youth Rishyacringa was—like Lycius—brought up on austere studies in a lonely hermitage, never having seen a woman; drought fell on the land, and the youth had to resign his chastity to cure the state; a maiden was prepared as his seductress (in earlier versions, the king's daughter played the role of temptress); as soon as the marriage was consummated, rain fell.[7] But in Keats's poem, the import of the hero's ceremonial marriage with the fertility goddess is ironically distorted. The epiphany, the showing-forth and recognition, is what Northrop Frye calls a "demonic epiphany," for the bride is shown to be bestial. The result of this recognition by the rational consciousness is not fertility but sterility.

In the mythical archetype, the mystic marriage takes place among the plant-life that is the fruitful aspect of the earth, and is accompanied by sacramental participation in the life-power through food. For her marriage, Lamia prepares a great feast—"the store thrice told of Ceres' horn"—and converts the banquet-hall of the palace into an artificial forest, "fresh carved cedar, mimicking a glade," branching aisles of trees and other vegetation creeping in "fretted splendour" through the panels. The mimicry here is an ominous note of the parodistic treatment of the ritual theme. The spherical tables with feet shaped like leopards' paws and with images of gods on them, the golden cups, the burning myrrh, the white robes of the guests, and the careful selection of a suitable garland for each of them, are reproduced in Lamia's banquet, and mirrors everywhere redouble the mimicry of illusion. The garland selected for Apollonius is of spear-grass and thistle, weeds of the waste land. The wreath for Lycius is, ironically, the vine and ivy of the thyrsus—attribute of Dionysos, intoxicated lord of life. Lamia's garland is of willow—for her misery—and adder's tongue—snake-emblem of the degraded goddess of generation. In this parody of ritual form, the symbolism of food and drink, bread and wine, is associated with violent disunion, mutilation of the body, and the sterilization of life by "truth."

The progress to the autonomy of the male consciousness required, Erich Neumann says, the " 'symbolic slaying' of the Great Goddess," and the "father's support of the son principle that has grown independent of the Earth Mother."[8] The anxiety caused by this conflict creates holocaust at the end of Keats's poem. The "father," by destroying the goddess, kills the "son" too. There is here a total disjunction between consciousness and its matrix in the unconscious. The result of this sundering is a tearing apart of the physical body, *spar-*

agmos and death, in a paralyzed nightmare world. Apollonius fixes Lamia with his lashless eyes and she withers, her own eyes recessing like a snake's. Lycius cries out in horror, but the old man is adamant in his fatherly self-righteousness: "And shall I see thee made a serpent's prey?" At the word "serpent," Lamia vanishes with a frightful scream.

> And Lycius' arms were empty of delight,
> As were his limbs of life, from that same night.
> On the high couch he lay!—his friends came round—
> Supported him—no pulse, or breath they found,
> And, in his marriage robe, the heavy body wound.
>
> (*Lamia* II.307-11)

THE LADY OF THE WILDS:
"LA BELLE DAME SANS MERCI"

In the ballad of the Belle Dame, Keats's plot appears as sheer enactment, stripped, as in a dream, of any rationalization or convention of causality. A wandering knight meets a beautiful fairy lady who feeds him, takes him to her "grot," makes love to him, and lulls him to sleep. In his sleep he has a vision of a charnel house crowded with dead knights, their "starved lips" gaping skeletally in the gloom, who have preceded him in the lady's arms. They cry to him that the Belle Dame Sans Merci has him "in thrall." The ballad has perhaps had more charm for generations of readers than any other of Keats's poems. And yet it is a most mysterious poem. Who is the Belle Dame Sans Merci? The dead kings and princes, when they cry their warning, seem to assume that she is a well-known personage whose name and sinister reputation will be recognized by the knight. Why does the reader acquiesce in the same assumption? Why does a ghastly vision of dead men succeed the rapturous experience of love? By what means does the lady keep her cast-off lovers in prison to starve to death? If she is "without mercy," why does she weep and "sigh full sore" at the prospect of sending the knight to the same doom?

Is she herself under some sort of enchantment or "thrall" which forces her to kill the men she has loved?

The love-encounter and the death-dream follow the changing seasons. It had been summer when the knight met the lady in the meads (Keats first wrote "wilds"), when he made garlands of flowers for her and she fed him the strange food of the wilderness. Only a day seems to pass for their love-making, but it is already late autumn when he wakes "on the cold hill's side." After his dream he is left loitering, purposeless and impotent, in the spectral fields of the dead year. With his haggard face and the "fever dew" on his brow, he too is obviously going to die (in the line "I see a lily on thy brow," Keats had first written, "I see death's lily on thy brow"). What "ails" the knight is clearly the same ailment from which all nature suffers. If one leaves off the framing stanzas at beginning and end that provide the autumnal setting, one realizes how essential to the poem's import the seasonal imagery is. Without it the central episode would be dissociative and arbitrary.

In *The Eve of St. Agnes*, while Porphyro is waiting for Madeline to awake, he plays upon his lute

> an ancient ditty, long since mute,
> In Provence call'd, "La belle dame sans mercy: . . ."
> *(Eve 291-92)*

Sir Sidney Colvin pointed out that Keats had been reading a fifteenth century poem of that title, by Alan Chartier, wherein "a gentleman finding no mercy at the hand of a gentlewoman dyeth of sorrow."[9] But the Belle Dame of Keats's ballad is no gentlewoman but a witch of the wilderness, and the knight dies not of sorrow because she refuses his love but because she makes love to him. Spenser's Phaedria has also been suggested as Keats's model for the Belle Dame. Phaedria invites the knight Cymochiles into her little boat, dresses herself in garlands, and sings enchantingly to him. They land on an island, where she takes the "wretched thrall" to a dale, puts him to sleep with his head in her lap, and maroons him there (*Faerie Queene* II.6). Similarly the beautiful witches Duessa and Acrasia seduce knights and lull them to unmanning sleep. Since Keats was steeped in Spenser, it is not unlikely that the form and details of these episodes should make a reappearance in the ballad of the Belle Dame. But there are essential differences. Spenser moralizes the issue: the knights, by yielding to the lust of the senses, lose their heroic consciousness of mission. They have to be rescued by other knights from sleep in the sensual illusion, and they return to their chivalric intent, having learned and taught a lesson of temperance or prudence. Keats's poem has the oneiric quality of pure presentation, without rationale at the conscious level to determine its movement. The vision of death that follows on the exquisite love-encounter is not a vision of punishment for lust but a stark insight into the physical horror and starved deprivation of the grave. And it is the seasonal imagery—the flowering summer and the cold autumn—that gives to both the love-rapture and the vision of annihilation their quality as natural absolutes, not moral contingents.

Robert Graves says that the "most important source of all" for the poem is the folk-ballad of *Thomas the Rhymer*. Thomas is taken by the Queen of Elfland on a milk-white steed to a garden, fed on bread and wine, lulled to sleep in her lap, and given the gift of poetic insight. But he is warned by her that he might be destined as a Sabbatical sacrifice to hell, going by the road that "lies out owr yon frosty fell"—which Graves identifies with the "cold hill's side" of Keats's poem. The Belle Dame, he says, is the hag Death, one of the triple forms of the "White Goddess," and—since Keats's brother Tom had died of tuberculosis a few months earlier—she is, he suggests, specifically the plague tuberculosis, which leaves "anguish moist and fever dew" on the brow of the sufferer.[10] But the Belle Dame is distinctly a sexual enchantress. There is no emotional reason why the plague tuberculosis should appear as a lady of ardent beauty, garlanded with flowers, and speaking love-language.

The parallel motifs in *Thomas the Rhymer* are, like those in similar episodes in Spenser, reverberations of Celtic mythology that recur again and again in the great mediaeval romances. The very abundance of parallels indicates that the dramatic situation in the poem is far less imitative or dependent upon a specific literary "source" than it is intuitive and hereditary. This view is borne out by the fact that the poem uses again, with the pictorial economy of dream, the ritual details that had articulated the major pattern of Keats's other poems; so that—if one were seeking "sources"—one could say that the closest literary source at hand was Keats's own poetry. His repetition of his own poetic dominants shows that the imagery of the ballad was coeval and imbued with the creative impulse itself.

The sleep of the hero in a covert glade or a "grot," his magical experiences beyond the threshold of consciousness, the food that is proffered at the verge of epiphany—these motifs go back to *Endymion* and earlier. So also does the evolving seasonal imagery with which the dramatic action turns and is webbed. The brilliant and equivocal anima-figure of the Belle Dame—the "dream woman" of the male psyche— is another apparition of the "immortal love," the Otherworld Bride, of *Endymion* and the narrative poems. As early as *Calidore* the world "thrall" was used for the spell in which the lover was bound.

We can read the ballad of the Belle Dame in terms of a purely subjective libido-symbolism—a reading in which the "dream woman" of love gives such exquisite rapture that none other can match or follow it and only the image of death approximates its ultimate quality. Such dreams and fantasies are common enough (particularly in adolescence and always dimly remembered) that their imagery has its own "universal" character. But the vision of death in the ballad is too fearsome a vision of the horrors of physical annihilation, the general human doom, to be entirely contained in such a reading. Also, from that point of view, the seasonal imagery of summer garlands for love and autumn dearth for the "death" that is emotional deprivation is only a gracefully accompanying but not essential metaphor, whereas the dependence of the poem's structure—its lustrous sense of completion and finish—on this imagery suggests that the landscape is part of the subject. And if we should inspect in ourselves, at any depth, *why* such imagery seems fitting, as metaphor, to the subject of love and death, we would find it to be not a metaphor but integral to the objective experience of these things as the continuities of nature. Under the abstract urban and academic conditions where most of our literary criticism and analytic psychology are generated, the intimate sense of external nature as sharing one dynamism and one reality with the individual human life is almost obliterated from our mental habits—though, being instinctively operative, it can revive in a more open environment. It was powerful in Keats, and this, it would seem, is the reason why he could canalize personal psychological impulses through the great traditional or "collective" images and dramatic structures.

FANNY BRAWNE AS THE "YOUNG WITCH"

Ernst Cassirer, in his volume on myth, says, "It is not by its history that the mythology of a nation is determined but, conversely, its history is determined by its mythology."[11] An individual application of this statement may be made of Keats's life, and particularly to his relationship with Fanny Brawne: that his personal history was determined by his mythology. His commentators have uniformly taken the opposite view: that the figures in his poetry are projections of his biography. An assumption about the nature of poetry is involved here: that poetry is a more or less direct mimesis of actuality, that it is versified personal experience. This is the most trivial form of mimesis and one which—as a theory of the creative work— has never been able to encounter, consistently and at significant depth, the real complexities of poetry, its aesthetic character at such, and its ability to "universalize" experience.

The determination of critics to find Fanny herself in the Belle Dame, Lamia, and others is to solve the problem of the creative process too easily, as an accident of the fact that the Brawnes rented Charles Brown's house: presumably if they had not, and Keats had not met Fanny, the poems would not have been written. It is also to assume that Fanny's character actually resembled that of the *femme fatale* of the poems, although the same critics assent to the proofs that this was not so. In fact, Keats would have forced any woman whom he loved into the mold of the fatal anima-figure of the poems, that he would have found in his life the image he carried in his mind.

Writing to the George Keatses soon after he first met Fanny, he drew this coolly anatomical portrait of her:

> Shall I give you Miss Brawn? She is about my height—with a fine style of countenance of the lengthen'd sort—she wants sentiment in every feature—she manages to make her hair look well—her nostrills are fine—though a little painful—her mouth is bad and good—her Profil is better than her full-face which indeed is not full but pale and thin without showing any bone—Her shape is very graceful and so are her movements—her Arms are good her hands badish—her feet tolerable—she is not seventeen—but she is ignorant—monstrous in her behaviour flying out in all directions, calling people such names—that I was forced lately to make use of the term *Minx*—this is I think not from any innate vice but from a penchant she has for acting stylishly. I am however tired of such style and shall decline any more of it—
> (*Rollins* II.13)

Since he told Fanny later that "the very first week I knew you I wrote myself your vassal," one feels that the equivocations of the passage are a smoke screen to conceal his feelings. Like Endymion and the other lovers in his poems, he was to keep his love in intense secrecy from the world—though there was no practical reason for secrecy. In his letters to other people (and even, at times, to Fanny herself) he threw up buffers of ridicule of love and lovers in order to protect that secrecy.

Fanny is from the first the Circean enchantress of the poems, exercising through her beauty a cruel and dangerous power.

> Why may I not speak of your Beauty, since without that I could never have lov'd you. I cannot conceive any be-

ginning of such love as I have for you but Beauty. There
may be a sort of love for which, without the least sneer
at it, I have the highest respect and can admire it in others:
but it has not the richness, the bloom, the full form, the
enchantment of love after my own heart. So let me speak
of your Beauty, though to my own endangering; if you
could be so cruel to me as to try elsewhere its Power.
(*Rollins* II.127)

The fatal enthrallment of his fictional lovers is transplanted
to his own situation: "You have ravish'd me away by a Power
I cannot resist . . . I cannot breathe without you." He has
been reading an oriental tale about a talismanic lady in a
paradisal garden who captures lover after lover in a basket,
then drops them heartlessly back to earth to live in melancholy
ever afterward, and he applies the figure to Fanny:

I have been reading lately an oriental tale of a very beau-
tiful color—It is of a city of melancholy men, all made
so by this circumstance. Through a series of adventures
each one of them by turns reaches some gardens of Par-
adise where they meet with a most enchanting Lady; and
just as they are going to embrace her, she bids them shut
their eyes—they shut them—and on opening their eyes
again find themselves descending to the earth in a magic
basket. The remembrance of this Lady and their delights
lost beyond all recovery render them melancholy ever
after. How I applied this to you, my dear; how I palpi-
tated at it; how the certainty that you were in the same
world with myself, and though as beautiful, not so tal-
ismanic as that Lady; how I could not bear you should
be so you must believe because I swear it by your-
self. (*Rollins* II.130)

This tale of ensorcelment by an otherworld love, of bondage
and fatal deprivation, follows the typical Circean pattern, the
pattern of the ballad of the Belle Dame. That it should have
affected Keats with fearful palpitations, which he could ex-
orcise only by assurance that Fanny was not supernatural but

"in the same world" with himself, suggests the chill power that the imaginative model had begun to assume over his life.

There is nothing in what is known of Fanny to support his suspicions of her virtue—but the otherworld enchantress of his erotic vision ensnared lover after lover and consumed them. Fanny was a sheltered, well-bred girl, but she was very young and she liked parties and dancing. Keats turns this into brutal reflections on her chastity. "My greatest torment since I have known you has been the fear of you being a little inclined to the Cressid," he says. "I cannot persuade myself into any confidence of you."

> How have you pass'd this month? Who have you smil'd with? Well this may seem savage in me. You do not feel as I do—you do not know what it is to love . . . I appeal to you by the blood of that Christ you believe in: Do not write to me if you have done anything this month which it would have pained me to have seen. You may have altered—if you have not—if you still behave in dancing rooms and other societies as I have seen you—I do not want to live—if you have done so I wish this coming night may be my last. I cannot live without you, and not only you but *chaste you, virtuous you.*   (*Rollins* II.304)

The excesses of such passages, their distraughtness and incoherence, are measures of a situation far from rational—an overwhelming unconscious compulsion. His poems to her are obsessed by the same theme:

> Ah! keep that hand unravish'd at the least;
>
> ....
>
> Save it for me sweet love! . . .
> Though swimming through the dance's dangerous wreath,
>   Be like an April day,
>   Smiling and cold and gay,
>   A temperate lily, . . .
>
> ....
>
> Why, this—you'll say—my Fanny! is not true;
> Put your soft hand upon your snowy side,

Where the heart beats: confess—'tis nothing new—
    Must not a woman be
    A feather on the sea,
  Swayed to and fro by every wind and tide?

....

I know it—and to know it is despair. . . .
                 ("To Fanny")

It was Dante's Francesca who gave him, in the sonnet "As Hermes once . . . ," the pale figure clasped with her lover on the eternal whirlwind of the underworld:

    Pale were the sweet lips I saw,
  Pale were the lips I kiss'd, and fair the form
  I floated with, about that melancholy storm.

One may note that Dante's Francesca was in hell for adultery. It is worth mentioning in this connection that Fanny Brawne was not the only Frances—it was also the name of Keats's mother. The dream-figure floating through the air, never becoming tangible except in the hero's sleep, disappearing when he waked, bound by divine chastity and meeting her lover only in the secret depths of the underworld—this figure, the goddess of *Endymion*, Keats had known long before he met Fanny Brawne.

He uses the food and nursing imagery for his love that he has used in his poems. "Knowing well that my life must be passed in fatigue and trouble, I have been endeavouring to wean myself from you . . . I cannot bear the pain of being happy." Again: "I am not strong enough to be weaned." His existence "hangs" upon her: "I am greedy of you." She is his "feast" that someone else is eating:

  Who now, with greedy looks, eats up my feast?

....

Let none profane my Holy See of love,
    Or with rude hand break
    The sacramental cake: . . .
              ("To Fanny")

The profoundly unconscious source of this eucharistic imagery, identifying the body of the beloved with the sacred food of life, is indicated by its insistence in metaphor and dramatic episode throughout Keats's work. Eighteen-year-old Fanny is only an unwitting *persona* of that obscure power.

Typically, in her role as the "young witch" who "entrammels" the hero in her sensual snare, she is accused by the poet of cruelly destroying his freedom. "I do not know how elastic my spirit might be, what pleasure I might have in living here and breathing and wandering as free as a stag about this beautiful Coast," he writes her from Shanklin, "if the remembrance of you did not weigh so upon me. . . . Ask yourself my love whether you are not very cruel to have so entrammelled me, so destroyed my freedom" (1 July 1819). This is the problem of Lycius in *Lamia*, restlessly ensnared in sense, his intellectual life cut off and his free concourse with men. It is also that of Endymion in the episode of the Indian maid, whom he accuses as his "executioner," who "stolen hath away the wings wherewith I was to top the heaven." What Keats means by his "freedom" is his creative activity of mind, his poetry itself. This is the subject of his second ode to Fanny:

> What can I do to drive away
> Remembrance from my eyes? for they have seen,
> Aye, an hour ago, my brilliant Queen!
> Touch has a memory. O say, love, say,
> What can I do to kill it and be free
> In my old liberty?
> ....
> When, how'er poor or particolour'd things,
> My muse had wings,
> And ever ready was to take her course
> Whither I bent her force,
> Unintellectual, yet divine to me;—
> Divine, I say! . . .
>
> ....
>
> How shall I do
> To get anew

> Those moulted feathers, and so mount once more
> Above, above
> The reach of fluttering Love,
> And make him cower lowly while I soar? . . .
>   ("What can I do . . .")

He uses here the image of flight which is so constantly the image of poetic imagination in his early verse, as in the figure of the magic charioteer in *Sleep and Poetry*. The quest-flights of his early poetry had as their goal Poesy itself, the "symbol essences" of all things, and even in *Endymion*, where the goal is an "immortal love," the goddess is subtly identified with the empyreal Muse who will teach the hero the poetry of cosmic essences. But in the narrative poems that succeed *Endymion* the erotic element always implicit in the quest becomes dominant; the heroic goal of Poesy is lost and sexual love is substituted for it. Under these conditions, the hero entoiled in the sensual snare again and again suffers violent death or is left aimless and impotent in a barren land. The problem of goal, erupting in Keats's personal life, becomes a ravaging and ruinous struggle between love and poetry, body and mind (creative energy).

He makes an immense effort to steel himself against Fanny's image and writes her a "flinty" letter from Winchester, in which he tells her he can only see her "through a mist" and confesses that he is "excessively unloverlike and ungallant."

> I cannot help it—I am no officer in yawning quarters; no Parson-romeo . . . I know the generallity of women would hate me for this; that I should have so unsoften'd so hard a Mind as to forget them. . . . 'Tis harsh, harsh, I know it—My heart seems now made of iron. . . . You see how I go on—like so many strokes of a Hammer—I cannot help it—I am impell'd, driven to it. I am not happy enough for silken Phrases, and silver sentences—I can no more use soothing words to you than if I were at this moment engaged in a charge of Cavalry—   (*Rollins* II.141)

At the end he asks her to forgive him "for this flint-worded Letter," and the torturing split in his sensibility becomes evident when he adds, "Even as I leave off—it seems to me that a few more moments thought of you would uncrystallize and dissolve me—I must not give way to it."

He adopts a snide and truculent attitude about love and women, writing to Taylor—shortly after the Winchester letter to Fanny—that "I equally dislike the favour of the public with the love of a woman—they are both a cloying treacle to the wings of independence" (*Rollins* II.144). His letters to his friends and to his brother and sister-in-law become increasingly cynical in tone, and he indulges himself in quoting at great length, to George and Georgiana, a gruesome passage from Burton's *Anatomy of Melancholy* in which the women whom men love are morbidly caricatured:

> Every Lover admires his Mistress, though she be very deformed of herself . . . gubber tush'd, rotten teeth, black, uneven, brown teeth, beetle-brow'd, a witches beard, her breath stink all over the room, her nose drop winter and summer, with a Bavarian poke under her chin, a sharp chin, lave-eared, with a long crane's neck, which stands away too, pendulis mammis her dugs like two double jugs, or else no dugs in the other extream, bloody-falln fingers, she have filthy, long, unpaired, nails, scabbed hands or wrists, a tan'd skin, a rotton carcass, crooked back, she stoops, is lame, splea footed, as slender in the middle as a cow in the wast, gowty legs, her ankles hang over her shooes, her feet stink, she breed lice, a meer changeling, a very monster . . . vile gate, a vast virago, or an ugly tit, a slug, a fat fustilugs . . . whom thou couldst not fancy for a world, but hatest, loathest, and wouldst have spit in her face, or blow thy nose in her bosom. . . .

"There's a dose for you—fine!!" he comments, "I would give my favourite leg to have written this. . . . This I think will amuse you more than so much Poetry" (*Rollins* II.191-92). In view of his overwhelming involvement with Fanny, the man appears to be at his wits' end. It was on a page-margin of this section of Burton that Keats wrote his disgusted comment on the "horrid relationship" between love of God and love of women: "there is nothing disgraces me in my own eyes so much as being one of a race of eyes, nose and mouth beings in a planet called the earth who all from Plato to Wesley have always mingled goatish, winnyish, lustful love with the abstract adoration of the deity."

And yet at the same time that he is suffering morbid disgust with the biological aspect of love, he is frantically demanding God-like (or infantile) monopoly over Fanny: "Do not think of any thing but me," he writes her.

> Have I any right to wish you to be unhappy for me? You would forgive me for wishing it, if you knew the extreme passion I have that you should love me—and for you to love me as I do you, you must think of no one but me. . . . Well may you exclaim, how selfish, how cruel, not to let me enjoy my youth! to wish me to be unhappy! You must be so if you love me—upon my Soul I can be contented with nothing else. If you could really what is call'd enjoy yourself at a Party—if you can smile in peoples faces, and wish them to admire you *now*, you never have nor ever will love me. I see *life* in nothing but the certainty of your Love—convince me of it my sweetest. If I am not somehow convinc'd I shall die of agony. . . . You must be mine to die upon the rack if I want you. I do not pretend to say I have more feeling than my fellows—but I wish you seriously to look over my letters kind and unkind and consider whether the Person who wrote them can be able to endure much longer the agonies and uncertainties which you are so peculiarly made to create. . . . For God's sake save me—or tell me my passion is of too awful a nature for you.   (*Rollins* II.290-91)

Denis de Rougemont speaks of the combination of "sensual fret" and "humanistic pride" in that form of love which demands a totality identifiable only with godhood or with death— a form of love exemplified in the myth of Tristan and in the myth under which Keats was laboring. "There is fret in it," he says, "because it depicts the sexual instinct being resented as a cruel fate and as a tyranny; there is pride, because the tyranny is imagined to become a divinizing force—setting man up against God."[12] This is the paradox both of Keats's erotic poems and of his "awful passion" for Fanny. Its irresoluble inner contradictions may be seen in his sonnet to her, where he demands a "whole," and "all"—down to the last "atom's atom" of body and soul—that no human being can give, except by dying, and where he conceives his own death as the result of her withholding:

> I cry your mercy—pity—love!—aye, love!
>   Merciful love that tantalises not,
> One-thoughted, never-wand'ring, guileless love,
>   Unmask'd, and being seen—without a blot!
> O, let me have thee whole,—all,—all—be mine!
>   That shape, that fairness, that sweet minor zest
> Of love, your kiss, those hands, those eyes divine,
>   That warm, white, lucent, million-pleasured breast,—
> Yourself—your soul—in pity give me all,
>   Withhold no atom's atom or I die,
> Or living on perhaps, your wretched thrall,
>   Forget, in the mist of idle misery,
> Life's purposes,—the palate of my mind
> Losing its gust, and my ambition blind!
>
> ("I cry your mercy . . .")

The last lines repeat the situation of the knight in the ballad of the Belle Dame, the alienated and impotent thrall of an inscrutable mistress who gives life only to give death.

The secrecy under which Keats kept his relationship to Fanny had no visible reason in his circumstances. Since so many other aspects of the relationship correspond, point by point, with the requirements of his myth, it is to be assumed that the element of secrecy—correspondent with that of the love-unions in his poetry from *Endymion* on—arose out of the same configuration. A letter of June 1820 to Fanny is full of injunctions to secrecy: his friends have all now become "tattlers and inquisitors . . . spying upon a secret I would rather die than share it with any body's confidence." "Your name never passes my Lips," he tells her, "do not let mine pass yours" (*Rollins*

II.293). The excessiveness of his behavior in this matter is brought out by the incident of the misdelivered letter—a note from Fanny—when Keats was ill at the Hunts'. The incident is recorded by Maria Gisborne:

> Yesterday . . . Mrs. Hunt came in to tea; she called to apologize for herself and Mr. Hunt, for not having kept their appointment on the Saturday before; they were prevented by an unpleasant circumstance that happened to Keats. While we were there on Thursday a note was brought for him after he had retired to his room to repose himself; Mrs. Hunt being occupied with the child desired her upper servant to take it to him, and thought no more about it. On Friday the servant left her, and on Saturday Thornton produced this note open (which contained not a word of the least consequence), telling his mother that the servant had given it to him before she left the house with the injunctions not to shew it to his mother till the following day. Poor Keats was affected by this inconceivable circumstance beyond what can be imagined; he wept for several hours, and resolved, notwithstanding Hunt's intreaties, to leave the house; he went to Hampstead that same evening.[13]

Keats's hysteria can only be partly accounted for by his illness, for he was acting within a pattern of compulsive secrecy that had obtained since the beginning of his relationship with Fanny. It was a relationship wrung from the deepest and most obscure chords of his being, whose exposure could bring only crisis.

There is clearly no outcome for this passion except death—the "mystic marriage" or ultimate form of "love-death"—and it is death that is obscurely desired under the name of love. Keats writes to Fanny:

> I have two luxuries to brood over in my walks, your Loveliness and the hour of my death. O that I could have possession of them both in the same minute. I hate the world: it batters too much the wings of my self-will, and

would I could take a sweet poison from your lips to send
me out of it.   (*Rollins* II.133)

After he went to Italy, dying, he wrote Brown that "the very
thing which I want to live most for will be a great occasion
of my death. . . . Were I in health it would make me ill." And
a little later: "If I had any chance of recovery, this passion
would kill me." This is essentially true. Once he had fallen
into the power of the Belle Dame, mistress of life and death,
she could only be his murderess. In the following holograph
lines, that are assumed to have been addressed to Fanny Brawne,
the beloved is directly accused of guilt for her lover's death:

> This living hand, now warm and capable
> Of earnest grasping, would, if it were cold
> And in the icy silence of the tomb,
> So haunt thy days and chill thy dreaming nights
> That thou would wish thine own heart dry of blood,
> So in my veins red life might stream again,
> And thou be conscience-calm'd. See, here it is—
> I hold it towards you.

V. The Passion of the Groves

IN KEATS'S GREAT ODES, the most conspicuous sign of a different spiritual climate is their tense. The tense of the erotic poems was the past: everything that happened was somewhere else and "long ago"—in Renaissance Florence or in ancient Corinth, in a feudal castle or in a world of faery where armored knights wandered about. But in the odes the tense is the present, projecting into the future. This is the tense of exigency and potentiality. Everything that happens is happening this instant or will happen directly. In the "Ode on Melancholy" we, the imaginary audience, are involved in the emergency—a true emergency, for something is to "emerge" from it, a transformation of our sense of the world. We are told not to go to Lethe to find the goddess Melancholy but to seek her in her dwelling, the "temple of Delight," and we are told what *does* and *will* happen to one who goes there. Elsewhere the forms of speech evoke scenes that exist in pure duration, as in the "Ode on a Grecian Urn":

> More happy love! more happy, happy love!
> For ever warm and still to be enjoy'd, . . .
> ....
> Who are these coming to the sacrifice?
> To what green altar, O mysterious priest,
> Lead'st thou that heifer . . .

or in an immediate futurity that is to be brought about by voluntary action, as in the "Ode to a Nightingale":

> Away! away! for I will fly to thee, . . .
> ....
> Already with thee! tender is the night . . .

and the "Ode to Psyche":

> I see, and sing, by my own eyes inspired.
> So let me be thy choir, . . .
>
> ....
>
> Yes, I will be thy priest, and build a fane
>   In some untrodden region of my mind, . . .

In "To Autumn;" "we," the imagined audience, are again brought into the emergent action, for we ourselves have only to "seek abroad" to witness with our own eyes the *anodos* and *cathodos* of a goddess. The most general observation one can make about the difference of spiritual climate between the erotic poems and the odes is that there is in the latter this new sense of an emergency that is creative, of an imminent change in perception by which all reality may be transformed.

The two sets of poems were written during approximately the same period. Keats seems to have thrown off the odes in quick, casual impulses at the center of those months when he produced the erotic poems, so that we cannot speak accurately of a decisive and chronologically fixed kind of intellectual "break-through." This whole florescence is so condensed in chronology—a matter of months—that to split it into intervals of an intellectual "evolution" following the calendar dates of the poems would be to falsify its psychological density. Considering the poems as closed aesthetic units, as we must consider them, we are yet looking on a contemporaneous series of moving equilibria—experimental arrangements, so to speak, whose differences of spiritual climate may be an effect of the type of arrangement itself.

The erotic poems are written as history. Event follows event in a fiction of historical time and after the last event nothing more can happen—history comes to an end in disappearance under impenetrable shadow (the end of *Endymion* and *The Eve of St. Agnes*) or violent death, alienation, impotence. The attitude that reflection takes upon such an end is one of irony. For this is not a tragic world in which the human spirit is triumphant even in destruction, but an ironic world where spirit is fatally wasted. (Where there is an apparent victory of desire over anxiety, as in *Endymion* and *The Eve*, the reflective attitude is still one of irony, if nostalgic irony—for the lovers vanished long ago in a dream of youth, and such things do not happen any more.) By irony, reflection externalizes itself from events—even if, and more necessarily, reflection finds itself mirrored in them as victim of the disaster. One of the effects of the ode form—the interiority of the form as a piece of "duration" rather than an extension of events in time—is a difference in the attitude or placement of the reflective faculty. Reflection is not now externalized "outside" the subject matter as in the attitude of irony. (Though there may be a technical kind of "irony" engaged in the complex architectonics of these poems, in their structural ambiguities and paradoxes, it is not irony in the larger and common sense that implies disinvolvement.) Reflection is now the hero of the drama—the one who cuts through conventional aspects of anxiety ("Melancholy") and goes straight into its "sovran shrine," the one who follows the ecstatic song of the nightingale into the forest and experiences a "mystic death" there, the one (in the "Grecian Urn") who stands at the crisis of intuition between time and duration and receives the astounding message that they are the same, the one who builds a temple in his brain for the marriage of Psyche and Eros, the one who (in "Autumn") celebrates the epiphany and withdrawal of the harvest goddess. Since what happens in these poems is the advent of a new form of perception, reflection is the center of that happening. With this psychic centering, there is a great increase of depth and range of content in the poems, for the content is no longer a fixed historical course but an involution of complexity—the mind folding inward upon itself in unexpected and complex figures.

Each of the odes is poised in a moment or episode of Keats's myth. In the sequence in which we shall review them ("Melancholy," the "Nightingale," the "Urn," "Psyche," and "Autumn") these episodes are: the hero's entrance into the shrine of the world-goddess, his "death" in the magic forest, his presence at a fertility rite danced by "marble men and maidens" (like the rites of Pan in *Endymion*), his ministration as priest at a "mystic marriage," and his attendance as celebrant on the epiphany of the earth-goddess and her withdrawal to the underworld. Expressly, the poetic procedure is that of incantation. Like the formula or spell recited in agricultural magic, medical magic, and love magic, the poem proceeds by naming and describing the attributes of a phenomenon of apparition ("Thou still unravish'd bride of quietness," "Thou wast not born for death, immortal Bird!," "Season of mists and mellow fruitfulness"). The psychology of the drama and even of the syntax is surprisingly like that of primitive magic. The following song from the New Hebrides, chanted by a man who wants a wife, has magical potency:

> The song cries, the song cries,
> The song cries, Let her be my wife!
> The woman who is there,
> The two women, they two
> Who are in the sacred stone,
> Who sit inside, who live in the stone,
> The song cries, Let both come out![1]

Here the singer does not address directly the women who live in the stone, but uses the song as an intermediary; it is not the person but the melodic set of words that has the compelling magic. Similarly, in the "Ode to Psyche," the formal set of words—the poem itself—has the power to compel the apparition of the goddess, for the poem is her temple constructed by the priest-poet in his "working brain," her shrine, grove, oracle, and choir. Again, in the "Ode to a Nightingale," the poem acts as the magical spell which takes the poet into the forest ("not charioted by Bacchus and his pards, but on the viewless wings of Poesy") and the presence of the "immortal bird." The following is an Old Irish mantic poem:

Good tidings: sea fruitful, wave-washed strand, smiling woods; witchcraft flees, orchards bloom, cornfields ripen, bees swarm, a cheerful world, peace and plenty, happy summer.[2]

This was chanted by a prophet as an augury: the desired aspect of nature is invoked as if present, and the magical function of the words is to make it present. The method of the ode "To Autumn" is the same. Even the syntax is like that of the Old Irish poem, additive assertions about the fruitfulness of the season, the apparition of the corn-maiden, and the creatures who make up her choir.

The incantation develops its theme in essentially the same way as Keats's Fragment of an "Ode to Maia": the invocation of the goddess, the reminder of how she has appeared at other times, the appeal that she can help the poet with her power now:

> Mother of Hermes! and still youthful Maia!
>   May I sing to thee
> As thou wast hymned on the shores of Baiae?
>   Or may I woo thee
> In earlier Sicilian? or thy smiles
> Seek, as they once were sought, in Grecian isles,
> By bards who died content on pleasant sward,
>   Leaving great verse unto a little clan?
> O give me their old vigour, and unheard,
>   Save of the quiet primrose, and the span
>   Of heaven, and few ears
> Rounded by thee, my song should die away,
>   Content as theirs,
> Rich in the simple worship of a day.

In all its simplicity the poetic situation in the "Ode to Maia" has the germinal characteristics of the great odes, the grammar of the vocative, imperative, and conditional establishing the mode of imminence. Keats inherited the literary tradition of the ode, but to write within a tradition is not simply to imitate an older literary manner (to use its conventions as pattern, allegory, or metaphor). The cantatory character of the form and the magical intent inherent in it are wonderfully suitable to the mythopoeic mentality, and gave Keats a means of developing his myth beyond the negative point it had reached in the erotic poems, where love led to death, and into a sphere of possibility, imminence, and transformation.

The Veiled Goddess: "Ode on Melancholy"

As this poem is ordinarily interpreted, it would seem to be concerned with a peculiarly personal quality of experience, involving intense emotional excitement and disorder through the deliberate exacerbation of sensitivity. According to the usual reading, the poem is a prescription for "intensity": the precocious hedonist or aesthete cultivates states of feeling in which pain and pleasure, joy and sadness, are experienced simultaneously. But if this were the chief import of the ode, it would be oddly at variance with the classical effect of regularity, balance, proportion, and controlled emotion in the handling of the poetic form itself. The reading obscures the traditional setting of thought which gave Keats his subject and which determines the meaning of the word "melancholy" as used in the poem. It obscures also the effectiveness of the poem's actual mechanisms. These mechanisms are the experimental, problem-solving ones of drama—of a purposive action unfolding through error and conflict toward a point of revelation or discovery. The action takes the figure of a quest, the purpose being to find Melancholy. The quest figure is set up in the initial phrase, warning against a false road, and is pursued to the recognition scene at the end where Melancholy is confronted face to face. This kind of structure itself presupposes that what is discovered in the last stanza will have a different quality and a different significance from what is known about the problem in the previous stanzas. In other words, the conflicting terms of the problem, the simple opposition of extreme emotions and feelings, must be somehow transformed at the end.

In Keats's erotic poems, anxiety is overwhelming: the image of sexual love—the central image of fertility, generation, and vitality—tends to become a malignant disguise of death. But the "Ode on Melancholy" takes anxiety ("the wakeful anguish of the soul") as its formal subject, so that poetic form itself enforces a new kind of equilibrium. Like *Hamlet* and *Job*, the ode is, in its slight lyric way, a dramatization of the existential condition. By its dramatic approach, it places anxiety under the aspect of experiment—that is, as not merely a static condition of suffering but as a theater of exploratory action and of revelation through stress and conflict. In its revelation of a traditional theme, its references are public and collective rather than precociously personal.

The ode was anciently a choral form, providing a dramatic musical setting for ritual or heroic theater, with the divisions of the chorus answering each other in strophe, antistrophe, and epode, as they interpreted some action being carried out simultaneously at the altar or on the stage. The triadic arrangement of the "Ode on Melancholy" (like that of the ode "To Autumn") preserves this choral structure with its dramatic illusion. Resonance between chorus and protagonist is established in the opening words—"No, no, go not to Lethe"—with their imperative of a quest to be undertaken and a false road to be avoided. The protagonist is a "you" ("thy pale forehead," "your rosary," "your sorrow's mysteries"), a public or universal persona whose engagement in a search for Melancholy presumes its representative importance and the collective concern voiced by the chorus. In the recognition scene at the end of the poem, the actor is no longer a "you" but a "he" ("seen of none save him"), a change corresponding with a shift in the verbs, from the imperative of immediate action to the tense of a conditional future—the tense of possibility or vision—and corresponding also with a change from the uncapitalized "melancholy" in the body of the poem, where the word refers to a state of mind suffered, to capitalization of Melancholy, who now, at the point of discovery, is recognized as a personage, a divine power austerely veiled. At this point the actor himself is transformed, from the collective "you," the existential sufferer of *Angst*, to the elect and heroic "one" who is capable of the vision in the temple. For this drama, the stanzaic divisions of the poem set up three planes of experience, corresponding with scenic divisions on a stepped stage: the underworld of Lethe and the grove of Proserpine; the natural and human world of April and mortal love; and the visionary temple where the protagonist is heroized. Following these divisions, the germinal idea of the poem—a search for Melancholy—is involuted upon itself, first, as a temptation to narcosis, then as a kind of psychognosis of the dynamics of anxiety, and finally as achieved gnosis in the presence of the unifying symbol which the poem has sought.

In the first stanza Keats borrows the baroque style of the pre-Romantics of the "graveyard school," but manipulates their type of mortuary meditation for a different purpose. Assuming with them, that metaphysical anxiety is the condition of serious reflection and that therefore it should be kept up, so to speak, he isolates the deathward gravity in this state of mind. Concentration on emblems of mortality provides a negative kind of intoxication, a "poisonous wine" that submerges the actual tensions of anxiety and drugs, "the wakeful anguish of the soul." The underworld of death, where the mind travels as it broods on temporal fatality, is full of treacherously sedative images. In warning against narcotic devotionals to a false iconography, the stanza treats them as a kind of Black Mass inversion of religious ritual and typology. "Make not your rosary of yew-berries" puns on formal meditation on the dolors of the Virgin. "Nor let the beetle, nor the death-moth be your mournful Psyche" puns on resurrection imagery: the beetle is the scarab inserted in the breast of the mummy, the moth is an emblematic form of the soul (psyche) released from the dead body; both are false representations of what he is searching for, because they are post-mortem symbols— only the living are capable of "wakeful anguish." The "ruby grape of Proserpine" is a ghostly simulacrum of "Joy's grape" in the last stanza, which the initiate of Melancholy burst against his palate fine: this is eucharistic imagery, miming the Mass and Dionysian intoxication, but the "grape of Proserpine"— nightshade—is a deadly narcotic. In the Orphic mysteries, the road taken by the initiate led toward Lethe, the water that deadens consciousness, and Proserpine's grove, but he was warned to avoid these; near them a branching path led to the well of Mnemosyne—the world's memory or *anima mundi*— and there the initiate was to go, to receive *more* consciousness. The warning against the path to Lethe in this stanza is modeled on the formula of the Orphic tablets: the candidate for "sorrow's mysteries"—the secret ritual operations requisite for the discovery of Melancholy—must take another path, demanding more strenuous consciousness.

Keats has taken with extraordinary literalness the problematic assumption that anxiety should be sought, and with the same verve of literalism he exhibits, in the second stanza, the polarized structure of anxiety—a state of mind tensed and stretched between positive and negative poles. It is from the tensions of the organic outer world, poised between generation and death, that anxiety takes a definite form; the symbols of death acquire their significance only in polarity with the symbols of generation, florescence, and love. In the first lines of the stanza, the "wakeful anguish of the soul" finds its correspondent image in the outer world, not in the fall of the year, season of mournful passage, but in the generative spring—a tense and ambiguous April, when the droop-headed flowers on the green hill are "fostered" by a "shroud" of rain, an image in which the expectancy of life equivocates with the shadow of death. The other images of the stanza form a complex variation on the theme of *Carpe diem*, whose imperative "Gather ye roses while ye may" is transformed from a hedonistic injunction to enjoy because life is short, into a purposive tensing of consciousness by the extremes of despair and ardor, the dynamic psychical reflection of the vitalities of the world in their most vivid and fragile form—the "morning rose," the "rainbow of the salt sand-wave," the "wealth of globed peonies," and the mistress with the "peerless eyes."

To borrow Francis Fergusson's terms for the moments of the tragic rhythm—Purpose, Passion, Perception—as the first stanza of the ode has set up the purpose of the quest, the second stanza defines the "passion" or "suffering." But as the "wakeful anguish of the soul" is deliberately sought by the protagonist in order to carry out his quest, he is not only patient but agent. He voluntarily assumes the stresses of anguish as a "way." This volitional aspect of the engagement changes the relationship of the ego to those conditions of existence—temporary transiency, the fragility of life, the decay hidden in vitality—out of which anxiety arises. These conditions are seized by the mind, not as levies externally imposed on life by its temporal character, but as the internal form of consciousness. The fatal terms of time are interiorized as duration, the depthless structure of the psyche.

The temple scene in the last stanza corresponds with the third moment of the tragic rhythm, that of perception. From the existential plane of organic life in its fervor and doom, where the passion takes place, the scene shifts to the plane of grace, of spiritual receptivity and "seeing." The transition is accomplished almost unapparently, through the equivocation of the pronoun in "She dwells with Beauty—Beauty that must die." The backward reference of "she" is to "thy mistress" in the previous stanza. But in the syntactical impulse of the third stanza it refers foward to Melancholy herself (who is not the same mistress as the one with the peerless eyes, for she is veiled). As, in Keats's other poems, the hero crosses a threshold—of the underworld or of a castle or palace—to enter the precinct of his "immortal love," the agonist of Melancholy who has deliberately assumed the suffering presupposed by his quest passes the threshold of her temple. In other poems the threshold crossing is frequently accomplished by the mechanism of a dream or trance—a release of instinctive impulses in the mind's "darkness"—but here it is achieved by "wakeful" anguish, the conscious mind strongly involved in the ritualistic discovery of a recognizable event.

The veiled figure of Melancholy is a figure who reappears in *The Fall of Hyperion* under the name of Moneta. The scene in the ode is a silhouette or reduced profile of the temple scene in *The Fall*, where the goddess stands in her shrine, robed in deep and awesome veils, as her votary—the dreaming poet—approaches. She tells him that he is "near cousin to the common dust" and that he will "rot on the pavement" where he stands, unless he can perform the strenuous ritual of her mystery, a rite that resembles the throes of both death and birth. This is, in essence, a sacramental reenactment of the universal pattern, the existential condition; by enacting it ritually and voluntarily, the probationer quickens in himself the sense of his relationship to the total of life, thus recentering his own life in that mysterious fullness. Given this background in *The*

Fall of Hyperion, the small silhouetted scene in the "Ode on Melancholy" comes into sharper outline. As a symbolic form, the temple itself—for cultures nourished in mythology—corresponds with the world-plenum; its axes are the four directions of the horizon; the altar or sanctuary at the center is the point where all directions converge and where the form and energy of the world are continuously renewed (in *The Fall*, the cosmic configuration of the temple is dwelt upon at length).

Melancholy and Moneta, as the same archetypal figure, are related also to Mnemosyne in *Hyperion*, the great robed goddess who superintends the ritual rebirth of Apollo. Mnemosyne—who in Orphic ritual met the initiate in the underworld, where he drank from her well the draught of immortal consciousness—was the mother of the Muses, of all the arts and disciplines of knowledge; as "Memory"—she was the consciousness of the world. In this relationship, both Moneta of *The Fall* and Melancholy of the ode are that world-memory by which individual consciousness is quickened and centered—and unless so quickened and centered, a "quintessence of dust." From the mysterious Moon-goddess of *Endymion*, who made mountains "rise and rise," governed the tides of the sea and all things animate and inanimate, but who was never able to appear in that poem except in her Kore form, Keats's poetry has been moving toward this "immortal love" through phases of erotic desperation.

The particular rite that the votary of Melancholy enacts is a food-rite. She is

> seen of none save him whose strenuous tongue
> Can burst Joy's grape against his palate fine;
> His soul shall taste the sadness of her might,
> And be among her cloudy trophies hung.

As in other sacramental scenes in Keats's poems, the food is the grape—the god-intoxicant of the rites of Dionysos and Orpheus and of the Christian Eucharist. The temple of Melancholy is the "very temple of Delight"—the circumference and center of the ardors of the world, and her sacred food, the grape, is of a kind that inspires not only heightened consciousness but a different quality of consciousness. The disciplined austerity of the food-rite is defined by the fact that the initiate takes only one grape on his "strenuous tongue" (as, in the Eucharist, the communicant takes only one sip from the wine-cup). The single grape, taken sacramentally, is the miraculous abundance of the food of life. The volitional character of what is done is important (as it was in the second stanza, where the votary of Melancholy voluntarily undertook the existential anguish): for this act of food-taking, which rehearses in mime the creative biological transformation of vegetable matter into human vitality, becomes by virtue of the participant's "strenuousness"—the tension of volition—creative at the level of knowledge, a transformation of consciousness.

The line, "His soul shall taste the sadness of her might," Keats had written as "His soul shall taste the anguish of her might." The earlier line preserves the "wakeful anguish" of the first stanza, and carries the theme of the poem more distinctly. "Tasting" is the most intimate and organic way that knowledge of the outer world is carried to the senses; scarcely any images or metaphors can be made out of the sense of taste because it is the most purely physiological of sense-experiences. Allied with the incorporation of food, it is the body's subtlest means of "knowing." By eating the grape, the initiate of Melancholy "tastes" the divine power of Melancholy herself, the primeval Moira in whom all divisions and oppositions, spans and boundaries, geneses and endings, have their single source. The recognition of this veiled figure, who provides the unifying symbol of the poem, is achieved not as an intellectual perception in abstraction from the senses, but as organic gnosis.

The poem as it is ordinarily read—as a prescription for emotional intensity by exacerbation of simultaneous extremes of feeling—tends, by its inattention to the mechanisms of the form, to give the last stanza a morbid significance, confusing the progression of the tragic rhythm with the death-wish that enjoys such curious critical popularity. The narcosis of despair (suicide) has been abjured in the first stanza, the second stanza is an imperative to vital engagement, and the ritual recognition in the third stanza is *sacramental* rather than *sacrificial*.

The trophy figure in the last line belongs to the mythological context Keats has used from the beginning of the poem, with its warning against the road to Lethe. As against Lethe, the forgetfulness into which the dead are eased, trophies dedicated in temples were memorials of the vigorous accomplishments of the living. Homer's heroes were constantly dedicating such trophies to the deities who gave them prowess, as the victors in the Olympic games dedicated armor, chariots, and rich drinking vessels as memorial trophies to be hung up in temples. A champion poet dedicated his book or poem as a trophy: so Hesiod dedicated his prize. Temple trophies were frequently statuettes of armed warriors or athletes donated by champions. The poets and musicians of Mount Helicon who won the prize there memorialized their achievement in the same fashion. In Keats's ode, the trophy that the hero dedicates in the temple is also of an ideal character—his soul—that is to say, a dedication of mind in its ideal capacity. The trophy figure corresponds with what Yeats called the "Mask," "that object of desire or moral ideal which is of all possible things the most difficult"—a "form created by passion to unite us to ourselves."

A DREAM OF STONE: "ODE ON A GRECIAN URN"

Very little of Dorothy Van Ghent's section on the "Ode on a Grecian Urn" reached the stage of sustained prose; most of it remains in a sheaf of handwritten notes.* Yet it is precisely what feels to the editor as a sibylline form that gives to these tiny leaves an aura of containing a central, perhaps very private, message about Keats, and about her relationship to Keats. For her the "Ode" is not, as it is for the vast majority of commentators, about the nature of "art." Rather it is about Keats's hero, who here more than elsewhere merges perilously,

---

* The underlined passages throughout this chapter are my summaries of Dorothy Van Ghent's arguments as I could best reconstruct them from her notes. J.C.R.

vulnerably with the poet, as he probes a journey from self-isolation yet probes it in the wrong way. The poem becomes the nightmare of the Odes, a communion with an object that beckons him erotically but departs from him as stone—a meditative counterpart to "La Belle Dame." Or rather, and this is really her point, the hero loses nerve in the face of the eroticism he has called up (stanza I) and escapes into a spirituality which is really a human thinness, an abstracting from life of its sexuality. The aphorism at the end is hollow because it is all intellect, all sublimed. Several times in the notes I found such words as "unfortunate," "terror," "terrible," "harrowing," "the gravity of the hero's situation." For her this is the crisis poem in Keats, a bold, incoherent failure, a near loss of persona and of personal control. It is an undesigned critique of "imagination," that too-highly acclaimed faculty that can lead one away from participation in life.

The eight extant typed pages are as follows:

For its size, the "Ode on a Grecian Urn" has probably had more exegetical attention than any other poem in the language. The interpretations vary a good deal, but certain assumptions are uniform. One is that the "I" implicit in the grammar (the person looking at the urn and addressing questions to it) is Keats. Another is that the urn's primary distinction and symbolism lie in its being a "work of art" which has survived from an ancient time; the relationship between the "I" (Keats) and the urn is therefore construed as an aesthetic one. A third general assumption is that the ode presents a coherent system of meanings—although, to explain that system, criticism has always had to bring to the poem convictions and modes of reasoning (especially about "truth" and "beauty") that do not inhere in the ode but have to be imported from outside, from speculations about what was going on in Keats's head or from the reader's personal philosophic or aesthetic stock.

An "I" in any projected situation—dream, fantasy, or lyric poem—is a persona, a dramatic "mask" playing a certain role, and cannot be accurately identified with the person who does the projecting. If the ode is taken as a piece of psychic action having the objective form of a small drama or "plot," the "I" may be detached from its confining reference to Keats and acquire wider dimension as a symbolic character, the hero of a tale. The plot of the poem is a version of the mythical and fairy-tale plot in which a hero goes to some venerable bird or animal or patriarch or sibyl for advice on how to defeat the evil of his predicament and set things right in the disordered kingdom. In the usual "aesthetic" reading of the poem, the relationship between the hero and the urn is fortuitous and passive. Constellated in a plot, the relationship is purposeful and perilous: the hero comes to consult the urn as Aeneas came to the Cumaean Sibyl and Oedipus to the oracle of Delphi—he has a serious problem and is in need of the urn's ancient widsom. The urn's role is thus not primarily aesthetic but practical. If the hero fails to understand the urn (and that is the major critical problem, concentrating in the famous aphorism in the last lines), the example of Oedipus suggests that the hero's "blindness" is a classic complication of a plot of this kind; he may have landed himself in a frightful pre- dicament of inner scission from which there is no recovery— at least not in the terms the poem sets. From this point of view, the poem does not present a coherent system of mean- ings—although possibly it presents two systems, the urn's and the hero's, which are not congruent. In the incongruence of these two systems lie the pity and terror of the plot.

To retrace the course of events in the ode: the hero's prob- lem is extremely grave. He lives in a world perplexed by ne- gations, haunted by sorrow, fever, and thirst, where existence is consumed in a meaningless process of dying, of passage, pain, and loss. It is a world of discontinuities, where truth is without beauty and beauty without truth (otherwise the state- ment at the end, that "beauty is truth, truth beauty," would not be positioned and phrased as a revelation). As truth and beauty are divided, subject and object are incurably separated from each other. The whole ode is riddled by that separation, with the hero cast fatally in the role of impotent spectator. He is perhaps the first "outsider" of modern literature. This defective situation, where there is no common construct for the "within" and the "without," provides this motive for his questioning of the urn.

The superb ancient form bears on its surface scenes of ancestral life, a ritual fertility orgy with lovers pursuing each other through a forest, a religious procession led by a priest to an altar in the woods where a heifer is to be sacrificed, and the little town from which all these people came. From these scenes the urn acquires its authoritative, oracular character, as a symbol of collective experience, legitimized by age, by its beauty and intactness, and by the fact that gods are present here. Like the Cumaean Sibyl and the priestess of the Delphic oracle, the urn is female, a kind of *anima mundi*—world-soul or world-memory (corresponding, in Keats's own work, to the goddess Melancholy in the "Ode on Melancholy," Mnemosyne in *Hyperion*, and Moneta in *The Fall of Hyperion*—poems having local plot-elements similar to the plot of the "Ode on a Grecian Urn").

Urn-shapes are unfathomably old in magical and religious symbolism. Such shapes are often represented as holding within the ovoid an upright man, naked or in sacerdotal garment and with a long beard (like the "mysterious priest" of the ode), or a cross—the abstract figure of man—indicating the four points of the compass and the navel of the universe, with the twelve signs of the zodiac, rivers and mountains and animals, and most frequently the Tree of Life with the serpent of the underworld coiled about its roots. Under this aspect, the urn-shape is a propaedeutic image of wholeness, embracing all nature and man, showing in mythologems the forces flowing through reality and the polarizations of life. The scenes on the Grecian urn have a comparable universality, representing, in the bacchic orgy and the sacrifice, life caught in moments of supreme significance. The powers thought of as divine enter into the urn to renew it and insure its continuance. There are moments when (to use Malinowski's phrase) it becomes "a blaze of reality," and, in the little town, the homely common paths of daily life are embraced by the visionary, maternal urn.

In the standard "aesthetic" reading of the ode the urn is

denatured, disinfected, of those associations of female function which urns naturally have, which they have had since pottery was invented, and which they continue to have in total disregard of literary tastes and psychological resistances. As to "uterine symbolism" as such, most people have never seen a womb, since the organ is not usually exposed, and it is doubtful if a universally symbolic form, like an urn, draws its associations from so recondite an instrument; but there has never been any doubt that man is born of woman, nor of what the swelling shape of the pregnant woman portends. And it is not true that Keats "paid no attention at all to the shape." The urn is called a "bride" in the first line, certainly with relevance to the sexual connotation of the shape, in the fifth line it is spoken of as a "shape" ("What a leaf-fring'd legend haunts about thy shape") and again in the last stanza ("O Attic shape! Fair attitude!"). If the shape made no difference, he could have placed the sculptured figures on a frieze, like the one in the Elgin Marbles where he had seen the heifer "lowing at the skies," and where they would have had more room—for this is an extraordinarily crowded urn. As it is, the urn gives the commanding form to the imagery of the poem, and there is no avoiding its symbolism as a shape.

The fertility orgy depicted on one side of the urn bears a direct relationship with that aspect of urn-symbolism which has to do with fecundity and birth; and relationship also with the female earth of which pots are made (the urn is of marble, but marble too is earth), for such rites were held when the earth was thought to need the human example of love-making in order to become fruitful, its common fruits of daily use to be stored again in the mothering urn. The sacrifice depicted on the other side is the natural counterpart of the scene of ritual love-making, and is related to that aspect of urn-symbolism which has to do with death; together they express the ritual laws governing all natural things.

If the title of the "Ode on a Grecian Urn" were changed to "Ode on a Greek Vase," one would become startlingly aware of a layer of meaning that had fallen away from the poem, for the word "urn" inevitably arouses an association with death. Used immemorially for burial, ossuary, or incinerary purposes (as Keats knew from Plutarch and others, the Athenians buried their dead in giant urns, *pythoi*, sunk in the ground), urns are still placed on graves, often with growing plants in them. Like the basil that flourished with peculiar luxuriance in the urn where Isabella interred the head of her lover, the plants growing in graveyard urns as well as in garden urns are reminders of that other indivisible emblematism of urns as shapes of earth made round to contain food-supplies and nourish life like the female belly. Sir Thomas Browne in his *Urn Burial*, discussing Roman ossuary urns found in Norfolk, says that the shapes vary, some having long necks, ears, and handles, "but most imitate a circular figure, in a spherical and round composure. . . . But the common form with necks was a proper figure, making our last bed like our first."

Thus the urn of the poem is a kind of *krater* or mixing-bowl of elemental symbols (comparable, on the natural level, to the "simple substances"—earth, air, fire, and water—anciently thought to compose the physical universe), symbols that are full of power, not secondary and derived effectiveness, derived from learning and thought, but the original, primitive power that shapes our deepest unconscious responses into images. Or it is a kind of Grail, *servator mundi*, a vessel of food and healing that has come down from ancient times and that is greatly needed in this schismatic world in which the hero lives, where there is grave peril of destruction of all that the centuries and millennia of human experience have built up. Or it is a kind of *thalamus* or bridal chamber, garlanded with forest branches, offering to the hero—who here plays the role of the conscious ego—a bride of ancient ancestry, the unknown psyche. Or is what W. B. Yeats called the "Mask"— "a form created by passion to unite us to ourselves." The hero's problem is division, of which he himself is the representative sundered fragment, standing outside with his burning forehead and parching tongue, racked by mortal anxiety, an erratic object in a disjointed world. His encounter with the urn—following the legendary paradigm of such encounters— should tell him who he is, his parentage, how he is related to the past and what resources he has inherited, what dangers he faces and what skills he has to face them with. What does he do with this privileged moment? That is the plot of the poem.

From here I have simply pieced together selected fragments.

The hero has come to the ancient urn to find some meaning in his mortal condition, some wisdom about life which will place him *in it*, so that he is no longer standing outside with his burning forehead and parching tongue, his "heart high-sorrowful," consumed in a meaningless process of dying, of passage and loss.

ON FIRST APPROACHING the urn, he thinks it will have a "flowery tale" to tell him, but the tale turns out to be not at all flowery.

> Thou still unravish'd bride of quietness,
>   Thou foster-child of silence and slow time,
> Sylvan historian, who canst thus express
>   A flowery tale more sweetly than our rhyme:
> What leaf-fring'd legend haunts about thy shape
>   Of deities or mortals, or of both,
>   In Tempe or the dales of Arcady?
>   What men or gods are these? What maidens loth?
> What mad pursuit? What struggle to escape?
>   What pipes and timbrels? What wild ecstasy?

While he seems to be asking for historical information—who are these people? what place is this? what is going on here?—it is perfectly obvious what is going on; and one does not need to ask the particular identity of the men or gods madly pursuing maidens through the woods to couple with them, or the names of the girls, for personal identity is precisely what is lost in the "wild ecstasy" of the group orgy and what the orgy, with its clamor of pipes and timbrels, is meant to obliterate. Nor does one need to ask where all this is taking place—Tempe or the dales of Arcady—for it could have happened in thousands of places in the Mediterranean world at any time over thousands of years, and Keats was well aware of the fact from his reading in eighteenth-century archeology and mythography. But the historical question is largely academic, for the urn is a fantasied urn (like the "dreamy urn" of the "Ode on Indolence," which is deliberately treated as a product of "dim dreams"). Rhetorically, the questions that are asked in this stanza contain their own answers, but they are also an expression of wonder at the strangeness of the scene. For it has arisen from an unmoralized part of the psyche that is unrecognizable as belonging to the personal self, and that indeed is not personal but collective and anonymous, like the figures on the urn. So a dreamer might ask himself, on waking, where the figures of his dream came from, how they could have entered his mind, and what in the world they could be doing there.

KEATS SCHOLARS have traced a number of possible models for the imagery of the urn, but have ignored the common ritual content of the supposed models. Among the "sources" that have been traced is the Townley vase, which shows a bacchic dance, the Borghese vase, with a bacchic dance and a piper under a canopy of leaves, the Holland House vase, showing a sacrifice; in the Elgin Marbles is a heifer being led to a sacrifice; Potter's *Antiquities*, one of Keats's books, contains a description of the festival of the Hyacinthia at Athens, with heifers sacrificed at altars made of turf, boys playing harps and flutes, choirs of young men, virgins, persons appointed to dance in the ancient form, and the multitudes so eager to participate that the city is "left empty and desolate"; Spence's *Polymetis*, another book Keats encountered very early, has a condensed version of a passage from Longus' *Daphnis and Chloe*, where, after a sacrifice to Pan, shepherds perform an ancient dance representing the god's pursuit of the maiden Syrinx (Keats could also have read Longus himself, in various contemporary editions which had illustrations of this and similar scenes). The common element among all these and the scenes on the urn is that they represent rituals for the renewal and insurance of all nature, vegetable, animal, and human. It is, after all, for just such a purpose that the hero has come to the venerable urn, to seek wisdom for the renewal of his own sadly depleted life. But the only significance that critical scholarship has attributed either to the supposed models or to the urn of the poem is that they represent an "ideal": youth, beauty, and radical innocence paralyzed in a "work of art" of a peculiarly petrifying medium—although what the scenes actually symbolize is a collective action intended to prevent life from becoming paralyzed and to keep it moving. To interpret the scenes in this way is to repeat what the hero of the poem does—confusing the import of the images with the stony medium in which they are transfixed.

The strangeness of this confusion, amounting, it would seem, to an antipathy for the urn's plainly stated meaning, may be illustrated more clearly by comparison of the first scene with the story of Krishna and the herd girls, which belongs to the same corpus of myth as the story of Bacchus' pursuit of Syrinx, Apollo's pursuit of Daphne (this tale, in Sandys' *Ovid*, has been cited as another model for Keats's lovers), and all the similar tales about Zeus and mortal women. In the familiar late classical stories, the god is after one woman, but the example of the shameless rapes committed by Zeus, the fact that Pan is part goat, and the orgiastic nature of bacchic ritual, indicate that the license of gods is unlimited—for their business is to fertilize life, not to moralize it. The stories of individual love affairs between gods and mortals derive from ritual episodes, probably performed as dances, like the shepherds' dance in *Daphnis and Chloe*, where one of the dancers takes the part of Pan and another of Syrinx—episodes symbolizing, not some fanciful romantic affair, but a real and collectively important event (or one that must be made to recur by the dance magic). In the story of Krishna and the herd maids, the god copulates with a thousand girls at once, which is only another way of showing the ubiquity of the divine embrace. The celestial shepherd wanders through the woods, "charming all with the music of his flute, wild creatures, demons, maidens. The peacocks dance for joy. The cows come running, the fresh grass still in their jaws, and the calves come all splattered with their mothers' milk. The beasts weep tears of joy when they hear the flute and the shepherd." The herd girls throng round the god, who "satisfies his thousand tender loves at one and the same time; each of them possesses him for herself alone, and all have him entire." The episode occurs in the forest, and as depicted in Indian art, the intertwining limbs of the girls and the god are like a greater luxuriance of plant growth, their arms like stems and their hair like vine tendrils. The pulsation of joy "pervades plants, animals, God, and man. Both blood and sap respond to the call of the holy Flautist." Like its parallels in classical myth, the symbol is rooted in instinct, which is why it recurs with endless variation in dream and poetry and art. As a psychic event, it serves to link up again the individual human soul—always threatened by alienation and sterility—with the natural, living world and with his own instinctive, creative resources. But imagine this forest of beings turned to stone, so that neither sap nor blood can flow, the girls frozen in abstract glacial chastity at the moment of embrace, the god impotent, the fertilizing meaning of the divine union falsified and denied. That is the way the hero of the ode interprets the similar scene before him.

THE INTERPRETATION which he puts upon the scene attempts to exclude both sex and death. The piper is said to "pipe to the spirit" only, but spirit (that part of experience which is *meaning*) when unsupported by nature is merely spectral and negative. The ditties have "no tone." Underneath this insistence on a happiness beyond nature ("all breathing human passion far above") is an evident repulsion against the magic the lovers are practicing, sexual magic of the most primitive kind, intended to reestablish the connection between the earth and the "dark" powers of human instinct, of the group, the powers of fertility in nature. But the hero, desperately seeking communication with those powers, at the same time tries to neutralize and disinfect them. Paralyzed in his imagination, the lovers might as well be sexless.

STRANGELY UNWILLING to recognize the direct symbolism of the image, he finds all its purport only in the medium—the stone in which it is carved.

> Heard melodies are sweet, but those unheard
>   Are sweeter; therefore, ye soft pipes, play on;
> Not to the sensual ear, but, more endear'd,
>   Pipe to the spirit ditties of no tone:
> Fair youth, beneath the trees, thou canst not leave
>   Thy song, nor ever can those trees be bare;
>   Bold Lover, never, never canst thou kiss,
> Though winning near the goal—yet, do not grieve;
>   She cannot fade, though thou hast not thy bliss,
>   For ever wilt thou love, and she be fair!

In the following stanza the lovers are "happy" because they are made of stone and unable to breathe or move. In Samuel Beckett's plays, where people are put in ashcans and urns for an eternity of degrading impotence, they are not happy but wretched. In the familiar anxiety dream when one is suddenly "turned to stone," the blood frozen and limbs petrified, the experience is one of nightmare horror. Only by a psychic deception can stony rigidity be considered a happy condition of life—but the mind is adept at such deceptions, as witnessed by the fact that critical scholarship has almost uniformly agreed with the hero, in effect repudiating the plain meaning of the urn in favor of a barren cerebral interpretation. The hero's spiritual predicament is clearly not entirely personal.

The piling up of grammatical negatives in the stanza reflects this denial: melodies "unheard," played "not to the sensual ear," "ditties of no tone," "thou canst not leave thy song," "nor ever can those trees be bare," "never, never canst thou kiss," "do not grieve," "she cannot fade," "thou hast not thy bliss." Everything here which seems to affirm a deathless happiness can use only forms of negation, but because the unconscious is engaged in this tortuous linguistic game too, the negatives double over on themselves, denying the very happiness ascribed to the petrified lovers—"thou hast not thy bliss"—and they have to be consoled—"yet, do not grieve"—

for the dreadful state imposed on them. In the third stanza the word "happy" is repeated six times, with a rather desperate effect of insistence on a series of untenable propositions: that breasts can pant "for ever" because unable to pant, that the piper's songs are "for ever" new because he has no breath to pipe with, that love "still to be enjoy'd" is happy because it can never be enjoyed.

> Ah, happy, happy boughs! that cannot shed
>   Your leaves, nor ever bid the Spring adieu;
> And, happy melodist, unwearied,
>   For ever piping songs for ever new;
> More happy love! more happy, happy love!
>   For ever warm and still to be enjoy'd,
>   For ever panting, and for ever young;
> All breathing human passion far above,
>   That leaves a heart high-sorrowful and cloy'd,
>   A burning forehead, and a parching tongue.

The stanza is somewhat asthmatic and short-winded, with no through-flow of syntactical rhythm, as if the hero himself, like the figures on the urn, were suffering a stoppage of circulation.

The notes suggest that by the end of stanza III the hero has, out of his own spirit of negation, of inhibition, driven himself beyond, "above," outside the sphere of love, has made himself inaccessible and immobile (like the urn itself). It is precisely the experience of self-isolation and undesired commitment to a vision of alienation and death that the fourth stanza records.

That he is engaged in an intrigue to denature the urn of all chthonic content gives to his case a peculiarly modern irony, not to say pity and terror. In this constellation, he plays the part of the ego, refusing to admit that the instinctive, collective elements of the psyche have anything to do with the self. They must be neutralized as shards of the antique. But even the antique must be forced to represent a purely cerebral "ideal": in the interests of "Beauty," there must be no birth, no sexuality, no death. As the lovers cannot mate, they cannot die either.

To admit the great chthonic magic of the urn would be

intellectually disastrous. This unwillingness, unformulated and devious, determines the tortuous course of the ode.

> Who are these coming to the sacrifice?
>   To what green altar, O mysterious priest,
> Lead'st thou that heifer lowing at the skies,
>   And all her silken flanks with garlands drest?
> What little town by river or sea shore,
>   Or mountain-built with peaceful citadel,
>   Is emptied of this folk, this pious morn?
> And, little town, thy streets for evermore
>   Will silent be; and not a soul to tell
>   Why thou art desolate, can e'er return.

As in the first stanza, the questioning form allows the images their own independent being, without the hero's trying to impose his interpretation upon them as he did in the second and third stanzas. They are, indeed, more powerful than he, because they have existed for aeons and have unfathomable roots in human experience. And now they exact the penalty of his hubris. For it is a kind of hubris that has possessed him—the hubris of the ego that considers itself alone and autonomous, existential, separated from the ancestral past, separated from its own instincts alien to mind, an outsider in a universe not made for it, victimized by mortal fate as by an enemy. He is beginning to suffer the reflex of his negations, a reaction that inevitably takes the form of revulsion. The emptiness and desolation of the little town are his own emptiness and desolation; all those people who streamed out of it to partake in their urgent, joyous festival really streamed out of himself, and now, because he refused to recognize them, not a soul will ever come back. It is his own refusal that has made the great numinous urn incommunicative now, a silent form, a "cold Pastoral!"

The psychic distancing, developed so evidently in the three middle stanzas of the "Ode," leads inevitably to a final stanza which accepts the resolution of a transcended, sublimated sexuality. We can imagine that Dorothy Van Ghent would have developed at this point her notes on nineteenth-century attitudes towards stone and sculpture. Keats handles his fear of mythic knowledge won through a yielding to desire by idealizing a transcendent immobility, perfect and impervious to change, as Baudelaire did in his poem "La Beauté," a poem that shows the Medusa-face of the urn of Keats's ode:

> Je suis belle, ô mortels! comme un rêve de pierre,
> Et mon sein, où chacun s'est meurtri tour à tour,
> Est fait pour inspirer au poète un amour
> Eternel et muet ainsi que la matière.
>
> Je trône dans l'azur comme un sphinx incompris;
> J'unis un coeur de neige à la blancheur des cygnes;
> Je hais le mouvement qui déplace les lignes,
> Et jamais je ne pleure et jamais je ne ris.
>
> Les poètes, devant mes grandes attitudes,
> Que j'ai l'air d'emprunter aux plus fiers monuments,
> Consumeront leurs jours en d'austères études;
>
> Car j'ai, pour fasciner ces dociles amants,
> De purs miroirs qui font toutes choses plus belles:
> Mes yeux, mes larges yeux aux clartés éternelles!

And in Hazlitt and Hegel sculpture is a representation of thought "abstracted" from life and from commerce with the whole personality. Says Hegel: "The spirit which sculpture represents is that which is solid in itself, not broken up on the play of trivialities and of passions." Sculpture charms the mind that is haunted by images and passions. Yet the charm contains the threat of the medusa and turns to stone the viewer himself. This means that the hero, anxious for a sculptured unity of vision, a perspective, denies his participation in his own life as well as in the collective mythic life, loses touch with the threatening but also life- and knowledge-giving fertility rites, refuses to join these rites, and sees only an "attic shape." The "unravished bride" is sublimed to the Medusa-stone.

This, then, is the context in which we are to read the last two lines of the poem. Just as the stone as stone represents unity, the ascribed message takes the form of a unity, an equation of two great principles which evidently have been sundered in the hero's world; and to that extent the utterance is appropriate; for a unifying grasp of life is what he seeks— a perception of an order of reality that is whole. However, in this kind of plot, the real burden of the oracle's meaning always rests with what the hero actually does, the kind of person he is, his attitudes, how he proceeds. He may have great skill, subtlety, and strength, together with the best intentions, and still go wrong, like Oedipus. Thus the oracular message of the urn comes to the urn as tragic knowledge, that is, knowledge abstracted from the context in life that could make it powerful.*

Ode to Psyche AND *To Autumn*

The "Ode to Psyche" and "To Autumn" present the hero in his most achieved condition of power and coherence. He enters completely into ritual, becomes genuinely and harmoniously entwined in mythic repetition and celebration. The first poem itself becomes the "magical potency" of incantation. The second nearly dissolves the voice of the hero altogether; it is a simple form of fertility ritual in which the earth-goddess

* Throughout her notes on the "Ode on a Grecian Urn" Dorothy Van Ghent implicity equates the hero's failure to confront and accept the power of sexuality, which could lead him to feel part of the cultural collectivity, with Keats's critics' refusal to see the same lived, mythic occasion and reality of the poem. Rather, she says, Critical reading tends, almost without exception, to treat the poem as a certain content of thought putting the question: What does the figured urn "mean"—that is, what does it mean conceptually? The problem is then to fit into that thought-content the ideas of "truth" and "beauty" in such a way that a more or less logical pattern is evident and so that the poem appears to present an ordered, coherent comment upon experience, a comment of a philosophical kind. This intellectual feat is not difficult, since concepts have an elastic way of adapting themselves to almost any logical arrangement one wants to make of them. For these critics, who see the poem in "aesthetic" terms, the urn has nothing to do with actual life, and the content of the scenes—what they are about their relationship with each other and the urn—is apparently of no moment. Thus the seriousness of the hero's problem, and the purposiveness of his action, are obscured.

ascends with fruits and then withdraws after the harvest. The urgency toward mythic knowledge and form relinquishes the bonds of the poet's insistent selfhood, his negation, his sexual fear. Or rather, the metaphor is not of severing but instead merging and subsuming the selfhood. In this the "Ode to Psyche" stands opposite to the tragic nature of the "Ode on a Grecian Urn" in which the voice is disembodied, the mind formulates and conceptualizes out of fear, and therefore the hero, as a hero, is passive before his fear. In "Psyche" the hero acts the sacer ludus which is the poem itself. If the urn symbolized a source of Dionysian fertility, the chthonic implications of which the hero rejected, in "Psyche" the hero actually becomes the fertility god, Dionysos himself. Unconflicted, he leaves behind the hero's "tearings-asunder." Indeed this fearlessness allows for the sexuality infused into the voice of the "priest."

These two poems reflect the archaic origins of poetry as magic; they recall Sappho's "Hymn to Aphrodite" to the point that perhaps the "Ode to Psyche" is a modern version of that poem. If Sappho has sought, for the sake of happiness in love, a life perfused with divinity, Keats's hero seeks that same life for the sake of rectifying the Romantic analysis of modern Western life, to recall and reinvest existence with the animating reunification of spirit and sense; on the level of art it means reinvigorating art with ritual power—from another point of view, allowing ritual to transform itself into an art conscious of its inhibiting social context. In an age of unbelief and anxiety, when collective sacramental forms have been rubbished off as delusions of antiquity, the poet—to find again a mode of union, between consciousness and nature, the spirit and the senses, the ego and the outer world—must create that union by the magic of the poem itself, which is both spiritual and sensuous, which recovers the shadowy images of dream and desire and brings them forth with "awaken'd eyes" into an objective musical order, and which unites the present with the past and men with men by the incantation of archetypal situations which are the primary forms of all life. This poem becomes an example of Socrates' "procreation in the beautiful"; unification is an activity: "since spiritual reality is never a *status quo*, a condition once given that remains settled, it must constantly be *re*created in the living present—that is, as action, an authentic drama. The magnetic pole of drama is not what exists but what does not yet exist, an emergent futurity." "Futurity" here does not, in other words, imply a want; it is not created by desire for what is absent, but instead desire becomes its own fulfillment, the eroticism that spills over in this poem proves the triumph of the act as ritual, of a hymn already granting the pleasurable power which it calls for. In this regard how extraordinary that modern criticism persists in locating the "true" vision of the poet in the other, alienated odes!

What follows are fragments on the "Ode to Psyche."

Though Psyche is the soul, her beauty is praised (the traditional praise of the bride's beauty in wedding-songs) in terms suitable for a love-goddess. She is called a "dove"—Aphrodite's bird. She is fairer than the moon—"Fairer than Phoebe's sapphire-region'd star"—and fairer than Venus—"Or Vesper, amorous glow-worm of the sky." This is because the poem has from the beginning been a celebration of union, and "soul" or "spirit" has already taken over characteristics of sense-life (through association with the sensuous imagery of the glade). Psyche in the arms of Eros has herself become Love. This movement toward identification of the senses and the spirit is elaborated in a different way in the last stanza, where the poet's mental act will create that forest, all that luxurious vegetation, and will administer the fertility ritual.

IN APULEIUS' STORY, the girl is forbidden to look upon the god; he comes only at night, in the darkness of simple instinct, for he is the ground of all being and therefore "invisible" to the watchful, measuring, calculating consciousness. He must not be looked at, that is, inspected mentally, but must simply be accepted, without curious prying, as a great god and beautiful. There is also a sinister sense to this story. Because her lover had forbidden her to look at him, Psyche thought he might be a monster: this is the "soul's" distrust of the sensual,

which has raised such profound tabus in the western imagi-
nation of love. He was actually of divine beauty, but her
mental prying, her failure to entrust herself to unconscious
life, resulted in deprivation and sterility. In the "Ode to Psy-
che," Keats creates the marriage anew, acting as its poet-priest.
He transforms the emblem of Psyche's lamp, that wrought
such harm, into a positive symbol of welcome, a "bright torch"
lit at the casement of the mind, "to let the warm Love in."

In the first line—"O Goddess! hear these tuneless num-
bers"—the initial address directly to the goddess herself is the
ancient poetic formula of epic and ode, which always called
upon the god or goddess to hear and to recognize the reverence
of the song, before the minstrel went on to other subject-
matter. "Tuneless numbers" are not an expression of the poet's
modesty; they are "tuneless" because they do not have ap-
propriate instrumental accompaniment—the accompaniment
of the lyre, anciently indivisible from the chanted poem, and
a necessary part of the poem's magical effect as incantation.
Now the poet has only vocal expression to offer, or the printed
page, for this is far from the days of the "fond believing lyre."

INSTEAD OF the prying lamp of the sinister story told by Apu-
leius, the bright torch of the poet's own psyche is set at the
casement of consciousness, open to the fertilizing "night" part
of the mind, where Love has its source and being. The union
of Psyche and Eros is a union of mind with instinct taking
place within the poet, through the virtue of the poem which
brings the whole being, conscious and unconscious, into the
vital unity of Act.

The lines,

> Surely I dreamt to-day, or did I see
> The winged Psyche with awaken'd eyes?

are a variation, with a difference, on the last lines of the
"Nightingale":

> Was it a vision, or a waking dream?
> Fled is that music:—Do I wake or sleep?

There, the mood of the last stanza was one of suspicion and disillusionment, raised by the "dull brain," the rational faculty prying at the vision in the shadowy forest and rejecting it as a cheat of fancy, a "deceiving elf." But here, the stress is on really seeing, with "awaken'd eyes"; though the poet first sees the two fair creatures embraced in the love-sleep, they will wake soon too, "at tender eye-dawn of aurorean love," and in the fourth stanza the poet rejoices that what he sings of he really sees—"I see, and sing, by my own eyes inspir'd." This motif of seeing and celebrating with "awaken'd eyes" is carried out in the "bright torch" of the final lines; the fire of creative consciousness is also holy ("Holy the air, the water, and the fire"), and lights the union of the senses and the soul.

THE NEGATIVES of the second stanza are very different from the negatives of the "Urn"; there they pronounced only separation and impossibility; but here, though the time of "antique vows" is long past, the poet by sheer thought (i.e., the poem) will actualize the union which modern life has discredited. He takes on the heroic role with firm positiveness of assertion:

> I see, and sing, by my own eyes inspir'd.
> So let me be thy choir, . . .

and he repeats the whole hieratic sequence; he will be voice, lute, incense from the censer, shrine, grove, oracle, and the "heat Of pale-mouth'd prophet dreaming." The "heat" of the poet-prophet corresponds with the "fever" induced by the writing of poetry, but here it is a positive attribute of inspiration. Inspiration is spiritual fire, like that on the altar, and like that of the "bright torch."

"YES, I WILL be thy priest," he says, "and build a fane In some untrodden region of my mind"; and goes on to describe in luxuriance the sacred natural forest where the poem started. But this is a forest of "branched thoughts," the sacred grove of the psyche which by its very name is dedicated to the goddess.

That these branching thoughts are "new grown with pleas-
ant pain" has a differently defined meaning in this context
from the pleasure-pain conjunctions in other poems; the rigor
and strenuousness of the thought that goes into the writing
of poetry—and that brings on "fever"—is compared with what
trees must feel in pushing out new branches, the pain that
accompanies natural growth. The goddess' sanctuary will be
dressed "with the wreath'd trellis of a working brain, With
buds, and bells, and stars without a name," for consciousness
is as creative as Nature; it works like a gardener, "Who breed-
ing flowers, will never breed the same." In contrast with the
paralyzed, lifeless boughs of the "Urn," that "cannot shed
their leaves," and therefore cannot ever bud with new leaves
either, all here, in the "working brain," is a busily breeding
fertility of fresh manifestations, new forms.

WHEREAS IN the "Urn" the ritual panel was frozen motionless
in its stony medium, here the figures can move through the
holy forest, because the forest itself is a region of the mind.
Its boughs are "branched thoughts"—the very nerve-patterns
of the brain, where the union of subject and object, the spirit
and the senses, will be consummated in the act of writing the
poem.

Dorothy Van Ghent's notes to "To Autumn," written down
as a short explication, give little hint of their completeness.
Together they do clearly indicate a reading of the poem, one
that, though in itself not startling, fulfills for us the promise
that the poem is that episode in the hero's myth in which he
is attendant as celebrant on the epiphany of the earth-goddess
and her withdrawal to the underworld.

The controlling ritual figure in the "Ode to Autumn" is one
many times represented on vases and metal or ivory seals of
the Aegean world: the *anodos* and *kathodos* of an earth-
goddess. This is the simplest form of fertility ritual. It omits
the *agon* altogether, and hence omits the hero with his "tear-
ings-asunder." It may possibly be more ancient than the drama
of the dying and resurrected god; for the mother (Ishtar, Cy-
bele, Demeter) came before the son-consort. She simply as-

cends out of the earth with the fruits of the season, and withdraws when the harvest is done and stored up. The "hero" in this ode has become a lyric voice only—a voice like that of the priest in the rites of Pan in *Endymion*, when he points out to the multitude the bounties that Pan has given:

> Are not our lowing heifers sleeker than
> Night-swollen mushrooms? Are not our wide plains
> Speckled with countless fleeces?

But there is a certain personalization of the voice in the ode, for the poet is speaking directly to the goddess, as if there were two people who might hold a dialogue; he asks, "Who hath not seen thee oft amid thy store?" and when he brings up the subject of the songs of spring, he tells her, "Think not of them." This personalization of the voice makes it possible for the reader to identify himself humanly with the speaker, to share in praising the goddess's work and in the sense of being blessed by her abundance—and (in the last stanza) to share as well in the quiet, implicit assent to her withdrawal, as all nature seems to be assenting through its music of farewell. These devices of the ode conjure up a complete ritual situation: the harvest scene, the goddess, the priest (poet), the chorus or "choir" of creatures in the last stanza, and the multitude (ourselves—for it is we who are referred to by "Who hath not seen thee oft amid thy store?").

In the poem all the stanzas are invocative; they "call on" certain phenomena—first the fruits, then the goddess, then the creatures. Webster defines invocation as the act or formula of conjuring, i.e., incantation. But here there are not spirits to be conjured out of their nature-dwellings, for everything that is invoked has primary, substantial, earthly existence: the food (first stanza), the life-energy that creates the food and motivates the harvesting (second stanza), and the beasts, birds, and insects who are dependent on it. The method is purely presentational, like that of the Old Irish poem that said: "orchards blossom, cornfields ripen, bees swarm, a cheerful world, peace and plenty"; but it is not merely descriptive (as if the artist were objectively—or "realistically"—setting down the details of a natural scene) for it is emotionally charged with a sense of miracle, that is, natural miracle.

The first stanza is a single syntactical unit, with no period-stops, but it is not a sentence; it starts off, "Season of mists," but there is no grammatical predicate, only naming—as Adam named the beasts. This is the method of the magician. The stanza is of morning (ripening, budding), as the sun conspires with the earth to make the fruits; the second stanza is of afternoon and drowsy siesta; the third, of the beginning of twilight. As there are mists and sun in the stanza of morning, there are "barred clouds" and a rosy radiance in the evening stanza. The barred clouds are of coming night; the mists that go with "fruitfulness" and "ripeness" also foretell winter and the death of nature. But a great "store" has been hoarded up from the harvest, as the cells of the bees are brimmed with honey; and all is divine—the day, with its last radiant glance, the evening when the creatures say farewell, and the night of patience.

Demeter was always a mellow, genial goddess, of the earth and earthy, holding her bowing stalks of full-headed grain. She is here a close "friend" of the maturing sun, who is masculine ("conspiring with him"). "Maturing" may be taken both transitively and intransitively; he helps to mature the fruits, and he is also getting old himself as winter comes on (in the last stanza, the day is "dying"). To con-spire is to "breathe together," act in harmony; it also means to agree in secret—for the power of these gods is mysterious power, they do by sheer being. Together with nouns—the naming of fruits—verbs and verbals dominate the first stanza—the naming of vegetational functions ("to load," "to bend," "and fill," "to swell," and so on). Both functions of the fruit-shapes are kinesthetic, acting through the imaginative sympathy of the body-sense of weight and motion. The phrase "load and bless" names a single function in two ways, a physical way and a spiritual way; the vines are made heavy with food-fruits, and blessed with productiveness; food is itself nature's blessing. Common human beings are almost never brought into the high ritual action of Keats's poetry, as an element of imagery;

but here the divine anodos takes place right around their "thatch-eves" and among their "cottage-trees": it is they who are blessed with all this abundance. Kinesthetically the fruits are shaped out into the rounded substantial form—"filled" from core to surface—that distinguishes Keats's imagery and his concretistic mode of thinking: heavy apples, swollen gourds, plumped hazel shells, brimmed honey-cells. As in the New Hebrides song-pattern, where one stanza is called the "base of the tree," another the "leaf," another the "bunch of fruit," so in this poem the first stanza might be called the "food," the second the "worker" or "harvester," the third the "creatures." Still through imagery of abundance and largesse, the last two lines—where the bees "think warm days will never cease" because more and more flowers are budding for these busy fertilizers, and their hives are brimful—suggest what the mistiness of the season suggests: that it is late, that warm days *will* soon cease, that night and death follow after "ripeness."

The earth-goddess has so far shown herself only as agency; now she appears as agent. The first stanza was concerned with her functions and the foods she produced; now she shows herself in person, as divine harvester. The major rhythm of the three stanzas is that of Nature itself, but it is also the "tragic rhythm" at its simplest—from fruitfulness, to reaping, to the barren stubble-fields from which life has slowly withdrawn. The figure of Autumn in the second stanza is not a conventional literary personification. In a personification, what is symbolically attributed to a figure (say, the scales with which Justice is shown) is literally true of what the figure represents (justice does weigh right and wrong). But one cannot say of the autumnal season that it sits on a granary floor, that it sleeps on a furrow, that it keeps steady its laden head across a brook. The figure of Autumn engages in activities appropriate to the season, but in which the *season* could not engage. She acts just like the human harvesters she presides over, visiting the realm of her ministry in the guise of her charges; she reaps, gleans, winnows, watches the cider-press. She has the form, in this stanza, of Kore (we cannot, I think, read the stanza without imagining a young, full-bodied peasant girl, her hair "soft-lifted" by the wind, falling asleep among field-poppies, robust enough to balance a heavy basket of grain on her head across the stepping-stones of a brook). Demeter and Kore were the same person; in vase-paintings or votive plaques where they are shown together, sometimes Demeter is a matronly figure and Kore a slender girl; but often as not, they are both young women and one cannot tell them apart. Kore was a late development out of Demeter, her myth (her rape by Hades and her sojourn in the unerworld) an elaboration of the *kathodos* or "going down" of the vegetation goddess in winter. Appearing here as the corn-maiden, she has all the mellowness, the earthy reposefulness, of her mother. She is as bodily substantial, "filled with ripeness," as the fruits of the first stanza, sure and lazy in her power. There is no haste, for she is the harvest itself ("the limbs of Demeter" the grain was called); she is "careless," "patient," drowsy, falls asleep over her work. In Christian symbology, death is called the "grim Reaper." There is no grimness about this reaper, although she is Persephone, bride of death, and the furrows that are now half-reaped will soon all be reaped, the ripe apples that bent the cottage-trees have been made into cider, and it is the "last oozings" which she watches.

The question—"Who hath not seen thee oft amid thy store?"—again brings in the common human element, the participation of mortal folk (those who live in the thatched cottages of the first stanza). Being rhetorical, the question asserts what it asks: it is literally true that anyone, everybody, may see the goddess, for she is found "amid her store" and her store is herself—the fruit, the flowers, the honey, the wine, the grain. But it is a magical formula also, like Sappho's calling on Aphrodite, "O come as I often saw thee," and like the demand of the New Hebrides sorcerer, that the woman come out of the stone to be his wife. The difference is that this goddess does not have to be called on to appear, she is already there, and the poet is talking to her: he does not say that anyone may find *her*, but that

> whoever seeks abroad may find
> *Thee. . . .*

The position of the pronoun at the head of the line, carrying a deliberately displaced stress, places her in full presence—as if she could answer in a dialogue, except that she is a divinely unconscious power and "drows'd with the fume of poppies."

The harvesting actions that are being carried out are slowed down to the warm somnolence of the late afternoon, the somnolence of power and repletion. The harvester sits careless on the granary floor—the wind does the winnowing; she leaves a furrow half-reaped—her hook "Spares the next swath and all its twined flowers." Though this is the hook of the reaper (the dread "scythe" of death) and though the word "spares" carries a suggestion that the cutting down of living growths is only temporarily withheld (even "swath" has a resonance of the "swatches" that wrap the dead), this harvester's hook is a genial instrument, not too thorough, sparing a swath of poppies (those "later flowers for the bees," of the first stanza) because the girl has fallen asleep. In its modulation of assonance and consonance, and of the long syllabic *morae* that take the accents, the line is one of the most beautiful in English verse. After being a reaper, the goddess is a gleaner (like Ruth in Boaz's field and in the "Nightingale"). These two lines also do an extraordinary work of kinesthesia by the arrangement of the words:

> And sometimes like a gleaner thou dost keep
> Steady thy laden head across a brook; . . .

Between "keep" and "steady" there is the necessary voice-pause that comes at the end of a line (that would have a beat in music), especially here because the syllables are long ones; the reader himself has to "keep/steady" the imaginative voice-pitch that holds over the pause, just like the girl who keeps the basket steady on her head as she takes another step in the brook. Finally she appears as a vintager, still wonderfully relaxed in her vigilance; and the line—"Thou watchest the last oozings hours by hours," with its long syllables, repeated diphthongs (that take a longer *mora*, or delay in the mouth, than vowels), the "s's" of "hours" that are delaying voiced consonants like the "z" of "oozings"—has the kinesthetic or bodily feeling of her patient watching over this last work of the receding year.

The unity achieved by the poem is the concrete natural unity of the temporal cycle, where the beauty of abundance is not divided from the truth of time, but one with it. A shift from lamentation to joy was integral to the Sacer Ludus. This movement is reversed in the ode, which ends with the *kathodos* of the goddess and the ritual music of lament. The sounds of mourning are shrill and high—the wailing of gnats, the bleat of lambs, the treble whistle of the red-breast, the twittering of swallows gathering for departure. But the long syllables still carry over the bodily feeling of completion and repose, so that the music of farewell becomes an act of celebration. The creatures who sing are those closely associated with human activities, with sheep-fold, hearth, and garden. Touching the stubble-plains with rosy hue, radiance glows over the last scene of this sacred drama, where all nature, including human nature, is drawn into the collective assent.

VI. The Succession of
the Gods: 1

Hyperion shows the Titans in pain and wrath immediately after the Olympians have usurped power. It stops abruptly on a line of asterisks at the moment when Apollo achieves godhood by a ritual rebirth under the ministration of a great matriarchal figure, Mnemosyne. Keats stopped working on this section of the epic in April 1819, and a few months later started again with a new title, *The Fall of Hyperion, A Dream*, and a completely new beginning. The poem now has a vision-framework. The poet dreams that he is in a forest glade where the remains of a divine feast are spread out, of which he eats. The sacramental food induces a vision of himself undergoing a ritual rebirth under the auspices of another great matriarchal figure, Moneta. Thereafter he is allowed to see the events which had begun unrolling in *Hyperion*. At this point, the vision-framework hooks on to the section that had been written earlier. The structure is circular: the dreaming poet is reborn to see the god of poetry being reborn.

The events in *Hyperion* appear from a dramatically objective point of view, under the fiction of events of a far-off time. The vision-framework of *The Fall* places them in the immediacy of the poet's personal experience; in order to see these events, he has to undergo the same ordeal of rebirth as did his hero, Apollo. Furthermore, by entering the poem as a persona, he is enabled to speak directly with the mysterious priestess who selects certain people to be reborn from death, and to discuss with her this very problem. Keats himself was very near death when he was writing *The Fall*.

We shall treat the two fragments as a single poem. It is a poem about giant nature-daemons. The connection between poet and giant was established very early, in the lines of *Sleep and Poetry* where Keats speaks of the poet as being like a giant who seizes the whole world and becomes immortal:

> Then the events of this wide world I'd seize
> Like a strong giant, and my spirit teaze
> Till at its shoulders it should proudly see
> Wings to find out an immortality.
> <div align="right">(<i>S. & P.</i> 81-84)</div>

In the same poem, poetry itself is a powerful giant, a reclining sculptural figure slumberous through sheer power:

> A drainless shower
> Of light is poesy; 'tis the supreme of power;
> 'Tis might half slumb'ring on its own right arm.
> <div align="right">(<i>S. & P.</i> 235-37)</div>

Among the "events of this wide world" which the giant poet will seize in order to become immortal are "the agonies, the strife of human hearts." In *The Fall*, Moneta says that the only human beings allowed to enter her immortal precincts are those who cannot "rest" because of "the miseries of the world":

> "None can usurp this height," return'd that shade,
> "But those to whom the miseries of the world
> Are misery, and will not let them rest."
> <div align="right">(<i>Fall</i> I.147-49)</div>

The cosmic giant that Keats very early associated with poetry becomes, in this epic about the god of poetry, a whole *dramatis personae* of giants. Since the poet must comprehend all the secrets of nature, the "symbol-essences" of earth, air, fire, and water, it is fitting that the *Hyperion* giants should be daemons of the elements, born of the union of sky and earth. As for the Olympian gods in the poem, one has no tendency to visualize Apollo—the only Olympian fully presented—as of merely human size beside the gigantic Titans; a sun-god has to be big enough to manage a very large planet. And as the hero who is to seize the events of the world—

Names, deeds, grey legends, dire events, rebellions,
Majesties, sovran voices, agonies,
Creations and destroyings, all at once—
     (*Hyperion* III.114-16)

he is that giant early conceived by Keats as the sovereign poet.
The chief ancient distinction between Titans and giants was
that the giants were children of earth, and the Titans children
of earth and heaven. Keats's Titans have the right parentage.
Coelus, the sky, is their father—it is he who speaks to Hy-
perion at the end of Book I and urges this "brightest child"
to strive like a god against the disaster that has happened—
and the earth is their mother ("While his bow'd head seem'd
list'ning to the Earth, His ancient mother, for some comfort
yet"). This genealogy is given in the creation myth that Oceanus
relates in Book II to warn the Titans against insubordination
to the laws of nature. Chaos was the first father, night the
first mother; from them came light, and light, engendering
upon its mother, darkness, produced the male heavens and
the female earth. Of these two the Titans—"the giant-race"—
were born.

From chaos and parental Darkness came
Light, the first fruits of that intestine broil,
That sullen ferment, which for wondrous ends
Was ripening in itself. The ripe hour came,
And with it Light, and Light, engendering
Upon its own producer, forthwith touch'd
The whole enormous matter into life.
Upon that very hour, our parentage,
The Heavens and the Earth, were manifest.
     (*Hyperion* II.191-99)

"The Titans cannot be very precisely delimited from the
Giants," Jane Ellen Harrison says. "They too are in some
sense Earth-born." According to Diodorus, their mother was
by some called Titaia—a title of earth—and others said that
they were sons of Ouranos, the sky (actually the aether), and

Ge or Gaia, also a name of earth. Hesiod calls them "the earth-born Titans." But in Homer and Hesiod they are always gods. Unlike the giants, they

> seem early to have left their earth-nature behind them and climbed one step up the ladder to heaven. Fertility-daimones they remain, but rather as potencies of sky than earth.[1]

The Olympians, who deposed them, are a highly humanized race of gods whereas the Titans are more purely powers of the elements. This is also Keats's characterization of the Titans, while he attempts in Apollo to differentiate the Olympian by passionate and mobile human characteristics. Keats gives his own interpretation of the deposition of Titans by Olympians: the new gods are more beautiful, and the "first in beauty should be first in might." "Beauty" is a very packed term in Keats, and cannot be taken at merely face value, as we have seen in trying to apply the beauty-is-truth equation to the "Grecian Urn," and in examining the sense of "things of beauty" in the opening of *Endymion*.

Since the narrative plan of *Hyperion*, and the intellectual or philosophical meaning Keats evidently wanted the poem to have, are built on the succession of one race of gods by another, it is of importance that we gather what we can, from the traditional mythological background, about this succession. The story of the Titanomachia is Olympianized myth; that is, it is a revision of earlier myth to fit the politics of a new breed of gods who had to establish their authority by subsuming older religious traditions. The Titans were fertility daemons associated with the planets and the weather, and when Zeus was established as supreme heaven-god and father-god, the degrading of the Titans had to be accounted for. The story was that the Titans had resisted his supremacy and been punished for their insurrection (the myth is analogous to the rebellion of the angels under Lucifer). The Titans "are constantly being driven down below the earth to nethermost Tartarus and always re-emerging."

The very violence and persistence with which they are sent down below shows that they belong up above. . . . Their great offence in Olympian eyes is that they will climb up to high heaven. . . . The fight between Titans and Olympians always takes place in mid-air. In the *Theogony* the Titanomachia is but a half-humanized thunderstorm, where Zeus as much and perhaps more manifestly than his opponents is but a Nature-Power.[2]

The difference between the war with the giants and the war with the Titans is that

The Gigantomachia stands for the triumph of the humanized Olympian over the powers of Earth . . . ; the Titanomachia stands for the Triumph, partial only, of Olympians over that higher form of Naturism which is Ouranianism.[3]

We shall want to gather together more of the implications of this succession of gods upon gods, adopted by Keats for his major narrative plan and repeated so often in ancient myth—which, in its variations on the scheme, was dramatizing an archetypal situation whose significance was psychological, social, and political as well as religious.

Keats scrupulously avoided allowing his Saturn to be implicated in the patriarchal cannibalistic scandals which were the most notorious events in the career of the Titan king, repeatedly recorded by mythographers. These scandals have an Oedipal quality that makes them particularly repugnant, and also, of course, they do not fit the serenely beneficent Titan character as Keats has designed it. But their striking presence in the legendary background suggests a question as to why Keats chose to make his Titans serenely beneficent. In legend, Ouranos imprisoned his Titan children under the earth to prevent them from claiming the divine kingship. But his son Kronos (Saturn) castrated his father at the urgency of his mother, Gaia, who gave him the scythe with which to do it. Kronos then married his sister, Rhea (the Greek name of Cybele), and swallowed his own children as fast as they were born. But Rhea substituted a stone, swaddled like a baby, for the child Zeus, who was hidden till adulthood and who then compelled Kronos to disgorge all the other children—the Olympians, who now took over the divine power. (The scythe and the stone have obvious associations, the scythe with the earth-mother as goddess of harvest, the stone with the meteorite or thunderbolt of the heaven-god.) The fact that Keats, instead of using this horrible history, made the Titans majestically beautiful set him a problem that has been noted by most of the readers of *Hyperion*—how to make their successors, the Olympians, more beautiful, in order to carry out the thesis of his narrative, that the "first in beauty should be first in might." He struggled to give Apollo a different kind of beauty so that his precedence over the Titan sun-god will be justified, but the Titans are already so aesthetically impressive that Apollo's competition is weak. If Keats had accepted the legendary character of the Titans as evil-doers, there would have been no problem. It would seem important to try to understand why he weeded the evil-doing out of the Titan myth and created for himself what turned out to be an insuperable difficulty in justifying the Titans' overthrow so that "the first in beauty should be first in might."

According to Harrison's reconstruction of the ritual circumstances in which the Titan mythology originated, the Titans were the same as the *Kouretes* or *Korybantes*, who were the priestly armed dancers attending the Great Mother and guarding the Divine Child, Zagreus, whose cult prevailed all down the coast of Asia Minor and flourished throughout historical antiquity.[4] In the myth of Zagreus (Dionysos), the Titan bodyguard went berserk, tore the child in pieces, put him in a cauldron on a tripod, and boiled him, piercing the limbs with spits. Their repast ended with the epiphany of the thunder-god, Zeus, who discovered what had been done and blasted the Titans with his bolt.[5] The child's torn limbs were collected, and he "emerged whole and entire." Plutarch, in explaining Orphic ritual, connects the characteristic mutations and resurrections of Dionysos with this story of the Titans' tearing the year-god to pieces and his restoration to life.[6] In

a cleaned-up variant of the Dionysos myth, making the dae-
mon a son of Zeus, there is no baby-eating; Zeus causes the
child to "enter his male womb" and be born again. Never-
theless, there is in this variant an equivalent entrance of the
son into the father's body and re-emergence, as the sons of
Kronos were disgorged—that is, born again. The horrendous
domestic cannibalism persists in legends of pre-Olympian fer-
tility heroes who were converted into sons of Zeus and whose
hubris caused them to act as if they were gods—as they orig-
inally were. Zeus was the father of Tantalus, who was pun-
ished by eternal hunger in the underworld for serving up his
son, Pelops, to the gods in a stew. Pelops was restored to life
(the rebirth motif, as in the story of the Titans eating Dionysos,
and Kronos eating his sons), and had two sons, Thyestes and
Atreus. Atreus killed Thyestes' sons and served them to him
at a banquet. These stories of kings who ate their own sons
express the royal situation in an annual or periodic kingdom
where the king was regularly killed and his successor en-
throned either as his reincarnation or as his son; their horrible
quality is an expression of fear of supersedure by an heir.

It is with the narrative scheme of the succession to the divine
kingship that we are concerned in Keats's epic—the displace-
ment of the old gods, the Titans, by the young Olympians.
Oddly, Keats partially muffles the paternal-filial relationship
between them. Oceanus asks the other Titans, "Have ye be-
held the young God of the Seas, My dispossessor?" as if Nep-
tune's uncles and aunts might never have seen their nephew
or been aware of his existence. Clymene speaks with aston-
ishment of Apollo, as if he were an utter stranger. But in the
same breath Oceanus, tracing the divine genealogy, says that
as the Titans were born of Heaven and Earth, the Olympians
were "born of us"; and Uranus, the ancient father-aether,
speaks of the father-son feud among his children and grand-
children:

> There is sad feud among ye, and rebellion
> Of son against his sire.
> (*Hyperion* I.321-22)

The schematic situation in Keats's epic is of the type of king-succession described by Raglan and others, the violent overthrow of fathers by sons (Oceanus' son has given him a "scalding in the seas," and the other Titans have suffered "buffets vile" from their progeny), with the reverse elaboration adopted from the myth of the Titanomachia—the retaliation of the fathers against the sons—however Keats intended to manipulate or revise the myth. The archetype in question is not father-son combat (this, with its Oedipus motif, is a special cultural elaboration), but cyclical rebirth. As the fertility god is reborn from a violent death, the king is reborn in his heir who takes his name, the name of the god—as the Egyptian kings who went through this type of ritual took the name of Horus, son of Osiris. Though Keats projects his narrative on the pattern of the violent succession of father by son, the Titans have to be beautiful and beneficent, even though this distorts their legend, because their beauty and beneficence give necessary ethical support to the fact that they have the role of fathers—whose sons, in duplicating their functions as planetary and weather daemons, are their reincarnations.

This view of the narrative seems to set aside Keats's progressive, humanitarian plans for the new gods, which we shall consider shortly, but only by going behind the intellectualized overstructure of the poem to the archetypal situation from which the epic and the traditions it employs are germinated. The rebirth ordeal of Apollo in *Hyperion* and of the Dreamer in *The Fall* are other elaborations of the general archetypal motif of rebirth contained in the narrative scheme of king-succession. The circular structure of the fragments is held to the central archetype in such a way that, like *Endymion*, it can have no "progressive" outcome but must simply move in its archetypal orbit. This may, in some degree, account for the fact that though Keats worked on the poem for over a year he could get no further ahead with it than to supply, in *The Fall*, another variant of the rebirth ordeal. When the Dreamer comes to the top of the terrible stairway and is allowed to see the ancient pageant of Titans and Olympians, he takes his place beneath the knees of the giant image of the father-god, Saturn. In the monomyth of the hero's rebirth, in order to be reborn he has to redeem the whole world, whose "symbolical deficiency" his mission was to correct—and the redemption of the world starts with the redemption of the parents. If Keats had allowed his Saturn to be the cannibal father he was in legend, he would have had a hard time setting him up as the presiding god-image in Moneta's temple.

A consideration of the intellectual superstructure of the poem provides an informative example of how rational "meaning"—the poet's evident intellectual, "progressive," intent, which he deliberately built into the poem—coordinates or fails to coordinate with the archetypal impulsion in the creative process. Various critics have noted the Wordsworthian, "humanitarian" drift of the poem. The speech of Oceanus in Book II, on the progressive improvement in the manifestations of deity—from "chaos and parental darkness," to the engendering of light, the formation of the heavens and earth, the birth of the "giant-race" of Titans, and finally to "a power more strong in beauty," namely the Olympians—is a decisive statement of the poem's intended intellectual import.

Keats's thesis of a progress in "beauty," by which the Olympians would be justified in taking over power from the Titans, required that he characterize the two generations of gods in such a way that Olympians would appear superior. He attempted to do this by contrasting a static regime with a dynamic regime.

> The days of peace and slumberous calm are fled;
> Those days, all innocent of scathing war,
> When all the fair Existences of heaven
> Came open-eyed to guess what we would speak.
> (*Hyperion* II.335-38)

As Titan king, Saturn's "godlike exercise" had been that of

> influence benign on planets pale,
> Of admonitions to the winds and seas,
> Of peaceful sway above man's harvesting,

> And all those acts which Deity supreme
> Doth ease its heart of love in.
> *(Hyperion* I.108-12)

And when he thinks of recapturing his throne, he describes his triumph again in terms of a great cosmic serenity:

> trumpets blown
> Of triumph calm, and hymns of festival
> Upon the gold clouds metropolitan,
> Voices of soft proclaim, and silver stir
> Of strings in hollow shells; and there shall be
> Beautiful things made new, for the surprise
> Of the sky-children.
> *(Hyperion* I.127-33)

"Progress" is unknown in the Titan world; "new" things are "beautiful things" already in existence—like sun and light and clouds and sea that are "new" each day and each moment. The descriptive metaphors associated with the Titans and their scene are those of a timeless dream, as in the superb passage about the dreaming oaks:

> As when, upon a tranced summer-night,
> Those green-rob'd senators of mighty woods,
> Tall oaks, branch-charmed by the earnest stars,
> Dream, and so dream all night without a stir,
> Save from one gradual solitary gust
> Which comes upon the silence, and dies off,
> As if the ebbing air had but one wave;
> So came these words and went; . . .
> *(Hyperion* I.72-79)

A body of ideas, involving the aesthetic principles and traditions of Keats's period, seems to have entered into his intellectual intention in the characterization of the Titans and Olympians and his thesis of a progress in "beauty." The profound influence of Winckelmann on aesthetic thought had set up an idiom for discussion of the arts which appears repeatedly through the period, as in the writings of Fuseli, Winck-elmann's translator, and the lectures of Flaxman and Hazlitt; one of the most influential of Winckelmann's arguments, his division of the history of Greek art into periods or styles, directly corresponds with the division of the periods of creation and manifestations of "beauty" outlined in Oceanus' speech in Book II of *Hyperion*. In contrast with the massive and changeless serenity of the Titan character, Keats's Apollo is described in terms of intense emotional expressiveness and a grace that is feminine, in accordance with Winckelmann's widely popularized interpretation of the aesthetic appeal and significance of the figure of Apollo in Greek art. In the statues of those gods, like Apollo and Bacchus, who were thought of as having eternal youth, the artistic ideal "consists in the incorporation of the forms of prolonged youth in the female sex with the masculine forms of a beautiful young man, which they consequently made plumper, rounder, and softer, in admirable conformity with their ideas of their deities." In the Apollo Belvedere, "the highest conception of ideal male beauty is especially expressed":

> the strength of adult years is found united with the soft forms of the most beautiful springtime of youth. . . . Health blooms in his youth, and strength manifests itself, like the ruddiness of morning on a beautiful day.

An "eternal spring plays with softness and tenderness" about his limbs, and "a heavenly essence, diffusing itself like a gentle stream, seems to fill the whole contour of the figure." His "soft hair is agitated by a gentle breeze, like the slender waving tendrils of the noble vine."[7] Keats, in introducing Apollo, enters immediately into an evocation of glowing roses, rosy clouds, and blushing maids:

> For lo! 'tis for the Father of all verse.
> Flush every thing that hath a vermeil hue,
> Let the rose glow intense and warm the air,
> And let the clouds of even and of morn
> Float in voluptuous fleeces o'er the hills;

Let the red wine within the goblet boil,
Cold as a bubbling well; let faint-lipp'd shells,
On sands, or in great deeps, vermilion turn
Through all their labyrinths; and let the maid
Blush keenly, as with some warm kiss surpris'd.
                              (*Hyperion* III.13-22)

Apollo appears "Full ankle-deep in lilies of the vale"; he has a "white melodious throat," "white soft temples," and "golden tresses famed, kept undulation round his eager neck." In a line that Keats wrote and rejected for the description of Apollo's rebirth ordeal, undergone beneath Mnemosyne's arms, the god is "roseate and pained as any ravish'd nymph."

The poem breaks off at this point, its fragmentary character indicated by asterisks—

                    At length
Apollo shriek'd;—and lo! from all his limbs
Celestial. . . .
                         (*Hyperion* III.134-36)

In English Romantic poetry, Wordsworth's pantheism provided him with a "universal" that was wholly concrete. Keats, in the "darkness" of extreme youth, philosophic ignorance, and lack of any compelling religious belief, had to grope in his own way for an emotional grasp of the "siege of contraries," and it was largely by unconscious processes that he created the figures of a drama which represented his own quest for a concrete, resolving unity, through the myth of the hero whose mission it is to "seize the events of the wide world," redeeming it from meaninglessness by poetic insight into a unifying and universal truth which would be "all ye know on earth and all ye need to know." The conceptualization at the end of the "Grecian Urn" is, precisely because it is abstract, inadequate. Death—which Keats, because of the character of his experience, had always felt at his pulses—is now becoming more and more immediate in this last year of his writing, and must also be seized in unification with the other events of the wide world and "agonies of human hearts." The Apollo of

Hyperion, being the god-poet, is conceived as the one who will do the "seizing"; it is his vocation "to feel the whole range of what man's soul in its utmost and secret corners has power to experience and to create." In other words, Apollo, as he is given in the poem, has the temperament for advancing straight into the heart of the "siege of contraries," like the hero of the "Ode on Melancholy"; and when this poetic temperament is re-examined in *The Fall*, in the character of the mortal poet, the Dreamer, the whole problem is reviewed in the same "sovran shrine" that was entered by the hero of "Melancholy"—the temple of the world-goddess. For after all, it is not merely to suffer the siege of contraries—"creations and destroyings all at once"—that is the hero's mission, but to resolve the contraries in union.

To do the seizing of the events of the wide world "like a strong giant," the febrile Apollo of the third book of *Hyperion* has to undergo a change of being. Therefore the apparently paradoxical situation that Middleton Murry points out when he asks: "Why should Apollo, who was already a god, endure such agony in order to become what he already was?" Apollo has to be reborn, not to become what he already was, which was the Romantic poet fevered by contradiction and chaos of sheer multiplicity impinging on his nerves, but to become the truly Apolline god of unity, measure, harmony. But the Titans already represent unity, measure, harmony. The Titans *are* Apolline. In Woodhouse's transcript of Keats's manuscript, the last line reads:

> from all his limbs
> Celestial glory dawn'd: he was a god!

The problem of immediate continuity here is one of visualization of this epiphany; it resembles the problem at the end of *Endymion*, where Endymion's epiphany as an immortal was side-stepped by having him vanish. What would this new sun-god, his limbs radiating celestial glory, look like? He would probably look like the dazzlingly beautiful sun-god who came before him, Hyperion. For there is only one kind of total change of being that Apollo can achieve by rebirth: from a fevered Dionysian character he can only change into an Apolline character, that is, a Titan. The intellectual intention of the poem—the theme of "progress"—is frustrated by the unconscious archetypal impulsion. The impasse reached at the end of *Hyperion*, where it is evidently impossible merely to turn Apollo into his opposite, a Titan, accounts for Keats's hopeless struggle with his poem, his breaking if off at this point where the god's epiphany in Apolline glory needs to be visualized. He rationalized his difficulty as a problem of poetic diction: he felt that *Hyperion* contained too many "Miltonisms." In starting it again in *The Fall*, using a Dantesque vision-framework and a more straightforward diction, he tried to clarify the myth that impelled him, by returning once more to spiritual beginnings—to the "house" or cosmic container, which is now Moneta's temple, where, under the gigantic and immobile image of the father-god, Saturn, the Dionysian poet-hero torn by the siege of contraries can bring his problem of transformation to the mother-goddess of life and death.

The god's changes into the elements and being born into all the forms of animate nature are a metaphor of his fertility function; he is not only the fertility daemon but he enters into, or *is*, the forms taken by the universe. In the third book of *Hyperion*, the craving of Apollo, before his rebirth, is to do precisely that. He cries to Mnemosyne:

> O why should I
> Feel curs'd and thwarted, when the liegeless air
> Yields to my step aspirant? why should I
> Spurn the green turf as hateful to my feet?
> Goddess benign, point forth some unknown thing:
> Are there not other regions than this isle?
> What are the stars? There is the sun, the sun!
> And the most patient brilliance of the moon!
> And stars by thousands! Point me out the way
> To any one particular beauteous star,
> And I will flit into it with my lyre,
> And make its silvery splendour pant with bliss.
>
> (*Hyperion* III.91-102)

When godlike power starts pouring into him from Mnemosyne, it is a psychic influx that takes the form of "knowledge enormous"—

> Names, deeds, grey legends, dire events, rebellions,
> Majesties, sovran voices, agonies,
> Creations and destroyings, all at once. . . .
> *(Hyperion* III.114-16)

These "agonies" and "creations and destroyings all at once" are similar to the "rendings asunder," the "destructions and disappearances and resurrections and new births" that Plutarch says were characteristic of Dionysos at Delphi and elsewhere. Then immediately Keats's Apollo goes through in his own person a "rending asunder," a death and a new birth, while Mnemosyne holds her arms over him, prophesying:

> Soon wild commotions shook him, and made flush
> All the immortal fairness of his limbs;
> Most like the struggle at the gate of death;
> Or liker still to one who should take leave
> Of pale immortal death, and with a pang
> As hot as death's is chill, with fierce convulse
> Die into life: . . .
> *(Hyperion* III.124-30)

Keats called this character Apollo, but the emotional attributes and the activities of the character—his craving to enter into everything that is, his undergoing ritual death and rebirth—are those of the mystery god Dionysos and all Keats's heroes. The unconscious situation in the substructure of *Hyperion* is clarified if we think of Keats's Apollo, before his rebirth, as not having the traditional temperament and function of Apollo at all, but those of Dionysos—the temperament and function of the typical hero in Keats's poetry and of the "Poetical Character" as he had described it, who has no "identity" himself because he enters into all things. The mission of this Dionysos-like character is to *become* Apollo by rebirth, that is, to free himself from "rendings asunder," by becoming Apolline like the Titans.

Keats has his Apollo playing the music of Dionysos, an

utterance full of sufferings and metamorphosis, wandering and distraction. A "living death was in each gush of sounds"; coming on the shifting wind, it "did both drown and keep alive my ears," Clymene says, to "make me sick of joy and grief at once." The suffering in the "rapturous hurried notes" overwhelms the joy, and Clymene becomes frantic: "Grief overcame And I was stopping up my frantic ears. . . ." The Dionysian and the Apolline were the two poles of Keats's psyche. Whatever causes may be adduced for the "fever" Keats experienced in writing, under the aspect of the present terminology it is the Dionysian "fever," as the music of the Apollo of *Hyperion* is the music of the Dionysian "siege of contraries," and as the temperament of the Dreamer in *The Fall* is the Dionysian one that cannot have "the pain alone, the joy alone, distinct," but is a "fever of itself." But Keats wanted to write without the "fever," because it was breaking down his health: "I want to compose without this fever," he said. In other words, he wanted to be, not the Dionysian poet writing out of the *dynamis* of the instinctive libido, out of dreams and images welling from the unconscious, but the Apolline poet writing the "ordered paean" under a "sober Muse." This problem is the one the Dreamer puts to Moneta in *The Fall*. As a matter of fact, Keats did write the "ordered paean" in his best poems. It was by the shaping principle of verse, the principle of order, symmetry, measure, number, limitation, that he was able to find, in composition, the Apolline character. The Apolline principle also determines the typically clear spatial form of his imagery, its concrete visual and tactile "identity," as well as his gift for images of pure repose, of stillness. These polar principles face each other in his poems as Apollo and Dionysos faced each other at Delphi, and as (in a curiously complex illustration of the Freudian axiom that, in the unconscious, opposites stand for each other) the Apolline Titans and the Dionysian Olympians face each other in his last epic. He drew on the fevered Dionysian temperament for the personality of his heroes, but he had them seek, as the goal of their quest, the immortal calm and "identity" of Apollo. In the "Ode on a Grecian Urn" the two principles stand implacably opposing each other, raised to consciousness as the time-bound hero with his phthistic flush and death-awareness, and the cold beauty of the marble urn. In *Hyperion*, he again opposes them, this time under the fiction of a legendary war and the displacement of one race of gods by a more beautiful race, and with the ingenuity of the unconscious he disguises one as the other, giving them the names of their opposites. But this ruse did not allow the narrative to go forward, so he tried to fight the problem through in *The Fall*, by bringing it to the oracular shrine of the ancient earth-goddess who had prophesied at Delphi while the two *Kouroi*, Dionysos and Apollo, rivaled each other for possession of the place.

The traditional Apollo is also the Olympian sun-god as well as the god of poetry and prophecy. In the symbolization of the two sides of the psyche, the "dark" side of instinct, the unconscious, dreams, imagination, and intuition, is naturally associated with night and lunar imagery, and the side of which the ego is aware, the "light" side of consciousness and reason, is associated with the sun and day. The two psychic phases, consciousness and unconsciousness, with their diurnal and nocturnal emblems, also are associated with male and female imagery. In Keats's poem, Apollo hasn't got hold of the sun yet, as his command of the sun has to wait on his rebirth, and the poem stops at that point. It is the point where this Dionysian character, who goes into frantic ecstasies of bliss and pain, weeping and rapture, and who has the effeminate nature of Dionysos is still tied to the mother: Mnemosyne is giving birth to him. This is to say, schematically, that the Apollo of the poem is still in the unconscious night-phase of the psyche, and wants to free himself from the unconscious and get command of the sun, as an ego in conscious control, as an "identity."

There was very little legendary matter connected with Hyperion, and Keats seems to have transferred to him the legendary conceptions about Helios, son of Hyperion. We see Hyperion in great trouble, at the moment before his "fall," when he is menaced by mysterious terrors. The splendid and masterly description of the sun, when Hyperion wants to drive it out during the middle of the night and it refuses to move, affords a strange correspondence with Apollo's trouble. As Apollo's need is to get command of the sun, so even Hyperion himself is frustrated in trying to drive the sun by his own separate and individual will when it is still night, frustrated by a principle older than himself, the cosmic order which ordained the hours of night and day, the hours and functions of the unconscious darkness and of the conscious will in its ego-separation.

> The planet orb of fire, whereon he rode
> Each day from east to west the heavens through,
> Spun round in sable curtaining of clouds;
> Not therefore veiled quite, blindfold, and hid,
> But ever and anon the glancing spheres,
> Circles, and arcs, and broad-belting colure,
> Glow'd through, and wrought upon the muffling dark
> Sweet-shaped lightnings from the nadir deep
> Up to the zenith, . . .
> . . . .
>   Two wings this orb
> Possess'd for glory, two fair argent wings,
> Ever exalted at the God's approach:
> And now, from forth the gloom their plumes immense
> Rose, one by one, till all outspreaded were;
> While still the dazzling globe maintain'd eclipse,
> Awaiting for Hyperion's command.
> Fain would he have commanded, fain took throne
> And bid the day begin, . . .
> He might not:—No, though a primeval God:
> The sacred seasons might not be disturb'd.
> Therefore the operations of the dawn
> Stay'd in their birth, even as here 'tis told.
> Those silver wings expanded sisterly,
> Eager to sail their orb; the porches wide
> Open'd upon the dusk demesnes of night;
> And the bright Titan, phrenzied with new woes,
> Unus'd to bend, by hard compulsion bent
> His spirit to the sorrow of the time; . . .
>   (*Hyperion* I.269-301)

The masculine quality of the imagery in this passage is as striking as the feminine quality of the imagery used to describe Apollo. From the point of view of this sun-symbolism, we may schematize the unconscious *quest* in the poem as a quest of the masculine impulse toward full conscious command, as the "strong giant" who can "seize the events of the wide world," despite the psychic gravity which binds consciousness to the ancient darkness. Even the sun was born out of that darkness, and can move only in its assigned hours and places— although, while it is yet stabled in the night, it is "not therefore veiled quite, blindfold, and hid," but "sweet-shaped light-nings" glance from its intertwining arcs, like "hieroglyphics" of a mysterious wisdom glowing in the "nadir deep."

The massive sculptural quality of the Titans of *Hyperion* is, in terms of imagery alone, the most striking aesthetic effect that the poem contrives. This effect has often been commented upon. I shall refer here only to Larrabee's discussion of the sculptural quality of the figures. "The pose of Thea," he says, "was sculptural: one hand on her heart and the other on Saturn's bended neck. She spoke sadly and then assumed an-other similar posture, kneeling to spread her hair as a mat for the feet of the god":[8]

> She touch'd her fair large forehead to the ground,
> Just where her falling hair might be outspread,
> A soft and silken mat for Saturn's feet.
> One moon, with alternation slow, had shed
> Her silver seasons four upon the night,
> And still these two were postured motionless,
> Like natural sculpture in cathedral cavern;
> The frozen God still couchant on the earth,
> And the sad Goddess weeping at his feet: . . .
> (*Hyperion* I.80-88)

In rewriting this section in *The Fall*, Keats leaves out the first passage quoted here, describing Thea as a "tall Amazon" with a face like that of a "Memphian sphinx" and so on, perhaps because he has just finished describing a great matriarch of the "ancient world," Moneta; but he picks up a verbal echo from the earlier lines about Thea, the word "stature," and converts it into "statuary":

> I mark'd the goddess in fair statuary
> Surpassing wan Moneta by the head, . . .
> > *(Fall* I.336-37)

The rewritten passage is this:

> She press'd her fair large forehead to the earth,
> Just where her fallen hair might spread in curls,
> A soft and silken mat for Saturn's feet.
> Long, long, these two were postured motionless,
> Like sculpture builded up upon the grave
> Of their own power. A long awful time
> I look'd upon them; still they were the same;
> The frozen God still bending to the earth,
> And the sad Goddess weeping at his feet;
> Moneta silent. Without stay or prop
> But my own weak mortality, I bore
> The load of this eternal quietude,
> The unchanging gloom, and the three fixed shapes
> Ponderous upon my senses a whole moon.
> > *(Fall* I.379-92)

The changes have not only emphasized the sculptural quality of the figures, but also their silent massiveness. The slight change from "Like natural sculpture in cathedral cavern" to "Like sculpture builded up upon the grave Of their own power" reflects the consistently darker emotional quality of *The Fall*: death is a more integral part of the subject matter of *The Fall* than it is of *Hyperion* (Saturn's cry—"there is no death in all the universe, No smell of Death,—there shall be death—" occurs only in the later, not in the earlier version). The device, in *The Fall*, of having the vision seen first-hand by the Dreamer makes possible the emotional intensification of the oppressiveness of the scene, for the Dreamer can tell how he felt bearing the "load of this eternal quietude" with its "three fixed shapes" upon his senses for a whole moon.

"Abstraction," along with "stillness" and "repose," is one

of the chief terms on which aestheticians rang the changes in describing the statues of the lofty style. In the context of this criticism, "abstract" or "abstraction" meant something practically equivalent to the "repose" and "loftiness" of these sculptures, their perfect spatial symmetry, their semblance of immortality and serene power transcending the passions of men. When Keats was working on *Hyperion*, he constantly referred to it as an "abstract poem," and its images as "abstract." The Titan imagery which constitutes the bulk of the poem is extraordinarily *concrete*, but "abstract" was the popular critical term for sculptural imagery of this order—the lofty style. He was working on *Hyperion* during his vigil at Tom's bedside, when he wrote Dilke,

> His identity presses upon me so all day that . . . I am obliged to write, and plunge into abstract images to ease myself of his countenance his voice and feebleness—so that I live now in a continual fever—it must be poisonous to life although I feel well. Imagine 'the hateful siege of contraries'—if I think of fame of poetry it seems a crime to me, and yet I must do so or suffer. . . . (*Rollins* I.369)

The "hateful siege of contraries" here is the opposition between the great Titan imagery—all the beauty and power that the giant "Poesy" stands for, the pure gifts of imagination—and the suffering and death that he sees in Tom's face—the "miseries of the world" that also got into the poem, along with the "fever" of the poet-hero. In a letter to Reynolds, written at the same time, he speaks again of the "feverous relief of Poetry" with its "abstractions"—namely the "abstractions" of *Hyperion*:

> This morning Poetry has conquered—I have relapsed into those abstractions which are my only life—I feel escaped from a new strange and threatening sorrow.—And I am thankful for it—There is an awful warmth about my heart like a load of Immortality. (*Rollins* I.370)

The "new strange and threatening sorrow" also got into the poem, for it is this that the Titans are overwhelmed by, with

their loss of immortality and first experience of mortal passion
and pain. The pressure tropes of the early part of the poem—

> O moments big as years!
> All as ye pass swell out the monstrous truth,
> And press it so upon our weary griefs
> That unbelief has not a space to breathe—
> *(Hyperion* I.64-67)

correspond with such phrases as "his identity presses upon
me so all day," and "there is an awful warmth about my heart
like a load of Immortality." Thea, when she is first described,
has her hand

> press'd upon that aching spot
> Where beats the human heart, as if just there,
> Through an immortal, she felt cruel pain.
> *(Hyperion* I.42-44)

Thea has a new and threatening load of *mortality* pressing on
her heart, while Keats speaks of a load of *immortality* creating
an "awful warmth" about his heart, but the tropes have a
similar character, and he is, after all, writing about divine
marble statues that have the same effect on him as seeing the
Elgin Marbles for the first time—

> Such dim-conceived glories of the brain
> Bring round the heart an undescribable feud.

In the context of the *Hyperion* fragments, the term "ab-
stract" or "abstraction" provides a curious and significant
illustration of the way a cultural current—in this case, the
contemporary aesthetics of sculpture—converges with the
deeper impulsions of an archetypal content; for the *Hyperion*
imagery is "abstract" also in the sense in which Keats used
that word for "beauty" ("the mighty abstract Idea I have of
Beauty in all things")—that is, they correspond with a pro-
found subjective content dynamically cathected with emotion.
Subjective contents emotionally charged are the most concrete
experiences that we have, simply because they are "felt life"
in contrast with the actually abstract character of most of our

observations of the external world, our routines of behavior, and the abstractions of reason or logic. "Consequitive reasoning," said Keats, could never reach truth because it could not be "felt on the pulses." Keats's "O for a life of Sensations rather than of thoughts!" and so many other things he said of this kind are pre-Bergsonian and pre-Proustian ways of saying, in the idiom of the early nineteenth century and of a very young man, what has since become a commonplace in our own analytical idiom. Roughly, "abstract" in the context in which Keats uses the word means "subjective," and as a subjective content with strong emotional cathexis the "abstract" corresponds in Keats with "Beauty" and the products of pure "imagination," for these products are internal to the psyche; they are *felt*, and therefore they are "true." It is in this sense that Keats could say again and again, in so many ways, that things of the imagination are "truth," as in his frequent variations on the idea of Adam's dream—"he awoke and found it truth"—for his own poetry was a development, under a growing craftsmanly technique, of subjective archetypal forms that were as "true" for waking consciousness as for the instinctive unconscious which gave them origin. It is in this sense also that one reads his famous statement about the "Negative Capability" of men of genius, who are content to catch "some fine isolated verisimilitude from the Penetralium of mystery"—that is, who trust the donations of the primary process of the psyche, instead of worrying them away with "consequitive reason." What Keats called the "abstractions" of *Hyperion* are of an equivalent order with what Blake called his "visions" and which he insisted were real as Keats insists that things of the imagination are "true"; as Keats uses the word "abstract," Blake uses the word "mental," when he speaks of "Mental forms creating," and "I will not cease from mental fight." This whole question, of the reality or truth of subjective and visionary experience, becomes the crucial question in the interview between Moneta and the Dreamer in *The Fall.*

The "concretism" of the kind of mythological thinking that is involved—which Cassirer says "demands the finite," the "definite plastic outline," "fixed determination and delimitation"—is everywhere notable in Keats's handling of the Titans and gives them that solidity and purity of image that makes them memorable. The distinction is brought out by comparison with Shelley's *Prometheus Unbound*, also a tale of the fall and redemption of man using a "giant" hero and classical mythological machinery: one cannot *see* Shelley's Prometheus or his Asia or other figures, because his imagery characteristically does not have plastic definition, and because the mode is allegory which diffuses the imagery in an intellectualistic content. Keats's means—besides the constant epithets of glyptic mass and weight, the marmoreal character and sculptural "stationing" of the figures—is linear and kinaesthetic, the movement of bodies through line-levels or angles, and images of muscular pull or strain or pulsation corresponding with felt body-dynamics. For instance, when Thea and Saturn are approaching the Titans' den in the mountains:

> Above a sombre cliff
> Their heads appear'd, and up their stature grew
> Till on the level height their steps found ease:
> Then Thea spread abroad her trembling arms
> Upon the precincts of this nest of pain,
> And sidelong fix'd her eye on Saturn's face.
>   (*Hyperion* II.86-91)

Keats uses the word "stature" in a peculiar way (again when Enceladus "lifted up his stature vast") to mean "figure" or "form" or "body." He seems to attribute to the word "stature" the implication of large size (perhaps because he was small in stature), and there is also the possibility that the word echoes with "statuary" in his mind as when he changed Thea's "stature" to "statuary." The coincidence of cosmic moving bodies with lines, to give visual definition, is not new in Keats's poetry: in *Endymion*, he improves on these lines from Thomson's *Summer*: "The horizontal sun, Broad o'er the south, hangs at his utmost noon," with "I, who still saw the horizontal sun Heave his broad shoulder o'er the edge of the world." Hyperion's cosmic movements—that is, those move-

ments that might be correlated with movements of the sun—
are given clarity of visualization by being placed on inclined
planes intersecting with horizontals. When the sun sets,

> Hyperion, leaving twilight in the rear,
> Came slope upon the threshold of the west.
> > (*Hyperion* I.203-4)

In re-writing these lines in *The Fall* and trying to take the
"Miltonism" out, Keats wrote: "Hyperion, leaving twilight
in the rear, Is sloping to the threshold of the West," spoiling
the clarity of the original image, as he frequently did in *The
Fall*, where his use of the present tense tended to be diffusive.
At the end of Book I, when Hyperion lifts his curved lids on
the stars, "And still they were the same bright, patient stars,"
his slow plunge into the night again makes a clear kinaesthetic
image linearly defined by a diagonal crossing a horizontal:

> Then with a slow incline of his broad breast,
> ....
> Forward he stoop'd over the airy shore,
> And plung'd all noiseless into the deep night.
> > (*Hyperion* I.354-57)

The cosmological places and figures in *Hyperion* have a high
degree of concrete definition and physically lucid relationship,
for the Titans are distinctly "shap'd and palpable" gods, and
the scenes of their action have, for the most part, the visual
clarity and precision of a "vision."

In all myth of this kind, the "fall" means the imperfection
of the human order, the contradictions and illusions and help-
lessness of men, the distortions of passion, the suffering and
pain of a time-bound world, and death. These are what we
see the Titans first beginning to feel, after their fall from the
tranquil, immortal state of Adamic man, when they were gods
of all the elements, as Adam was a nature-god in Eden, living
in a state of perfect harmony with creation, and as Blake's
Adamic man, Albion contained all the "Starry heavens" in
his own mighty limbs. Nevertheless, it is still as sculptures
that the Titans are represented: Moneta refers to the giant

statue of Saturn in her temple as "this old Image here Whose carved features wrinkled as he fell." The remark could be interpreted as meaning that when Saturn fell, and his features wrinkled with the immediate marks of time and mortality, his image in the temple reproduced the changes in the fallen god. It may mean this, but it also means that the image in the temple is Saturn himself—just as literally as the old god sitting "quiet as a stone" in the sunken vale is Saturn—and that he was already a "carven image" when he fell, a statue-god animated with the divine life. It is in the "lofty style" that the Titans fall. When they begin to feel the mortal anguish of their state, their suffering is represented, not in the "expressive" mode of the "graceful" or "beautiful style," like that of the rather hysterical Apollo of Book III, but with the emotional reserve and restraint that sculptural aesthetics ascribed to the statues of the "lofty" period. The most famous and widely repeated and paraphrased of Winckelmann's interpretations, where he laid down the attributes of the grand or lofty style, was that of the Laocoon group—actually a late Hellenistic piece, but thought by Winckelmann and other art critics up to the appearance of the Parthenon figures to belong to the earlier period. The agony of Keats's Hyperion takes the metaphor of a huge coiling serpent, and he suffers it like Laocoon, showing his suffering only by massive muscular resistance rather than by expressive violence. Hyperion is wound like Laocoon with the serpent of agony:

> At this, through all his bulk an agony
> Crept gradual, from the feet unto the crown,
> Like a lithe serpent vast and muscular
> Making slow way, with head and neck convuls'd
> From over-strained might.
>
> (*Hyperion* I.259-63)

Hazlitt knew that the Laocoon was a late and inferior piece, and the changing current in criticism appears in the passage of his essay *On the Fine Arts* where, still in the idiom of the Winckelmann tradition, he speaks of "the most perfect of the antiques" as being those "which affect the least action, or violence of passion," and says that he prefers these "models of internal grandeur to the violent distortions of suffering in the Laocoon."⁹ Keats has his Laocoon-serpent writhing about Hyperion, not externally, but internally, as a spiritual anguish suffered with the rigor of the true "lofty style." The same kind of handling—of an austere suffering taking a kinaesthetic metaphor—appears in the lines:

> And the bright Titan, phrenzied with new woes,
> Unus'd to bend, by hard compulsion bent
> His spirit to the sorrow of the time.
> (*Hyperion* I.299-300)

The sculptural description of Thea as a goddess of the "infant world," with a face "large as that of Memphian sphinx Pedestal'd haply in a palace court," contains the lines:

> But oh! how unlike marble was that face:
> How beautiful, if sorrow had not made
> Sorrow more beautiful than Beauty's self.
> (*Hyperion* I.34-36)

Keats, in the conception of the powerful arbiters of taste in his own time, was of the underbred "Cockney school," a livery stable keeper's son who naturally kept bad companions, was low in his manners, licentious in his morals, an apothecary's apprentice who had better stick to his pills and poultices than try to write poetry. He was "little Johnny Keats, five feet high," and as for his verse, "The driveling idiocy of this manikin!" Byron exploded. He was the complete and utter opposite of those ancient artists and poets who were given the surname "godlike," and might have their own statues placed beside those of the great heroes and the gods themselves. But little did society know who he really was or who his companions were:

> The roaring of the wind is my wife and the Stars through the window pane are my Children. . . . I feel more and more every day, as my imagination strengthens, that I do not live in this world alone but in a thousand worlds. No

sooner am I alone but then shapes of epic greatness are stationed around me, and serve my Spirit the office which is equivalent to a King's body guard. . . . Think of my Pleasure in Solitude, in comparison of my commerce with the world—there I am a child—there they do not know me, not even my most intimate acquaintance. . . . Some think me middling, others silly, others foolish. . . . I am content to be thought all this because I have in my own breast so great a resource. (*Rollins* I.403-04)

The resource in his own breast was the mythological theme of the poet's rebirth as an immortal, bringing about the redemption of the world. In the archetypal or unconscious structure of *Hyperion*, the poet-hero Apollo is destined, by a death of his former self and rebirth as his opposite, to an epiphany in celestial glory as a gigantic Apolline marble man in the grand style. In *The Fall*, the Dreamer—the mortal poet—takes up Apollo's shriek of agony and ascends the terrible stairway of rebirth, knowing what it is "to die and live again." The Dreamer is a more shadowy *persona* than Apollo, because he is the "I" of the poem, and the "I" as hero tends to be faceless. But his quest is the same as that of the "I" of Keats's very early poetry, either to die as a "fresh sacrifice" to "the great Apollo" in the god's own sanctuary, or to "find out an immortality" as the giant Poesy himself. The Dreamer, after his ordeal, is given a place in the temple, "beneath this statue's knees"—the vast marble knees of the father-god, Saturn. In terms of the primary pattern of Keats's myth, the dreaming mortal poet, like the great poets of ancient times, takes his place in his own right in the sculpture-gallery of the gods (as Dante took his proud place among the great poets and philosophers in the Elysian Fields of Limbo).

VII. The Succession of the Gods: 2

THIS TRANSFORMATION of the hero's soul requires descent to the deepest sources of being, to the most profound reservoirs of creative energy, which, in their instinctual springs, are felt to be the same obscure power from which all existence draws its form and animation. The descent is made through dream. *The Fall* is deliberately cast into the form of a dream—*The Fall of Hyperion, A Dream*—the aged convention of vision-poetry, which Keats no doubt adopted under the immediate influence of Dante's visionary *cathodos* and *anodos*, which he had been reading during the year when he was working on the epic. *The Fall* starts:

> Fanatics have their dreams, wherewith they weave
> A paradise for a sect; the savage too
> From forth the loftiest fashion of his sleep
> Guesses at Heaven: pity these have not
> Trac'd upon vellum or wild Indian leaf
> The shadows of melodious utterance.
> But bare of laurel they live, dream, and die;
> For Poesy alone can tell her dreams,
> With the fine spell of words alone can save
> Imagination from the sable charm
> And dumb enchantment. Who alive can say
> "Thou art no Poet; may'st not tell thy dreams"?
> Since every man whose soul is not a clod
> Hath visions, and would speak, if he had lov'd
> And been well nurtured in his mother tongue.
> Whether the dream now purposed to rehearse
> Be poet's or fanatic's will be known
> When this warm scribe my hand is in the grave.
> *(Fall* I.1-18)

The lines about savages having their dreams "in the loftiest fashion of their sleep," dreams which, could they find communicable symbols to give them "melodious utterance" so that they could be written down on "vellum or wild Indian leaf," would also be poetry, suggest an intuition of the fact that the "loftiest fashion" of the "dreams" of primitive people actually do take a *mythos* form that is analogical to the *mythoi* of the great poetic fictions.

It is not only *The Fall* which is a "dream": the scenes, the figures, and the action of *Hyperion* also are dream-imagery. The passage about the dreaming oaks is used as an extended simile, but it sets the scenic quality of the poem:

> As when, upon a tranced summer-night,
> Those green-rob'd senators of mighty woods,
> Tall oaks branch-charmed by the earnest stars,
> Dream, and so dream all night without a stir, . . .
>
> *(Hyperion* I.72-75)

As the oaks dream, the rocks of the Titans' den seem "ever as if just rising from a sleep":

> Crag jutting forth to crag, and rocks that seem'd
> Ever as if just rising from a sleep,
> Forehead to forehead held their monstrous horns; . . .
>
> *(Hyperion* II.10-12)

The crags are horned animal shapes, hewn with the magnificent dolor of nightmare like the prostrate giants "shrouded" and immobile in the cave. As the scene itself dreams or sleeps, so Saturn is first seen sleeping in the sunken vale, his head towering into cloudy strata of dream-forests—"Forest on forest hung about his head Like cloud on cloud"—as, in *The Fall*, his head will tower so high above his giant knees that the face is invisible—"What image this whose face I cannot see For the broad marble knees?"—for, in dreams involving psychic conflict with the father, the father-imago takes strange disguises or is faceless. In the night-shrouded den of the Titans, Ops, the queen, is

> all clouded round from sight;
> No shape distinguishable, more than when
> Thick night confounds the pine-tops with the clouds.
> *(Hyperion* II.78-80)

A rather startling association is suggested by the phrase "no shape distinguishable." Milton, whose poetry was, like Shakespeare's, second nature to Keats, uses a similar phrase when he speaks of an awful and amorphous figure at the entrance of the hell-abyss—a figure that "shape had none distinguishable." It is the figure of Death. Keats's Ops, the mother-goddess, with her "blackfolded veil," her "pale cheeks, and all her forehead wan," and "hollow eyes," is the subterranean Rhea, Cybele, Hecate, Mors, queen of death. Her amorphousness and dead pallor are attributes given to the dead in dreams— for though the dream-dead appear to be alive, they always have something oddly abnormal about their "shape," and extreme paleness is the dream-symbol of their changed state. This Ops becomes doubled in Moneta of *The Fall,* with her veils that "curtain'd her in mysteries," and her "wan face" that is blanched by eternal death:

> Then saw I a wan face,
> Not pin'd by human sorrows, but bright blanch'd
> By an immortal sickness which kills not;
> It works a constant change, which happy death
> Can put no end to; deathwards progressing
> To no death was that visage; . . .
>
> ....
> beyond these
> I must not think now, though I saw that face.
> *(Fall* I.256-63)

One wonders why the poet says he "must not think now" beyond the awesome deathly attributes he has described, "though he saw that face." The phrases imply an intensity of feeling that seems to suggest more than their fictional content: for he *had* seen that awesome face before in his "dreams"— the black-veiled Cybele dreamed by Endymion in the labyrinthine abyss, "veil'd Melancholy" of the ode, who actually has "no shape distinguishable"; Ops in the phantasmal pit where the Titans are strewn like gigantic tomb-stones; and also Mnemosyne of *Hyperion* (in *The Fall*, the Dreamer keeps calling Moneta by the name of Mnemosyne, "Shade of Memory," for the poet can't seem to keep them separated in his mind). When Mnemosyne, a vast "robed form," appears under the heavy dream-forests of *Hyperion*, Apollo says something very much like what the Dreamer says about Moneta, that he had "seen that face" before:

> "Goddess! I have beheld those eyes before,
> And their eternal calm, and all that face,
> Or I have dream'd."—"Yes," said the supreme shape,
> "Thou hast dream'd of me; . . ."
> (*Hyperion* III.59-62)

Mnemosyne's answer is the fictional equivalent of what had happened to the poet himself, in those "dreams" that became poems: the majestic robed form is an archetypal figure that Keats "dreamed" again and again and that moved through his psychic drama from beginning to end. Finally, as the scene of *Hyperion* is not only a dream-scene, but the "branch-charmed" oaks themselves "dream all night without a stir," and the cavern rocks "seem ever as if just rising from a sleep," and as the characters are "large-limb'd visions" who dream their own action as Apollo dreams Mnemosyne, so the Titan life in its divine state was a life of dream—those "days of peace and slumbrous calm" that are lost when human reality pours upon the Titans its "disanointing poison."

In *The Fall*, the succession of divine kings is beheld by the Dreamer as a dream within a dream, as Endymion's experiences were those of a dreamer dreaming of himself dreaming. This recession of dream behind dream, like the sliding open of panel behind panel in the mind, is the psyche's representation of its own mode of disclosure of its more profound impulses and forms. In a certain generalized sense, almost all Keats's poetry could be taken as an indirect discussion of the process of creative thought from the early trance poetry on.

There is Madeline's dream of an immortal love in *The Eve*; Isabella's dream; Lamia's dream which she can "send" where she wishes, even build a palace in Corinth with it, and which ends in the sparagmos of nightmare; and the dream of the knight-at-arms in "La Belle Dame," "the latest dream I ever dreamt" because it too ends in a nightmare *sparagmos* which leaves him a mere ghostly revenant. Finally there is the dream of the "Ode to a Nightingale"—"Was it a vision or a waking dream?"—and that of the "Ode to Psyche"—"Surely I dreamt today or did I see . . . ?"—and that "goddess of the infant world," Autumn, asleep on her furrow in the universal harvest, who dreams in a divine repose like that of the Titan world when the gods knew naught but "peaceful sway above man's harvesting." It is for this reason that he can so often say that the dreaming characters in his poems awoke and found their dreams to be "truth," for the poems that form themselves out of the deeper "dream"-impulses of the creative process are "true" inasmuch as they originate in universal instinctive responses to life, and also "true"—that is, objectively and concretely existent—as "Adam's dream," for, under the craftsmanly technique of one "well nurtured in his mother tongue," the poem stands self-substantial outside the poet as a work of art, quite as Eve stood self-substantial outside Adam when he woke from his generative sleep.

In speaking of the donations of the unconscious in Keats's writing—what he called "dream"—we must keep in mind the fact that, in the Romantic period, there was no reliable collective framework, religious, philosophic, or social, for the thought of a gifted poet. Keats spoke frequently of his intellectual "darkness" (he wanted to get Hazlitt as his teacher in philosophy to lighten that darkness); "I am very young and ignorant," he said, with only "seeds of light in a great darkness." But the real darkness was not so much his personal lack of intellectual training as the spiritual poverty and incoherence of his time. Young and ignorant, child of an age of revolt, Keats had the same blind, lonely, and terrible mission as the other great Romantics—to bring the esemplastic energies at the root of all feeling and conception into conscious coherence with objective experience. He tried to do so through a drama of archetypal forms moving in a traditional dramatic order of conflict and resolution, a myth inclusive of his personal conflicts and the elemental forms of nature and human life—as Wordsworth, though in terms of so different a temperament, tried to do something of the same kind, with his pantheistic identification of the "Powers" in external nature with poetic imagination, the "Powers" in the soul. Northrop Frye has characterized the Romantic theme as that of "the boundaries of consciousness"—the mind's passage between the depths of "felt" or "subjective" life and the forms of conscious observation and reason (not a new poetic experiment: Dante was concerned with it in the *Vita Nuova* and in his exchange of dream-sonnets and *canzoni* with his friends, a practice which laid a basis of poetic technique for the great visionary convention he used in his *Commedia*). Keats's poetry has been described as "a discovery of the mind made upon itself"—a sensitive phrasing for the kind of experience registered in the "Ode to a Nightingale," where the hero, in coming back from the magic grove to isolation and exile in the rationalistic wasteland, asks, "Was it a vision or a waking dream?" as well as for Endymion's alternating dreams and rude awakenings to "nothingness," and for the dream-sequences of *Lamia* and "La Belle Dame," where actuality enters as alienation, death, or exile, the *sparagmos* of nightmare. Doubt of the truth of the vision, that appears in Keats as often as his insistence on its truth, is a reflection of the overwhelming strength of the pretensions of rationalism to interpret "reality." From this arises the difficulty in Keats of the hero's "return" from his ordeal with a redeeming boon for the world, an insight gained at immense psychological danger and expense. The assumption of the nature of reality that was the "known" or the "given" in Keats's culture was so aggressively at odds with the Romantic mission that the hero often doubts his discovery of his own mind and felt identity and gives himself over to the "real" or "profane" death, the dreary desert of positivism and moralistic atheism which is all the modern hypothesis of reality affords. But it seems quite clear that Keats's ability to find traditional symbols and aesthetic communication for an archetypal psychic content was his salvation as poet—that, as Jung says of the potentialities of the "active phantasy" of the artist, his myth gave him his unity as a creative individual (that organization of the contrary states of the soul for which Blake made his life-long "mental fight"). It would seem that Keats's myth, and his craftsmanly control of it, endowed his perceptions with a dignity and universality that made him a poet of distinctly more classical caliber, despite his youth, comparative ignorance, and small output, than any of the other English Romantics.

Looked on in terms of the traditional monomythic quest-drama, *Hyperion* is plotted on a descent (a fall) into a dark region of mysterious and terrible powers, a region of suffering and death, where an *agon* is to take place in the form of a father-son combat (the *Titanomachia*), with a ritual death and rebirth of the principal character, Apollo, through the maternal offices of an ancient earth-goddess (Mnemosyne, the *Anima Mundi*, who in Orphic mythology guarded the subterranean wellspring of consciousness), whereupon the hero has a glorious epiphany in godlike power to redeem the world. This characteristic monomythic pattern is what the *Hyperion* fragment actually does present in the substantial form in which we have the poem, *whatever may have been Keats's intention for the continuation of the narrative* (we have extremely little evidence of what his intention may have been). To look upon the fragment in this way is to see it as dramatically consistent with the whole body of Keats's work, although, in this view, we have to disengage the monomythic core from the displacements of the fiction (for instance, the descent to the abyss is displaced from the hero onto his antagonists, the Titans). The ritual structure is a good deal clearer in *The Fall*, with its more detailed traditionalism and use of ritual motifs similar to those Keats had repeatedly used in his other poetry—the taking of the sacramental meal and the god-intoxicant drink, the vision-inducing sleep in a green glade of the magic forest, the waking in the temple precincts, the death-struggle, the climbing of the terrible stairway of rebirth under the ministrations of a great priestess in her "sovran shrine." It is, I think, fundamentally for this reason that *The Fall* appeals to readers of Keats as a somehow remarkable "breakthrough" into a new poetic zone, even though, in rewriting lines from the old *Hyperion*, he often fumbled them. *The Fall* is not really a new and different poetic zone—it is still the same *mythos* that Keats had been trying to write all his life—but the profound, death-driven seriousness of his effort now to discover his own meaning, through the inherited forms of the great tradition of ritual myth, is felt in the somber authority of the imagery and in the verbal timbre of the new poem.

The dark abyss of mysterious and terrible powers, where the initiation of the monomythic hero usually takes place, is, in *Hyperion*, conceived of as the earth itself, the place of mortal suffering. This earth, where the Titans have "fallen" to suffer like mortal men, is a place of ancient heavy forests— immense, misty, dark, and "cumbrous" as the primordial forests of creation—and "sunken" vales so deep and overshadowed that the "healthy breath of morn" does not reach there, nor any light of day or of the stars ("Far from the fiery noon, and eve's one star"). It is a place of vast subterranean caverns and stony pits—phantasmal hell-tombs filled with the "solid roar" of unseen primeval cataracts plunging into spaceless depths ("Pouring a constant bulk, uncertain where"), roofed by animal-shaped crags grappling with locked horns like terrible petrified totems of the night ("Crag jutting forth to crag, and rocks that seem'd Ever as if just rising from a sleep, Forehead to forehead held their monstrous horns"). There are dungeons like the metallic entrails of mines, where, in an anxiety-dream of fearful frustration and impotence of the will, a man might dream himself so rigidly imprisoned that muscles and jaw were clamped as if by rigor mortis; he could feel the convulsions of his heart beating against the vein of stone—

> pent in regions of laborious breath;
> Dungeon'd in opaque element, to keep
> Their clenched teeth still clench'd, and all their limbs
> Lock'd up like veins of metal, crampt and screw'd;
> Without a motion, save of their big hearts
> Heaving in pain, and horribly convuls'd
> With sanguine feverous boiling gurge of pulse.
> (*Hyperion* II.22-28)

On this earth where the Titans have fallen, everything is "dead" or takes a rigidified, strangled or "smother'd" form of burial and death. In the sunken vale, the leaves are dead and the stream that goes through it is deadened; Saturn sleeps like a stone, and his old right hand lies nerveless and dead. When he wakes, he cries that he is "smother'd up and buried." In "all the gloom and sorrow of the place," the rigid sculptured group made by Thea and Saturn stands frozen in stone for a whole month, while the moon goes through its four slow alterations. (Later, in *The Fall*, the Dreamer has to bear this ponderous image of death on his senses for a whole month, while he grows gaunt and ghostly. In terms of the typical anxiety-dream of "turning to stone" a deadly, icy numbness ascends his limbs, stifling, suffocating, and almost puts its "cold grasp" on his throat—but he suddenly escapes from it, as one escapes from the classical nightmare of petrifying impotence by waking up.) The other Titans are "scarce images of life"—which is to say that they are images of death—lying petrified on slaty ridges "stubborn'd with iron," each one "keeping shroud," in a blind night that is like a "chancel vault"; while Ops, the pale black-shrouded queen of death, broods shapeless over them.

The Titan of the sun, Hyperion, has not yet fallen with the others, for the ancient cosmic laws still hold, day and night yet succeed each other—but in the one long descriptive passage where we see Hyperion trying to command his planet to move, it is unable to move even though it wants to, and remains immobilized and impotent like everything else in this terrible night of the fall. In the sun-palace, once blazingly resplendent, monstrous phantoms of nightmare have taken over. Hyperion cries out:

> O monstrous forms! O effigies of pain!
> O spectres busy in a cold, cold gloom!
> O lank-eared Phantoms of black-weeded pools!
> (*Hyperion* I.228-30)

But—as with the Dreamer in *The Fall*—the strangling grasp of anxiety seizes his throat so that he cannot speak, while

> the Phantoms pale
> Bestirr'd themselves, thrice horrible and cold;
> And from the mirror'd level where he stood
> A mist arose, as from a scummy marsh.
> *(Hyperion* I.255-58)

Then another vast hell-image of torture slowly emerges out of the mist and scum, and encircles him in its coils—the ancient infernal serpent of demonic mythology:

> At this, through all his bulk an agony
> Crept gradual, from the feet unto the crown,
> Like a lithe serpent vast and muscular
> Making slow way, with head and neck convuls'd
> From over-strained might. . . .
> *(Hyperion* I.259-63)

These "horrors portion'd to a giant nerve," and the imagery of the Titans' fall as a descent into abysses of the interior of the earth, no doubt are partly indebted to the infernos of both Milton and Dante, as well as to the classical Tartarus where the Titan rebels were punished, and there are traces also of the daemonic imagery of *Macbeth* and *Measure for Measure.* At the end of Book II, when Hyperion appears at the entrance to the cavern, and a strange splendor starts to pervade "all the beetling gloomy steeps, All the sad spaces of oblivion" that have been "Mantled before in darkness and huge shade" (in terms of the sun-god's cosmic movements, this is the rising of the dawn) he looks very much like Milton's magnificent fallen angel: "Regal his shape majestic, a vast shade In midst of his own brightness"—for, after all, the Titan "rebel crew" of classical fantasy are the direct mythological predecessors of the rebel crew of angels in Christian demonology. But we are concerned not so much with the literary indebtedness of the imagery as with its psychological character, and a poet owes a good deal more to his own psychology than he owes to his literary tutors, no matter how much he may have learned from them. The strangely significant thing about Keats's inferno imagery is that his fiction in *Hyperion* makes the subterranean hell-world of the Titans not the usual mythological conception of a place for the punishment of daemons and the damnation of the ungodly—like Milton's and Dante's hells, and like the ancient Tartarus—but a conception of the earth itself as the place of ordinary, inevitable, universal human suffering. The Titans suffer infernally in nightmarish abysses, not because they are "bad"—for they obviously were "good," divinely generous, beneficent, before the Olympian usurpation—but because they have suddenly become like ordinary human beings, enduring the contradictions of fear and hope, dreams of serenity and dignity and fruitful function, and realities of bitter agony, impotence, and death—in short, the *Angst* of mortality.

The equation between the fall of these gods and the "fall of man"—meaning man's own loss of divine harmony with himself and with nature—is carried out with great deliberateness in the poem. When Thea is first seen, she is experiencing for the first time the painfulness of having a merely human heart:

> One hand she press'd upon that aching spot
> Where beats the human heart, as if just there,
> Though an immortal, she felt cruel pain.
> *(Hyperion I.42-44)*

When Hyperion tries to exert his sense of the godlike power of conscious will, and the sun will not move for him, the ancient parent, Coelus, says to him out of the regions of space, "Divine ye were created," but now the sun-god's actions are

>   even as
> I see them, on the mortal world beneath,
> In men who die.
> *(Hyperion I.333-35)*

As, in Christian mythology, the great cosmological change that came about with the Fall was that human pain and death entered the universe, so, in this poem by a poet with an essentially pre-Christian mentality, the great change in the Titan universe is that human pain and death have entered it. In the sun-palace, the "blaze, the splendour, and the symmetry" have been overwhelmed by a dark mist, and Hyperion cries that all he can see is "darkness, death and darkness." (Death, daemonically oppressive in *Hyperion*, grows even more somber in *The Fall*. Saturn cries that once there was "no death in all the universe, No smell of death"—and now, *"There shall be death."* Whereas in Mnemosyne's face Apollo was able to read "knowledge enormous," in the face of Moneta— another goddess of universal "memory," but with a name that makes Memory a *warner*—the Dreamer reads not only knowledge enormous but specifically knowledge of death, eternal pain, and death without end.) The original divine character of the Titans has been "disanointed" simply by their becoming human and destined to death; not "sin" but the *Angst* of mortality is their "sickness unto death." This aspect of the imagery of the poem—human pain, sickness, and death— corresponds with Keats's cry in the Burns sonnet: "Pain is never done!" and with "the agonies, the strife of human hearts" which the very young poet of *Sleep and Poetry* envisioned as part of his task of exploration into all the forms of life, and finally with those "miseries of the world" which emerge with such intensity of feeling in the crucial passage of *The Fall*, the poet's interview with Moneta.

Apollo is to be "reborn" as the new sun-god, and with his solar functions he will also be god of divination and prophecy, music and poetry. The "Apolline" attributes are, by definition, those of light and reason, order, law, symmetry, harmony. In other words, the "Apolline" attributes correspond psychologically with the "solar" nature of consciousness. In his true or "reborn" character, Apollo will be consciousness itself, but the holistic consciousness that is not only the light of reason but the psychic capacity for divination—that is to say, instinct and intuition—and the arts of the imagination, music, and poetry. But Apollo as we see him before his rebirth is not this holistic character. He is a gifted youth with a Dionysian temperament, torn asunder by violently opposing emotions, waiting "in fearless yet in aching ignorance" in a blind, instinctual darkness: "For me, dark, dark, And painful vile oblivion seals

my eyes." There is a threshold that must be crossed between
this darkness and the solar light. The figure at the threshold
is the ancient goddess Mnemosyne. It is from Mnemosyne
that he must obtain the consciousness that will make him the
divine Apollo.

The rebirth sequence is handled in two ways, one psycho-
logical and one physical, the two symbolizations poetically
reinforcing each other. The psychological symbolization of
the rebirth is contained in the lines where Apollo stands in
front of the silent goddess, desperately demanding that she
speak and tell him how to obtain the "solar" nature that he
intuitively knows he should have, and then suddenly becomes
aware that she is already giving it to him, through a mute
influx of a new kind of psychic being:

> Mute thou remainest—mute! yet I can read
> A wondrous lesson in thy silent face:
> Knowledge enormous makes a God of me.
> ....
>   as if some blithe wine
> Or bright elixir peerless I had drunk,
> And so become immortal.
>   (*Hyperion* III.111-20)

(In *The Fall*, the Dreamer will drink of that "bright elixir
peerless" not metaphorically but actually, when he eats of the
divine meal in the grove of the gods; and the psychological
symbolization of rebirth will be repeated, in almost the same
terms, when from Moneta's "electral" brain the Dreamer re-
ceives an influx of archetypal "memory" that gives him "power
. . . of enormous ken, To see as a god sees.")

Keats's physical symbolization of the rebirth uses certain
formal or ritual traditions. After Apollo has drunk in "knowl-
edge enormous" from Mnemosyne's face, and says that this
knowledge "makes a God of him," he still has to go through
a terrible physical ordeal that is an ordeal of death and birth
at once, before he is really the divine Apollo. Mere psycho-
logical acquisition of knowledge is not enough; there has to
be a real physical change in his whole being—the body, the

muscles, the cells themselves have to respond to the need for radical transformation; the whole person has to be changed in his habits of feeling and his habits of action. While Apollo keeps his eyes "stedfast" on Mnemosyne's face,

> wild commotions shook him, and made flush
> All the immortal fairness of his limbs;
> Most like the struggle at the gate of death;
> Or liker still to one who should take leave
> Of pale immortal death, and with a pang
> As hot as death's is chill, with fierce convulse
> Die into life: . . .
> . . . .
> During the pain Mnemosyne upheld
> Her arms as one who prophesied.
>   (*Hyperion* III.124-34)

What occurs at the end of *Hyperion* is an epiphany, a "showing forth" of the god in his divine person after he has been "born," with Mnemosyne assuming the magical, ritual posture with arms upheld "as one who prophesied." In *Hyperion*, the physical throes of actual childbirth are represented more clearly than in *The Fall*. In *The Fall*, the nightmare ordeal of the stairway represents the rebirth from death into life, whereas in *Hyperion* Apollo actually goes through the convulsions of birth, "wild commotions" shaking him like the convulsions of death.

> Or liker still to one who should take leave
> Of pale immortal death, and with a pang
> As hot as death's is chill, with fierce convulse
> Die into life: so young Apollo anguish'd; . . .
>   (*Hyperion* III.127-30)

The only attribute of Mnemosyne, besides her large stature and solemnity of countenance, that is physically visualized in the third book of *Hyperion* is her robes. Apollo says,

> How cam'st thou over the unfooted sea?
> Or hath that antique mien and robed form

> Mov'd in these vales invisible till now?
> Sure I have heard those vestments sweeping o'er
> The fallen leaves, . . .
>   Surely I have traced
> The rustle of those ample skirts about
> These grassy solitudes, . . .
>   (*Hyperion* III.50-57)

In *The Fall*, it is again the robes—the veils—of Moneta that are her most clearly visualized attributes, inspiring holy fear in the Dreamer. Her veiling robes are again and again mentioned: she is "the veiled Shadow," "the tall shade veil'd in drooping white," whose breath when she speaks moves "the thin linen folds that drooping hung" about her, again she is "the tall shade in drooping linens veil'd," and the Dreamer has "a terror of her robes,"

> And chiefly of the veils, that from her brow
> Hung pale, and curtain'd her in mysteries
> That made my heart too small to hold its blood.
>   (*Fall* I.252-54)

Seeing his terror, the robed form "with sacred hand Parted the veils."

Using new personae, the Dreamer and Moneta, in a new dramatic visualization, *The Fall* is another *anamnesis* of archetypal scenes and figures that had been recurring in Keats's poetry all his writing life. The "dream" starts in a glade of the magic forest, now more awesome, more austerely magnificent, than any of Keats's other glades, for this one belongs to the greatest and most ancient of the gods.

> Methought I stood where trees of every clime,
> Palm, myrtle, oak, and sycamore, and beech,
> With plantane, and spice blossoms, made a screen;
> In neighbourhood of fountains, by the noise
> Soft showering in mine ears, and, by the touch,
> Of scent, not far from roses. Turning round,
> I saw an arbour with a drooping roof
> Of trellis vines, and bells, and larger blooms,

Like floral-censers swinging light in air;
Before its wreathed doorway, on a mound
Of moss, was spread a feast of summer fruits,
Which, nearer seen, seem'd refuse of a meal
By angel tasted, or our Mother Eve; . . .
                    (*Fall* I.19-31)

This is a forest of no region on earth, but a "cosmic" forest,
an Eden-grove where grow all the original major species of
trees "of every clime." Fountaining invisibly nearby is fertil-
izing water. There is the arbor with its roof of trellis vines
and bells and other blooms, like the arbor in the Garden of
Adonis and the arbor created by the "working brain" in the
"Ode to Psyche," but on a grander scale, for angels or pri-
meval matriarchs like "Mother Eve" have apparently been
having their dinner here. The arbor is clearly a rustic shrine
(as the arbor the poet creates in "Psyche" is the goddess's
"temple"), and the mound of moss in front of it is a primitive
altar spread with the remnants of the vegetarian foods of the
"pure kinds" that were the most ancient food-sanctities of-
fered to earth-goddesses, to the Semnae (the Eumenides), and
to Demeter at Eleusis. The divinities to whom this sanctuary
belongs have naturally been using the mossy altar as a dining-
table, because that was what such an altar was for—to set
forth the special foods reserved as offerings to earth-goddesses
so that they might eat and renew the bounty of the earth.

   In the following lines, where the Dreamer describes the
"feast of summer fruits," one of these earth-goddesses, Pro-
serpine, is mentioned in passing:

For empty shells were scattered on the grass,
And grape stalks but half bare, and remnants more,
Sweet smelling, whose pure kinds I could not know.
Still was more plenty than the fabled horn
Thrice emptied could pour forth, at banqueting
For Proserpine return'd to her own fields,
Where the white heifers low. And appetite
More yearning than on earth I ever felt
Growing within, I ate deliciously;

And, after not long, thirsted, for thereby
Stood a cool vessel of transparent juice,
Sipp'd by the wander'd bee, the which I took,
And, pledging all the mortals of the world,
And all the dead whose names are in our lips,
Drank. That full draught is parent of my theme.

(*Fall* I.32-46)

In strictest archeological fact, the Dreamer is performing a sacrilegious act in eating of the leftovers of the divine dinner, for food-sanctities such as these were not to be shared by votaries. The sacramental or "Mystic Meal," in which votaries shared, was a totally different ritual, associated particularly with Orphism and later with the Grail ritual. But poetry is not archeology, and Keats telescopes the two rites. Why should the Dreamer eat at all before having his vision of the temple? It is a question that applies to all the feast-sequences in Keats's poetry, feasts or the taking of special foods before some profound emotional or spiritual revelation. Throughout tradition, there is a great deal of precedent for fasting, rather than eating, as a preparation of the senses for spiritual experience; but Keats always involves his heroes in food-rituals. It was the "domineering potion," the drink from the "cool vessel of transparent juice," that made the Dreamer fall unconscious on the grass and have his vision, for this was a divine drink that would naturally be very intoxicating to a mortal; but the Dreamer also ate a great deal, "ate deliciously," from a magical food supply that "Still was more plenty than the fabled horn Thrice emptied could pour forth." The most significant psychological and spiritual aspect of the whole poem, both the *Hyperion* fragment and the fragment of *The Fall*, is the aspect of transformation of personality, the transformation of Apollo, the transformation of the Dreamer. The food taken by the Dreamer at the mystic meal is a transformative food; that is to say that it is sacramental. By the food-sacrament, the votary absorbs the divine *mana* (or grace) into himself, and thus undergoes a radical change in his spiritual receptivity; the Dreamer has to be changed in this way before he can see the temple, and before he can undertake that other and terrible change experienced in climbing the stairway. By sharing the food of the divinities of the magic grove, food of the vegetarian "pure kinds" nature gives, he eats at the eternal natural source from which life is sustained and renewed. This food, though it is only leftovers, "remnants," "grape stalks," "empty shells," is nevertheless of a magical copiousness, like that of the "fabled horn thrice emptied," the cornucopia, and like that "Food of Life" supplied with miraculous renewal from the holy vessel in the ritual of the Grail.[1] It is the "inexhaustible dish," representing "the perpetual life-giving, form-building powers of the universal source";[2] and it is here associated with the primal vegetational scene, the green glade of the forest, that has occurred so often in Keats's poetry under varying aspects. It is associated also with an approach to an ancient earth-goddess, mother and food-source of all that lives, who holds "enwombed" in the "dark secret chambers of her skull" the mystery of the eternal transformation of the buried reed into food, of death into life.

Having fallen unconscious after the mystic meal, the Dreamer wakes up to find himself in a totally different place; he is no longer in the magic grove but is standing on a marble pavement in front of a huge temple. This apparent awakening from sleep is one of those dreams within dreams that occur so frequently in *Endymion*, the sliding open of another panel in the mind upon more profound depths of vision.

> I look'd around upon the carved sides
> Of an old sanctuary with roof august,
> Builded so high, it seem'd that filmed clouds
> Might spread beneath, as o'er the stars of heaven;
> So old the place was, I remembered none
> The like upon the earth; what I had seen
> Of grey cathedrals, buttress'd walls, rent towers,
> The superannuations of sunk realms,
> Or Nature's rocks toil'd hard in waves and winds,
> Seem'd but the faulture of decrepit things
> To that eternal domed monument.
>
> (*Fall* I.61-71)

The chief aspect of this introductory description of the temple is the effort to find metaphorical means of expressing the cosmic quality of the place, its immensity—it is so big that it could contain the clouds and the stars of heaven—and its infinite age—the most ancient English cathedrals and Fingal's Cave, a cathedral made by nature in the beginnings of time, would seem poor time-doomed ruins, "the faulture of decrepit things," in comparison with the "eternal domed monument."

After the Dreamer has inspected the strange vessels and linen robes and holy jewelries on the pavement at his feet, he turns to look at the temple more closely:

> Turning from these with awe, once more I rais'd
> My eyes to fathom the space every way;
> The embossed roof, the silent massy range
> Of columns north and south, ending in mist
> Of nothing, then to eastward, where black gates
> Were shut against the sunrise evermore.
> Then to the west I look'd, and saw far off
> An image, huge of feature as a cloud,
> At level of whose feet an altar slept,
> To be approach'd on either side by steps,
> And marble balustrade, and patient travail
> To count with toil the innumerable degrees.
> Towards the altar sober-pac'd I went,
> Repressing haste, as too unholy there;
> And, coming nearer, saw beside the shrine
> One minist'ring; . . .
>   (*Fall* I.81-96)

The significant features in this description are the rows of columns stretching north and south to such a distance that they end in "mist of nothing"; the black gates standing to eastward that are "shut against the sunrise evermore"; the placing of the altar and the image of Saturn, "huge of feature as a cloud," to westward; and the stairway with marble balustrade leading up to the altar by "innumerable degrees," a stairway so immense that the task of climbing it seems almost impossible to the Dreamer—"prodigious seem'd the toil."

The temple and the Dreamer's experience there may be considered in terms of an archetypal image of mythopoeic thought. Joseph Campbell says of the ancient temples and shrines of cultures "still nurtured in mythology," that the temple signifies "the miracle of perfect centeredness . . . the place of the breakthrough into abundance." Such temples "are designed, as a rule, to simulate the four directions of the world horizon, the shrine or altar at the center being symbolical of the Inexhaustible Point." The aim of the person who enters the temple compound and proceeds to the sanctuary "is to rehearse the universal pattern as a means of evoking within himself the recollection of the life-centering, life-renewing form."[3] The hero "goes inward, to be born again." "The temple interior . . . and the heavenly land beyond, above, and below the confines of the world, are one and the same." That is why the entrances to the temple are guarded by terrible apparitions: "they are preliminary embodiments of the dangerous aspect of the presence."[4] Almost all this description of the mythopoeic image-cluster of the hero's entering a temple applies to Keats's temple. The Dreamer enters the temple to be "born again," and the ordeal he goes through there is specifically focused as a "life-centering, life-renewing act." It is to find out who and what he is that he consults Moneta ("What am I then?") and she tells him in her own words that he is "dust and ashes unless immortal": he is "near cousin to the common dust," and unless he can "mount up these immortal steps," he will "rot on the pavement." The temple "simulates the four directions of the world horizon," with its north-south range of columns, its gates shut to eastward, and the giant image and the altar to westward; its cosmic immensity identifies it with "the heavenly land beyond, above, and below the confines the world"; Moneta embodies "the dangerous aspect of the presence," with her terrifying deathly pallor, her tyrannous attitude and fierce threats.

The confrontation between Moneta and the Dreamer is a repetition of the confrontation between "veil'd Melancholy in her sovran shrine" and the hero of the "Ode on Melancholy," though in the ode the confrontation is a single dramatic moment condensed into six lines. Here it is extensively dramatized in various actions and dialogue, and the lines of the ode, "His soul shall taste the sadness [anguish] of her might And be among her cloudy trophies hung," are illuminated by the anguish of the Dreamer's ordeal and what happens to him afterward. Her altar is a horned one: the Dreamer speaks of "the horned shrine," and again, "I look'd upon the altar, and its horns Whiten'd with ashes." The horned altar, wherever Keats discovered it, is of the so-called "Mycenaean" type, seen on Cretan seals showing the shrine of the "Mountain Mother," Cybele.[5] The "lofty sacrificial fire" that is burning on it, clouding the whole shrine with smoke, is fed with "faggots of cinnamon," and "heaps of other crisped spicewood," and Moneta speaks of the "gummed leaves" she is burning.

The steps leading to the altar are of particular interest, for it is by the physical ordeal of climbing the stairway that the Dreamer's spiritual ordeal of learning "what 'tis to die and live again" is represented. The stairway is a tremendous one, so vast that the Dreamer feels that it is impossible to climb; when Moneta threatens him with death if he doesn't climb it before the "gummed leaves" are burnt, he speaks of

> the tyranny
> Of that fierce threat, and the hard task proposed.
> Prodigious seem'd the toil; . . .
> *(Fall* I.119-21)

Enormous stairways leading up to altars are not a feature of any ancient temples Keats could have read about or seen representations of. Though he is notably accurate in his use of such archeological materials as were available to him (his accuracy clearly being the result of a strong bent of mind toward certain kinds of ritual imagery which fitted his own psychological needs, and which, from his earliest reading, became a natural part of his mental equipment), this stairway seems to be his own invention. But it is an invention which uses the same kind of depths/heights, descent/ascent dynamics that is a characteristic of his imagery in other poems and in those passages of his letters where he speaks about the ordeal of writing "great" poetry. For example, he says that "the high Idea I have of poetical fame makes me think I see it towering too high above me," and elsewhere compares himself to Shakespeare's cliff-hanging samphire-gatherer—"I am one who gathers samphire dreadful trade"; or in the sonnet on the Elgin Marbles, where the monuments of ancient art appear to him to be "pinnacles and steeps of god-like hardship" that tell him he "must die." Now, in *The Fall*, that "death" takes place on another "steep of godlike hardship," a giant stairway, and the prodigious toil of climbing it is still connected with the ideal of great poetry, for this is precisely the subject of Moneta's discourse with the Dreamer. The ritual action of ascending the stairs, the "words of power" uttered by Moneta before a lofty "fire altar" in a building which itself "represents the structure of the universe," are means of bringing about a comprehensible relationship—a relationship that can be grasped both intellectually and instinctively—between the Dreamer and the "mysterious characteristics and hidden potencies" of the world. One of the most mysterious characteristics of the world is that man is born to die. One of its most hidden potencies may be that he dies to be born.

Let us reread some of the passages we have been considering, so that we may see them in their sequence. We left the Dreamer standing on the pavement below the mighty stairway, looking up at the altar and "one minist'ring" beside it. Then "there arose a flame," and a magical incense pervades the air:

> When in mid-May the sickening east wind
> Shifts sudden to the south, the small warm rain
> Melts out the frozen incense from all flowers,
> And fills the air with so much pleasant health
> That even the dying man forgets his shroud;
> Even so that lofty sacrificial fire,
> Sending forth Maian incense, spread around
> Forgetfulness of every thing but bliss,
> And clouded all the altar with soft smoke; . . .
>
> (*Fall* I.97-105)

The extended comparison between the magic incense and the breath of flowers in May under "the small warm rain" is Dantesque in its structure; typically Keatsian as the image is, it is a curious instance of what is also a typically Dantesque use of closely observed nature-imagery. The word "Maian" is an adjective formed from Maia, mother of Hermes, to whom Keats had written the beautiful small "Fragment of an Ode to Maia," a poem that contains the same fresh vernal associations as the long simile here. Functionally, what the extended simile does is to associate the revival of vegetation in May with a dying man's return to health, so that he "forgets his shroud," which is the effect of the incense on the Dreamer; and this effect is immediately dramatized in the Dreamer's escape from imminent death by his ascent of the magic stairway.

He hears terrible words uttered out of the cloud of smoke:

> From whose white fragrant curtains thus I heard
> Language pronounc'd. "If thou canst not ascend
> These steps, die on that marble where thou art.
> Thy flesh, near cousin to the common dust,
> Will parch for lack of nutriment—thy bones
> Will wither in few years, and vanish so
> That not the quickest eye could find a grain
> Of what thou now art on that pavement cold.
> The sands of thy short life are spent this hour,
> And no hand in the universe can turn
> Thy hourglass, if these gummed leaves be burnt
> Ere thou canst mount up these immortal steps."
> I heard, I look'd: two senses both at once
> So fine, so subtle, felt the tyranny
> Of that fierce threat, and the hard task proposed.
> Prodigious seem'd the toil; . . .
> (*Fall* I.106-21)

And then he has the familiar classical nightmare of turning to stone, when nerves and muscles seem literally petrified in impotence before some veiled and monstrous danger, and one utters a shriek of terror inside the dream and makes an intense effort to move some part of the body in order to wake up. It is a typical anxiety dream, and the anxiety is here the fear of death:

> the leaves were yet
> Burning—when suddenly a palsied chill
> Struck from the paved level up my limbs,
> And was ascending quick to put cold grasp
> Upon those streams that pulse beside the throat:
> I shriek'd; and the sharp anguish of my shriek
> Stung my own ears—I strove hard to escape
> The numbness; strove to gain the lowest step.
> Slow, heavy, deadly was my pace: the cold
> Grew stifling, suffocating, at the heart;
> And when I clasp'd my hands I felt them not.
> One minute before death, my iced foot touch'd
> The lowest stair; . . .
> (*Fall* I.122-33)

Since there is a great goddess watching this nightmare from the top of the stairway, a figure that is at present only a terrifying "veiled Shadow," it is of interest to cite a note from Neumann's *The Great Mother* on the Medusa aspect of the "Terrible Mother." Medusa, who turns men to stone if they look on her, is one of the most primitive forms of the earth-goddess preserved by mythology. In her snake-tangled hair, she bears the serpent-companion of the most ancient chthonic deities, and she combines both the deathly associations of the underworld goddess, and the frightful tabu peculiar to female magic that is reflected also in such grim stories as that of Actaeon's being torn to death by his hounds when he looked on Artemis-of-the-Wild-Things (a Greek form of Cybele, the Mountain Mother). Neumann says: "The petrifying gaze of Medusa belongs to the province of the Terrible Great Goddess, for to be rigid is to be dead."[6] The Dreamer's nightmare of turning to stone is obviously, in its context, a death-fantasy, and in combination with the veiled and deathly pale figure of the goddess watching him, it is a scene that stands in analogy with the myths of the Medusa and the terrible Artemis.

But the Dreamer does escape this death, by making an immense effort to perform the ritual command laid upon him:

> One minute before death, my iced foot touch'd
> The lowest stair; and, as it touch'd, life seem'd
> To pour in at the toes: I mounted up,
> As once fair angels on a ladder flew
> From the green turf to heaven.
> *(Fall* I.132-36)

It is like the last-minute escape from the typical petrifying nightmare, when the body is finally able to make some movement and the mind emerges suddenly from its horrible vision of impotence. The Dreamer doesn't really have to climb the stair at all; what he has to do is make the colossal effort of will to break through the rigid iciness enough to put his foot on the lowest stair, and the magic stairway itself speeds him upward like an escalator—or like Jacob's ladder. The ascent of the stairway is like the adventure of the Symplegades, the Clashing Rocks; it is accomplished in a timeless instant or not at all. The Dreamer has escaped real or profane death (rotting on the pavement, as Moneta says) by a ritual or mystic death performed as a turning-to-stone nightmare, and his ascent to the top is a mystic rebirth involving a total metamorphosis of the material body in defiance of gravity.

At the top he approaches what Northrop Frye would call a "point of epiphany," the horned shrine and the holy power standing beside it:

> "Holy Power,"
> Cried I, approaching near the horned shrine,
> "What am I that should so be sav'd from death?
> What am I that another death come not
> To choak my utterance sacrilegious here?"
> Then said the veiled shadow—"Thou hast felt
> What 'tis to die and live again before
> Thy fated hour. That thou hadst power to do so
> Is thy own safety; thou hast dated on
> Thy doom."
>
> *(Fall* I.136-45)

Here, where the ritual of the "second-fate" or "later-doomed" is referred to directly in Moneta's words, what is substituted for the "passing through the robes" is a classical Freudian birth-fantasy—the image of the stairway ("And yet I had a terror of her robes"). The extraordinary character of Keats's use of typical dream-material is that the fantasy images correspond or correlate so precisely with historical and proto-historical ritual, and that he has such purposive control of the archetypal dream material that he is able to coordinate it with "learned" information (such as the rite of the second-fated), with intellectual intention, and with progressive dramatic movement.

The Dreamer is a *mana*-personality, a hero in the myth-ological tradition, because he has had the power to escape death and to live for a supernal vision of the world. His situation is analogous to that of Dante, who also escaped from a close brush with death to live for a supernal vision. Now the Dreamer asks Moneta to clear away the film from his mind so that he may understand why he has been saved from death and allowed this high privilege:

> "High Prophetess," said I, "purge off,
> Benign, if so it please thee, my mind's film."
> > *(Fall* I.145-46)

(The request is similar to that which Dante so often makes of Virgil, and later of Beatrice.)

The scenic situation at this point is that the Dreamer is now standing beneath the knees of a vast statue. He is "safe" there—"Thou standest safe beneath this statue's knees," Moneta tells him. As yet he does not know that the statue is Saturn, and he asks Moneta about it:

> Majestic shadow, tell me where I am:
> Whose altar this; for whom this incense curls:
> What image this, whose face I cannot see,
> For the broad marble knees; and who thou art, . . .
> > *(Fall* I.211-14)

The fact that the father-god's face is invisible is a typical dream-trait of the father-imago, in dreams whose psychological impulse is toward "atonement" with the lost father, or—to use a term preferable in this mythological context—"redemption" of the father as a primary act in the redemption of the dreamer himself and of the defective reality in which he exists. The dream either occludes the face of the father entirely, as it often occludes the facial features of dead people, leaving a blank for them—to be filled in, as it were, like a blank check—or else it substitutes someone else's face, that of a well-known gangster, or a Rembrandt head, or of one's psychoanalyst. (Nevertheless, it may be noted, the lower parts of the father-image here are immensely large—the "broad marble knees" under which the Dreamer finds himself "safe.") Later in the Dreamer's vision, Saturn's head becomes more clearly visible, with

> snowy locks
> Hung nobly, as upon the face of heaven
> A midday fleece of clouds.
> (*Fall* I.452-54)

—a classically "cosmic" description of the father god. Moneta answers the Dreamer's question about the place, the altar, and the statue by telling him that the temple is all that is left from the ancient war of the "giant Hierarchy," and that "this old Image here, Whose carved features wrinkled as he fell, Is Saturn's," while she herself, Moneta, is "left supreme, Sole priestess of his desolation." This congeries of images makes up the psychological family, the father-god, the mother-priestess (actually a goddess too, being a Titaness), and the dreaming son. The father-god is at the moment totally silent and immobilized as a statue, and partly invisible. The Dreamer, though he is "safe," is a small, helpless, and rather sick character. Moneta treats him with matriarchal tyranny, telling him the truth about himself without equivocation, that he is "a dreaming thing, A fever of thyself," and that he "venoms all his days" by mixing up joy and pain instead of keeping them distinct the way people with any identity do. Nevertheless she has treated him mercifully by admitting him to the Elysium garden and then saving him from death at the foot of the stairway—though she refers to him brutally as "such things as thou art." The Dreamer admits his unworthiness, his sickness, and the favor she has done him by "medicining" him, the sickness itself not being of an ignoble kind but the kind that dreamers and visionaries are prone to:

> "That I am favoured for unworthiness,
> By such propitious parley medicin'd
> In sickness not ignoble, I rejoice,
> Aye, and could weep for love of such award."
>   (*Fall* I.182-85)

Meanwhile Moneta goes on tending the sacred fire, feeding it with faggots of cinnamon and spicewood, as the Roman Vestals tended the ever-burning fire.

Then she cries out that "the sacrifice is done," and turns to the Dreamer to give him the supreme favor of letting him see into her brain—as Apollo into Mnemosyne's—where the pageant of an ancient history unrolls, the history of creation and of the gods of the universe, contained in the world's "memory," the Anima Mundi:

> "My power, which to me is still a curse,
> Shall be to thee a wonder; for the scenes
> Still swooning vivid through my globed brain,
> With an electral changing misery
> Thou shalt with these dull mortal eyes behold,
> Free from all pain, if wonder pain thee not."
> As near as an immortal's sphered words
> Could to a mother's soften, were these last:
> But yet I had a terror of her robes,
> And chiefly of the veils, that from her brow
> Hung pale, and curtain'd her in mysteries
> That made my heart too small to hold its blood.
> This saw that Goddess, and with sacred hand
> Parted the veils. Then saw I a wan face,
> Not pin'd by human sorrows, but bright-blanch'd

> By an immortal sickness which kills not;
> It works a constant change, which happy death
> Can put no end to; deathwards progressing
> To no death was that visage; it had pass'd
> The lily and the snow; and beyond these
> I must not think now, though I saw that face—
> But for her eyes I should have fled away.
> They held me back, with a benignant light,
> Soft mitigated by divinest lids
> Half closed, and visionless entire they seem'd
> Of all external things;—they saw me not,
> But in blank splendour beam'd like the mild moon,
> Who comforts those she sees not, who knows not
> What eyes are upward cast.
>   (*Fall* I.243-71)

The Dreamer strains his eyes to search out from Moneta's brow what is taking place behind it, and compares his effort to that of one who would grope in the depths of a mine, "to search its sullen entrails rich with ore."

> I ached to see what things the hollow brain
> Behind enwombed: what high tragedy
> In the dark secret chambers of her skull
> Was acting, that could give so dread a stress
> To her cold lips, and fill with such a light
> Her planetary eyes; . . .
>   (*Fall* I.276-81)

Flinging himself "with act adorant at her feet," he cries out, "Shade of Memory!" and begs her to let him behold "What in thy brain so ferments to and fro." The idiom through these lines is significant: Moneta's brain is conceived of as the "entrails" of an earth-cavern, as a womb ("what things the hollow brain behind enwombed"), as a death's-head ("the dark secret Chambers of her skull") with the "cold lips" of the dead and looking out through "planetary eyes," and as a place of chemical "fermentation," like a retort. The image-base of this idiom is the age-old archetypal identification of the grave with the womb, as a place where the mysterious fermentation of birth goes on—in this case transplanted inside the skull of Moneta, as her "memory."

The archetypal figure embodied in Moneta had been haunting Keats's poetry from *Endymion* on, but this is by far the longest and most detailed presentation of the figure, and, as a dramatic character, she completely dominates *The Fall*, as the Moon dominates *Endymion* but under disguises and "splittings." Moneta's deathly paleness is given extraordinary emphasis in the description, in such a way as to make her a remarkable example of the "white goddess" whose appearances in legend and poetry Robert Graves has so variously illustrated in his book by that title. On paleness as an attribute of persons seen in dreams, Theodore Reik says: "The feature of paleness . . . appears frequently in dreams to signify that a figure is dead; persons who are deathly pale . . . represent dead persons or death itself."[7] Moneta's eyes are "planetary," and they seem to the Dreamer "visionless entire . . . of all external things"; looking out from her "hollow brain" and "the dark secret chambers of her skull"—with its "cold lips"— they have the character of the eye-craters in a death's-head. The terrible white veils worn by Moneta are another of her "spiritualizing" characteristics, and they are associated with her deathly pallor in giving her that form of the "white goddess" which is Death. They also enter into context with the ritual of the second-fated who had to "pass through the robes": the goddess "with sacred hand Parted the veils." Her "globed brain," her "sphered words," her "planetary eyes" are all "cosmic" characteristics that associate her with the Moon in *Endymion*, who was psychologically blocked from appearing there in the fullness of her triple divinity because it was her erotic phase (constantly confused, to Endymion's distress, by her virginal phase) that predominated in the narrative of that poem.

The Dreamer addresses Moneta as "Shade of Memory!" and later she is twice called "Mnemosyne" ("Then came the griev'd voice of Mnemosyne . . .") and, in the second canto,

> Mnemosyne
> Was sitting on a square edg'd polish'd stone,
> That in its lucid depth reflected pure
> Her priestess-garments.
>   (*Fall* II. 50-53)

The Fall contains certain repetitions, obscurities, and confu-
sions in the writing that probably would have been eased out
if Keats had been able to work on it longer, but nevertheless—
even as a confusion in the first draft—the identification of
Moneta with Mnemosyne is distinct and significant. We have
no means of knowing whether, had Keats been able to con-
tinue with the rewriting of *Hyperion*, in its new framework
of *The Fall*, he would have had Moneta herself taking Mne-
mosyne's place in giving rebirth to Apollo—an adjustment
suggested by his suddenly beginning to call Moneta Mne-
mosyne—or would have found some other means of clarifying
the narrative relationship between these two goddess-figures
who are obviously only one figure: one figure, that is, with a
certain significant shifting in the balance of attributes, for
Mnemosyne appears more as a forest-goddess or "earth-god-
dess," maternal and all-knowing but without the tyrannous
traits of the "terrible mother" Moneta shows, and without
the death-symbolism so marked in Moneta. Lemprière speaks
only of the name "Moneta" as the "surname of Juno among
the Romans." Keats makes functional use of the implications
of the name—the "Warner" or "Advisor" (Moneta was Juno
in her oracular capacity)—in the chief scene of *The Fall*, where
she warns and advises the Dreamer about his feverishly con-
fused personality, in fierce and brutal terms. Being able to
impart her own divine all-knowledge to the Dreamer, by let-
ting him see within her brain ("whereon there grew A power
within me of enormous ken, To see as a god sees"), as Mne-
mosyne did to Apollo, she has, like Mnemosyne, the character
of Sophia or Wisdom; and as she not only advises the Dreamer
on what makes a "great" poet, but is also the source of the
poem in the most concrete sense—for it is from her that he
gets the dream or vision that makes up the poem—she is the

Muse, as the Moon was the Muse of *Endymion*, and as Mne-
mosyne is "mother of the Muses."

After Moneta's "fierce threats," her words soften to a
"mother's,"—

> As near as an immortal's sphered words
> Could to a mother's soften,
>   *(Fall* I. 249-50)

even while the Dreamer still has "a terror of her robes." There-
after—after the goddess "with sacred hand Parted the veils"—
she is what can only be described as the *Mater dolorosa*, the
"sorrowing mother" who wept at the death of Thammuz and
of Adonis, accompanied by the ageless lamentations of sor-
rowing women who followed her processions. Her great eyes
have a "benignant light" like that of the moon:

> But for her eyes I should have fled away.
> They held me back with a benignant light, . . .
>   they saw me not,
> But in blank splendour beam'd like the mild moon,
> Who comforts those she sees not, who knows not
> What eyes are upward cast. . .
>   *(Fall* I. 264-71)

and it is with "griev'd voice" that she speaks, in words that
have the timbre of an ancient tragedy. The Dreamer wonders
what can "touch her voice With such a sorrow." In the nar-
rative sequence of the poem, the ancient tragedy over which
Moneta broods is the deposition of the Titans. This is what
Dante, with his four-fold interpretive system, would have called
the allegorical (i.e., historical) subject of the poem. At the
moral level of the same system of interpretation, the tragedy
held in Moneta's memory is the fall of creatures with godlike
attributes to the human state—in analogy with the fall of man,
so "like an angel," and yet a "quintessence of dust." But at
the level of anagogy, the ancient and endless tragedy mourned
by this Mater dolorosa is human suffering and death—the
miseries of man, forever "deathwards progressing."

It is true that the Dreamer is struggling for some kind of

primary knowledge of himself, both as a poet and as a human being who is representative of other human beings inasmuch as he has to face death—the poet, because he is a maker of cognitive and comprehensible forms, having a particularly urgent need for grasping primary reality in terms of form. This struggle for understanding, through Moneta's help, may be considered as a struggle for consciousness, although, since the word is subject to the loosest of usage, it might better be expressed as a struggle for some kind of radical transformation of all his perceptive faculties, conscious and unconscious. However, this struggle is a dramatic situation taking place between two characters, the Dreamer and Moneta, and it does not make one of the characters, Moneta, herself a symbol of "consciousness." She is only what she is dramatically, in the specific context of the poem, as the mother-goddess image was for ancient cultures only what it was in specific contexts of magical drama and religious drama—not a symbol in an allegory but a presence as concrete as the earth that gives food, the female who is impregnated (whether by wind or water or man) and brings forth life, and the death that all men owe, but that they see conquered when the corn of wheat buried in her is transformed into abundant life.

We shall return now to the controversial passage where Moneta and the Dreamer discuss what he is, how he differs from non-dreamers, and why he has been saved on the stairway. The passage has become, for Keats's critics, the key-passage for the interpretation of the poem, because it evidently attempts to put the Dreamer's quest into a conceptual form— the form of *dianoia* or "thought." But *dianoia*, excerpted away from the structural *mythos*, cannot stand for the *mythos* as the import of a poem, as we have seen in the discussion of the "Ode on a Grecian Urn," where the conceptualizing lines, "Beauty is truth, truth beauty, That is all ye know on earth, and all ye need to know," are an example of *dianoia* that fails to integrate with the poem's *mythos*. The first-draft tentativeness of the writing in the present passage is indicated by the repetition of the extended image in lines 194-198, later on in lines 216-220:

> The tall shade veil'd in drooping white
> Then spake, so much more earnest, that the breath
> Mov'd the thin linen folds that drooping hung
> About a golden censer from the hand
> Pendent—

which is repeated eighteen lines later as,

> Then the tall shade in drooping linens veil'd
> Spake out, so much more earnest, that her breath
> Stirr'd the thin folds of gauze that drooping hung
> About a golden censer from her hand
> Pendent; . . .

The Dreamer has just mounted the terrible stairway, and has asked Moneta, "What am I that should so be saved from death?" to which she has replied,

> "Thou has felt
> What 'tis to die and live again before
> Thy fated hour. That thou hadst power to do so
> Is thy own safety; thou hast dated on
> Thy doom."
>
> *(Fall I.141-45)*

He then asks her to "purge off his mind's film" and tell him what his situation is:

> "None can usurp this height," return'd that shade,
> "But those to whom the miseries of the world
> Are misery, and will not let them rest.
> All else who find a haven in the world,
> Where they may thoughtless sleep away their days,
> If by a chance into this fane they come,
> Rot on the pavement where thou rotted'st half."
>
> *(Fall I.147-53)*

Since the Dreamer has managed to "usurp this height," he is evidently one of those to whom the miseries of the world are real ("are miseries") and who therefore cannot "rest" in apathy ("thoughtless sleep away their days") or "find a haven in the world" while those miseries exist. The Dreamer wonders why others are not here with him:

> "Are there not thousands in the world," said I,
> Encourag'd by the sooth voice of the shade,
> "Who love their fellows even to the death;
> Who feel the giant agony of the world;
> And more, like slaves to poor humanity,
> Labour for mortal good? I sure should see
> Other men here: but I am here alone."
>
> (*Fall* I.154-60)

In terms of scene, the Dreamer standing alone before Moneta's "horned shrine" is in the same dramatic position as the hero of the "Ode on Melancholy" standing alone before the other veiled goddess in her sovran shrine, "seen of none save him" who can perform the strenuous food-ritual as the Dreamer has performed the strenuous stairway-ritual. Moneta tells him why he is here alone. It is precisely because he is a visionary, a "dreamer weak." Her distinction between the Dreamer and other men is approximately the same distinction Keats had made a year earlier in his letter about the Poetical Character, a character that has no identity as other people have; but in that letter the distinction was made as a matter of professional definition, without affect, and without assigning superior or inferior value; whereas in the poem there is evident anxiety, for Moneta's words are plainly accusatory, and superior value is assigned to the "other" people, in relation to whom the Dreamer is weak and unworthy:

> "They whom thou spak'st of are no vision'ries,"
> Rejoin'd that voice—"They are no dreamers weak,
> They seek no wonder but the human face;
> No music but a happy-noted voice—
> They come not here, they have no thought to come—
> And thou art here, for thou art less than they.
> What benefit canst thou do, or all thy tribe,
> To the great world? Thou art a dreaming thing;
> A fever of thy self—think of the earth;

What bliss even in hope is there for thee?
What haven? every creature hath its home;
Every sole man hath days of joy and pain,
Whether his labours be sublime or low—
The pain alone; the joy alone; distinct:
Only the dreamer venoms all his days,
Bearing more woe than all his sins deserve.
Therefore, that happiness be somewhat shar'd,
Such things as thou art are admitted oft
Into like gardens thou didst pass erewhile,
And suffer'd in these temples; for that cause
Thou standest safe beneath this statue's knees."
                              (*Fall* I.161-81)

The related distinction made in Keats's letter on the poetical
character is this:

> A Poet is the most unpoetical of any thing in existence;
> because he has no Identity—he is continually in for—and
> filling some other Body—The Sun, the Moon, the Sea and
> Men and Women who are creatures of impulse are po-
> etical and have about them an unchangeable attribute—
> the poet has none; no identity. . . .   (*Rollins* I.387)

Men and women who are creatures of impulse have an un-
changeable attribute, i.e., identity, because they are moved by
simple, undivided feeling straight to unequivocal action, as
the sun, moon, and sea move unequivocally in their functions.
But the Dreamer and all his "tribe" experience feeling ("joy
and pain") as a complex. Nevertheless, though the Dreamer
is temperamentally impotent to do any "benefit to the world,"
it is this "unworthiness" in him which allows him the gift or
power to enter the Eden grove and the temple—that is, to
dream, to explore unconscious contents of the psyche through
such manifested images as those of the grove, the temple,
Moneta herself, and the statue of the father-god beneath whose
knees he "stands safe." The other people, who have identity
and are not subject to the siege of contraries, "have no thought
to come," since they do not "dream"—which amounts to the

truism that non-dreamers are non-dreamers. If we refer these lines back to the exordium of *The Fall*, where the writer says that fanatics and savages "have their dreams," but that "Poesy alone can tell her dreams" because poets, unlike savages, have been nurtured in a literate tradition, and further, that it will only be known after the writer's death ("When this warm scribe, my hand, is in the grave") whether "the dream now purpos'd to rehearse Be poet's or fanatic's"—we are faced with the proposition that *The Fall of Hyperion: A Dream*, including what Moneta says about inferiority and the unworthiness of dreamers, if it is not the work of a fanatic, is the work of a poet. But Moneta goes immediately on to say that dreamers are *not* poets, that they are the sheer opposite of poets.

First the Dreamer thanks her for letting him have this dream:

> "That I am favour'd for unworthiness,
> By such propitious parley medicin'd
> In sickness not ignoble, I rejoice,
> Aye, and could weep for love of such award."
>
> (*Fall* I.182-85)

And then begin the lines that Woodhouse said "Keats seems to have intended to erase":

> So answer'd I, continuing, "If it please,
> Majestic shadow, tell me: sure not all
> Those melodies sung into the world's ear
> Are useless: sure a poet is a sage;
> A humanist, physician to all men.
> That I am none I feel, as vultures feel
> They are no birds when eagles are abroad.
> What am I then? thou spakest of my tribe:
> What tribe?"
>
> (*Fall* I.186-94)

Moneta answers:

> "Art thou not of the dreamer tribe?
> The poet and the dreamer are distinct,

244

> Diverse, sheer opposite, antipodes.
> The one pours out a balm upon the world,
> The other vexes it."
>   (*Fall* I.192-202)

We shall not assist at the fruitless argument as to the significance of the passage in isolation from the *mythos* in which it exists. Since the *mythos* of *The Fall* is the same plot we have been observing in its various phases or dramatic moments throughout Keats's previous poetry, we cannot agree with those critics, who, in one way or another, find in *The Fall* a completely new poetic sensibility. The controlling motif of *The Fall* is, indeed, transformation—transformation by rebirth into a new kind of being—but this has been the controlling motif of Keats's poetry from the beginning. The whole action of *The Fall* is a transformative action: the ancient divine agencies, the Titans, are transformed into mortals; Apollo, the protagonist of a new divine order, must, to become a god, undergo a reverse transformation; the Dreamer's visionary capacity is transformed, first by the food he eats in the Eden grove, and again, more profoundly, by his rebirth from death in the crisis of the stairway. The discourse which then takes place between Moneta and the Dreamer concerns the reason for this transformation and a question which arises naturally in metamorphic circumstances—the question as to *what he is*. The reason given by Moneta for the Dreamer's change of being is precisely the fact that he is a Dreamer: he is able to imagine ("dream") himself other than his own imperfect reality, in a dream that uses the dramatic transformation symbols of the grove, the temple, the stairway, and the vision of his anti-self or ideal self, the Apolline sun-god. The question of the Dreamer's identity ("What am I then?") is implicit in this set of dramatic circumstances, and is consistent with the heroic quest throughout Keats's poetry. Endymion asks the same question—"What is this self? Whence came it?"—and as Endymion commits himself to the quest for an immortal identity, so Apollo and the Dreamer make the same plunge into mystery to find out who they are—dust or ashes unless immortal.

In Keats's *Fall*, the Dreamer seeks transformation of the divided self into the unified self—of the "dreamer" into the "poet"—as, long before in *Sleep and Poetry*, the poet had sought transformation from blind and fumbling apprenticeship into the giant Poesy who would "seize the events of the wide world" and thus "find out an immortality." *Endymion* similarly sought transformation of his "triple soul," anguished by self-division, into that immortal identity in which he would learn the language of the universe from a goddess-muse. As with the other poems, the *dianoia* or meaning of *The Fall* can only be referred back to its dramatic action, the quest for transformation into a new state of being, one in which the Dreamer would know unequivocally who and what he was.

Whereas at the psychological level the transformation motif refers to transformation of personality, as it does in *The Fall*, at the mythical level it refers to "god-renewal," as it does in *Hyperion*. *The Fall* provides the psychological dimension of meaning for the death and rebirth ritual that is dramatized in the mythical dimension in *Hyperion*. The correspondence between what happens to the god Apollo and what happens to the mortal Dreamer is emphasized by the access of godlike power in the Dreamer's mind, a power of "enormous ken, To see as a god sees." This achievement is won at the cost of that dread initiation into the dark, the chaotic, the inhuman side of life which, at the mythological level, is death and, at the psychological level, is the unconscious. The Dreamer's "death" is dramatized at the foot of the stairway, but it is the other, the psychological, aspect of the dark and uncontrollable side of life which forms the subject of his discussion with Moneta afterwards. In opposing the "dreamer" to the "poet," Moneta focusses Keats's apprehension of the unconscious sources of his poetry and his anxiety for emergence into conscious control of his mental life. We have seen again and again that "poetry" represents for Keats not merely literary expression as such but a complete cognitive relationship to life in all its primary forms—to the elements of earth, air, fire, and water, to the planets and the stars, to the vegetation of the earth, to the phases of the mind in sleep and waking, to love, to death, and to the "agonies of human hearts." "Poetry," "identity," "immortality," are the terms he uses for this state of cognition, varying under different dramatic determinations. The *Hyperion*-myth of the sungod's rebirth as an Apolline and conscious god, the hero-poet, is the mythical elaboration of the poet's own desire for cognitive grasp of his human condition, poised between life and death, sleep and waking. As the sun moves on its arc within the larger curve of universal space, so the conscious mind moves within the larger and containing psychic space of the unconscious. It is to this matrix or "mother" or consciousness that the Dreamer turns with his question, "What am I?" for though she herself is unknowable, she contains all psychic potency.

"When the hero-quest has been accomplished, through penetration to the source," says Joseph Campbell,

> the adventurer still must return with his life-transmuting trophy. The full round, the norm of the monomyth, requires that the hero shall now begin the labor of bringing the runes of wisdom, the Golden Fleece, or his sleeping princess, back into the kingdom of humanity, where the boon may redound to the renewing of the community, the nation, the planet, or the ten thousand worlds.[8]

Appendix. *"Ode to a Nightingale"*

THE "Ode to a Nightingale" has the ancient form of redemptive mythos, a "night journey" undertaken blindly, with the guidance only of an instinctive creature of the forest, to find a source of life-giving power in a maimed and diseased world. Because the poem speaks in the voice of an "I," it has usually been read as an intensely personal description of mood, but this is to ignore the universal or collective nature of its controlling symbols—the forest, the mantic bird, the "night journey" itself; from these, the "I" acquires a collective role,* and we shall speak of him here impersonally as the hero. The action moves with exquisite simplicity and regularity in the ternary rhythm natural to this kind of mythos: a gradually defined Purpose, a Passion suffered at the heart of the night forest, and a Perception or anagnorisis brought about by the song of the "immortal bird." Because the poem is realistic in its assumptions and perfectly naturalistic in its method, it ends with an ironic movement of return to the depleted and alienated world of the "sole self."

That world is a barely human collection of stunned and crippled objects, twitching limbs, phthisic lungs, pale eyes without luster of hope or desire or memory, a world that can neither breathe nor breed and that has no insight beyond its own despair. We should consider this strange place rather closely, for from its condition arises the motivating purpose of the hero's venture into psychic darkness. In the third stanza he stops for a moment on the edge of the forest to look back on the sick city from whence he came:

The weariness, the fever, and the fret
  Here, where men sit and hear each other groan;

* Just as, in the "Ode to Psyche," the "I" deliberately assumes the collective role of priest, chorus, and all the other instrumentalities of the goddess's ritual.

Where palsy shakes a few, sad, last gray hairs,
    Where youth grows pale, and spectre-thin, and dies;
      Where but to think is to be full of sorrow
        And leaden-eyed despairs,
    Where Beauty cannot keep her lustrous eyes,
      Or new Love pine at them beyond to-morrow.

In terms of factual health statistics, the description is scarcely representative of a normal cross-section of the population, for here are *only* old men dying in the palsy of age and young people who will never live to maturity.

It is true that Keats's was a special experience of ravaging disease in his own family, together with haunting apprehension of a similar personal doom—though long before his brother Tom's gruesome illness and death he had written to his friend Reynolds that he saw "too distinct into the core of an eternal fierce destruction" (*Rollins* I.262). This too-distinct vision may, in part, have been a result of his surgical training at Guy's Hospital, an experience in disease from which may also have arisen that other early statement that he would refuse a Petrarchal coronation because women have cancers. The Hospital was in a slum area of London where the images of the streets—dark crooked lanes overshadowed by grimy brick—repeated the hospital atmosphere of infection and despair. But the symbolism of the city ravaged by an anomalous disease is by no means peculiar to Keats. The sick city had been a major symbolic property of the later eighteenth-century poets who were his first teachers, and who contrasted the suffocating life of the streets with the magically rejuvenating harmonies of the forest, and the symbol was refashioned with more cruel aptness by nineteenth- and twentieth-century writers.

The London described by Dickens is a vast ghetto where human life is distorted into anarchic forms parodying the human, where even human speech—the minimal measure of community—has degenerated into spastic gesture and harelipped mumble. This condition Dickens saw as the effect of a disease disorganizing all reality and stemming from some hidden crime against nature that lurked at the core of modern life, secretly metastasizing. Dostoievsky's Petersburg and Kafka's anonymous middle-European city are stifling slums for the sick, the deformed, the impotent, the manic-depressive. In Camus' *La Peste* the city is literally plague-stricken and barricaded by government edict behind walls, with its infected rats and mounting corpses and night convoys to the quicklime pits.

In the ancient sick city of Thebes, the source of infection was one person's crime, and with the disclosure and banishment of the criminal public health was restored. But in Dickens's London and Dostoievsky's Petersburg, though the dramatic demands of narrative may require a single major criminal culpable before the law, implicitly the guilt is distributive, for its source is a common spiritual infection, a sick way of life. In Kafka's *The Trial*, the foul unbreathable air, the dinginess and fatuousness of the characters, the irrelevance of all action, are symptoms of a degeneracy so pervasive that it is not even regarded as abnormal: "guilt" for the condition cannot be traced, for it is inscrutably inherent in the fundamental assumptions of a culture.

Keats's ode contains oblique suggestions as to the cause of the disease wasting the world, but here also the cause is so deeply inherent in fundamental assumptions about the nature of reality that it is taken for granted; it controls the idiom of thought. In the fourth stanza, "the dull brain perplexes and retards" the hero's venture into the magic forest in quest of life; and glancingly in the preceding stanza the rational or "thinking" faculty is associated with the general condition of sickness, impotence, and despair:

> Where but to think is to be full of sorrow
> And leaden-eyed despairs, . . .

In the final stanza, skeptical rationality dismisses the whole expedition under the nightingale's guidance as a "cheat" and deception, and with the return to reason the hero is thrown back on the "sole self," alone and palely loitering in a death-stricken world. As the sick city is separated from the burgeoning springtime life of the forest, so the hero is divided within himself by a radical discontinuity between the thinking "brain" and the whole dense massive structure of feeling, intuition, and instinct. The result of this inner division is what might be called a crisis of identity, the typical crisis of nineteenth- and twentieth-century heroes.

Since the essential virtue of the intellect (Descartes' "I think, therefore I am") is involved in any questioning of the assumptions of the poem, the sick world of the ode would appear to be irredeemable from within—that is, by any action undertaken on its own premises. In this wasteland, a movement toward redemptive action can occur only through invasion by some power from "outside." The messenger or embodiment of that power is the nightingale. Unlike Coleridge's *Rime of the Ancient Mariner*, where a bird is the precursor of redemptive action, but which uses a great deal of supernatural machinery to carry out the action, Keats's poem is faithful, throughout, to the natural order of experience. The nightingale is only a familiar creature of the woods, almost domestic, whose song the hero has doubtless heard innumerable times before, but without ever feeling the peculiar drugging intoxication and the urgency of a summons that he feels now. His action, in following the bird into the forest, against the perplexing and retarding bias of the "dull brain," must—in view of the anarchic discontinuities and disintegration of the ordinary daylight world he leaves—be conceived as a powerful, instinctive impulse of the will to live. This is critically important, in reading the poem as a consistent piece of action, with an initiating purpose that evolves with dramatic logic through the organization of the parts, the "beginning, middle, and end"; for the poem has generally been read in modern criticism as an expression of "the death wish"—an interpretation which strangely ignores the fact that it is death, physical and spiritual, that characterizes the world from which the hero issues.

In myths, fairy tales, and legends of a redemptive pattern, where all life may be threatened by a deficiency—mysterious failure of the rains or rivers so that the land lies sterile, a scourge of mice sent by a witch to devour the corn every year, whole cities and villages wiped out by an enchantment that

makes them invisible—the stalemate of impotence and hope-
lessness is broken through by some abrupt apparition of an
improbable character, a unicorn of a fairy hound perhaps, a
headless knight who carries his head in his hands and delivers
a challenge to combat, or an insignificant creature like a frog
who breaks into human speech and demands a grotesque for-
feit. These apparitions act as conductors of a tremendous
psychical energy invading personality as if from the "outside,"
shifting and warping the total common reality off its base,
shattering routines, forcing the abandonment of *idées réçues*,
and plunging life into the unknown. This irruption of un-
known power is always perilous, for life-renewal invariably
demands a "death." The nightingale of the ode acts as such
a symbol of transformation.

Birds have a unique authenticity as transformative symbols
or catalysts of spiritual change. They have always been sanc-
tities, not themselves as "gods" (although Horus wore the
head of a hawk, Zeus appeared in the form of a swan, and
the Holy Ghost in that of a dove) but rather as *numina* or
bird-spirits, sharing the instinctive life of all earthly creatures,
living in trees, eating earthworms—but having an unearthly
power that other creatures lack, their wonderful power to fly.
Their cries have all the subtle, complex range of speech, con-
veying to each other an immense variety of intelligence, and
not only do they converse but they sing. Other animals make
the functional sounds they have to make, but birds seem to
sing because they want to, shaping their songs at will and
with an incomparable range of effect, inventing new ones, and
delivering themselves utterly into the music. Uncontaminated
by the anxieties and spiritual perversities that waste the human
world ("what thou among the leaves hast never known"),
they are nevertheless closely associated with human life, ar-
ticulating in their songs and flights the natural rhythms by
which human behavior is regulated—seasonal changes, the
rhythm of day and night, sleeping and waking. The periodic
nature of their migrations, and the local pattern of their habits
in mating, brooding, hatching, feeding, can be read infallibly
for predictive signs of human welfare, the bounty or failure

of crops and weather. These familiar patterns, together with their strange capacity for awareness of events—like storms and earthquakes—before they happen, have immemorially offered men a natural means of divination, as well to farmers, hunters, and sailors today as to Hesiod and Homer, Jason and Odysseus, and the prophets Calchas and Tiresias who read bird auguries before Troy and Thebes.

Still contained within the naturalistic conditions of the poem, the nightingale of Keats's ode bears all the primordial *mana* of the bird-image, and it is for this reason it is able to magnetize so powerfully the psychic latencies of the modern hero's (and the modern reader's) averted nature. But because it is a nightingale, it has its own special *mana* as well. In the old savage story, the Greek girl who was changed into a nightingale had been driven to frenzied revenge for a barbaric crime committed by her husband, and killed her own child and fed the limbs to him. Ever since, the ecstatic song of the bird has harbored that incredible pain. Because of the incantatory habits of the species in the mating season, the nightingale has always been a love emblem in story and poetry, as in the lyrical debates of the twelfth-century Courts of Love.

The first effect of the nightingale's song is to put the hero of the ode into a state of numbed shock:

> My heart aches, and a drowsy numbness pains
>   My sense, as though of hemlock I had drunk,
> Or emptied some dull opiate to the drains
>   One minute past, and Lethe-wards had sunk: . . .

This can scarcely be said to be a usual effect of hearing a nightingale sing, but it is a recognizable and familiar psychic event that often seems to occur causelessly or through an apparently insignificant cause like the bird's song here, when energy is suddenly drained away from the conscious mind and concentrated just beyond the boundary of awareness, in some turbulent activity of the unconscious that is sensed only as depression and a kind of helpless paralysis of ordinary mental functioning. As a rule, we try to distract ourselves from this unintelligible state, cursing it as an inconvenience and a bore—

although it is a way in which the deepest needs and demands of our natures, those we habitually evade, are signaled to us. The mystic understands this condition, and the tradition of mysticism has evolved disciplines for suffering through it, attentively and assentingly, recognizing it as that necessary numbing assault upon the rational mind and the ego that must be borne in order that the deeper self may speak. Artists have always respected such signals as normal mysteries of creativity. Significantly, both mystics and artists are disciplined to project such states of mind upon or into "images"—specific figurations that focus the energy of the unconscious so that the conscious personality may use it in a positive way—just as, in Keats's poem, the nightingale affords a focus for the obscure, desperate life-longing of the hero.

A major aspect of the poem's structure as well as of its subject matter is the way in which the creative process—"Poesy," which will take the hero on its "viewless wings" into the forest, in the fourth stanza—works. But this is the creative process in a more encompassing sense than what we usually mean by it when we associate it rather exclusively with the artist; it is an exploration of that darkness of the soul which is the source of all creative energy, an exploration traversing paths of instinct common to all men.

Assent is necessary, a kind of faith in the substance of things unseen and unknown. The second stanza of the ode, describing the wonderful wine, marks that movement of assent to forces other and greater than the chill, small actualities of the "sole self":

> O, for a draught of vintage! that hath been
>   Cool'd a long age in the deep-delved earth,
> Tasting of Flora and the country green,
>   Dance, and Provençal song, and sunburnt mirth!
> O for a beaker full of the warm South, . . .

"Man, being rational, must get drunk," Byron said, epigrammatizing the difficulty of post-Enlightenment man in finding again the lost connection with his own unconscious. To break through to the instinctive sources of creativity, Hart Crane used whisky and Ravel's *Bolero*, played over and over hypnotically on a phonograph record (a twentieth-century mechanization of the nightingale's song). Rimbaud used drugs, absinthe, and willed psychic dissociation in order to discover that "*Je est un autre*"—that the self has mysterious dimensions in an "other" which the ego does not recognize as its identity. Coleridge's *Kubla Khan*, an opium reverie, ends with a classic description of the artist's—or dervish's or prophet's—intoxicated state of "possession" by the unconscious:

> Weave a circle round him thrice
> And close your eyes with holy dread,
> For he on honeydew hath fed,
> And drunk the milk of Paradise.

The "draught of vintage" in the second stanza of the ode is only an imagined, a wished-for one, but the extended image—celebrating collective, instinctive life, country dance and song in the season of the new vintage, under the warm Mediterranean sun—affords a sensuous correlative of the psyche's assent to the unknown and emergent, the *autre*. In Coleridge's poem, the intoxicated poet or dervish, drunk on "honeydew" and the "milk of Paradise," is an image of man become god (he has eaten the food and drunk the drink of gods)—that is to say, of a person totally overwhelmed by the unconscious, swept out of time and common life into the frightening, vertiginous, masterless realm of spirit. Coleridge was helpless to bring from that vision any positive significance or discipline for conscious life; he was unable even to finish the poem, for the casual visit of the man from Porlock knocked it flat. Indeed, the violently daemonic character of the vision seems to have debilitated his poetic imagination from then on. Rimbaud's experiments and Hart Crane's desperate compulsions led to the same open but untraversable end—open *behind* or *below* consciousness but without access back to the controls of formal art—and the result was destructive; one abdicated to the primitive, and the other committed suicide. Keats's assent to the unconscious as the source of his poetry had always the motivation of an effort to regain, for conscious life, the creative vitalities of the source, and his extraordinary sensibility to inherited forms of myth gave him those formal structures of plot which insured control of his experience. In contrast with Coleridge's drunken dervish, whirling in a sealed, magic circle and having no end but to whirl there, the wine image of the second stanza of the ode is a popular revel, celebrating what is common to men—the fruits of the earth, the warmth of the sun, the lustiness of the body, the mirth of the mind—and the image is used as part of a psychic progression to a deeper experience of the redeeming energies latent in the common soul.

The purposive direction of the action is at this point still obscure, for all the hero wants at the moment is to get away from the deathly anxieties of the sick city, to "leave the world unseen, and with thee fade away into the forest dim"—

> Fade far away, dissolve, and quite forget
> What thou among the leaves hast never known,
> The weariness, the fever, and the fret. . . .

The purpose cannot as yet be clear, inasmuch as the action of the poem consists in a gradual mutation of consciousness, a series of discoveries of depth upon depth of the self. The first stage of that process is not a stage of "knowing" but a necessary movement into "unknowing." The purpose is taken care of, not by the hero, but by the nightingale, emissary of powers greater than himself and his guide through the lost ancient paths of racial experience.

So far the grammar of desire has taken tenses of "as if" rather than of direct action, but in the fourth stanza the lines suddenly glow with decision, and the tense changes to that of will—"for I will fly to thee"—and of exultant physical immediacy—"Already with thee!"

> Away! away! for I will fly to thee,
> Not charioted by Bacchus and his pards,
> But on the viewless wings of Poesy,
> Though the dull brain perplexes and retards:
> Already with thee! tender is the night, . . .

Psychologically this is a crucial moment, when the "I" enters as a positive actor into his own vision, for it marks the mobilization of all the forces of the personality, both conscious and unconscious. It is that dynamic, combining state of creative emergency ("emergency" in the sense that what "emerges" into awareness from the depths of self is the unforeseen, the unplanned, the unknown) that Coleridge described in his famous definition of the unifying imagination. Keats's word for this activity was "Poesy." By its nature, a poem seeks unity; it is a mode of developing unity out of disparate and estranged psychic elements. The purpose of unification or integration, generic to poetry, is specifically and at the level of plot the motivating purpose of the action in the "Ode to a Nightingale," for the hero's very life—threatened with disintegration in the sick city—depends on finding a unifying organization or identity between the estranged parts of himself. The dynamic effect of "Poesy," as it liberates those instinctual energies which the "dull brain" distrusts and tries to inhibit, is represented in the fourth stanza as a sudden physical action, taking the hero bodily into the forest, for not the "brain" only but the whole physiological being is involved in this venture of discovery. As a subjective phenomenon, taking place in the darkness of the unknown, Poesy has "viewless wings" like its objective counterpart and natural image, the invisible bird hidden among the leaves, singing a song of seductive sweetness and inexhaustible creative vitality.

Up to this moment, the images of the poem have been those of daylight—sunlight casting "shadows numberless" in the plot of beechen green where the nightingale sings, the "sunburnt mirth" of country revel, and the spectral daylight that exposes the doomed creatures of the sick city; but now suddenly, when the hero enters the forest, it is night, and he must feel his way like a blind man.

Already with thee! tender is the night,
　And haply the Queen-Moon is on her throne,
　　Cluster'd around by all her starry Fays;
　　　But here there is no light,

Save what from heaven is with the breezes blown
    Through verdurous glooms and winding mossy ways.

Darkness is stressed again in the next stanzas:

> I cannot see what flowers are at my feet,
>
> ....
>
> But, in embalmed darkness, . . .
>
> ....
>
> Darkling I listen; . . .

In a civilization overwhelmingly engrossed by abstraction, our eyes (we are told) account for ninety per cent of the stimuli to which we react; in a civilization completely rationalized, we would not need taste and smell at all, and would have but minimum mechanical use for hearing and touch. The eyes do not "feel" anything, having no physical contact with their stimuli, but busily abstract the shapes of the world into intellectual data; whereas the other senses, that have remained far more primitive in function, are specifically the conductors of feeling and thus are much more closely allied with instinct. In the ancient classical tradition, the arch-seer, the greatest poet, and the king who experienced the human condition most profoundly, were blind men. The darkening of the visual sense implies a corresponding enlargement of the primitive sensitivities of feeling, instinct, and those non-rational cognitive faculties we call insight and intuition. In the night forest of the ode, the hero has to rely on touch, the smell of the plants, and listening. The darkness also implies an encompassing and penetrating mystery, both within the human being and in outer reality, the *autre* with which the rational mind cannot deal and where the ego loses its way—the "winding mossy ways" of the forest are designed to make it lose its way, so that the self, by simple trust, may find access to greater powers than itself. And, with entrance on an unknown way, the darkness implies peril, that peril of utter obliteration of self or "loss of soul" which primitive man, and the primitive in man, most fears—a peril which the hero will encounter in the sixth stanza of the ode, the "death" stanza.

But a little moonlight, barely guessed at, enters the forest through blown leaves. These subtle glimpses of the moon and stars, shining above the night forest, reinforce the sense of an intuitively directed quest or purpose, however unconscious and unknowable until revealed of its own obscure psychic momentum. And like a touch of illuminating grace from the interior of the night and the perilous darkness, the presence of the moon relates the hero's lonely venture with the great dependable sidereal rhythms; just as the bird, with whom the hero has a consistent "I-thou" relationship almost like dialogue, connects his isolated spiritual expedition with the instinctive rhythms of animal life and the green world.

Now, in the fifth stanza, he has come to a place of abundance and power, where one can almost hear the seeds stirring, moving toward germination. It is a glade at the heart of the forest, like the Garden of Adonis in *Endymion*, where life continuously pours forth in diversity and fullness. The stanza marks the first of the graduated series of perceptions, or psychic transformations, wrought in the hero under the nightingale's guidance: the simple, primary perception of the *there-ness* of the earth, inexhaustibly fecund source of life, and of his own *there-ness* in immediate sensuous relationship with the earth. Primitive as the perception is, it is of utmost importance for the modern hero with his existential despair and his problem of "identity." Significantly, it is a perception brought about nonconceptually (he cannot see, and the dull brain no longer perplexes and retards), but only by those senses by which we first know reality. The stanza is written with exquisite naturalistic purity, being merely a naming of the plants, a simple inventory of their particularity, their *there-ness*, in the way that Adam might have counted them over by night in a forest glade very much like this one:

> I cannot see what flowers are at my feet,
>   Nor what soft incense hangs upon the boughs,
> But, in embalmed darkness, guess each sweet
>   Wherewith the seasonable month endows
> The grass, the thicket, and the fruit-tree wild;

White hawthorn, and the pastoral eglantine;
    Fast fading violets cover'd up in leaves;
        And mid-May's eldest child,
    The coming musk-rose, full of dewy wine,
        The murmurous haunt of flies on summer eves.

And yet with this simplicity, and in so small a scope, the authenticity of the detail involves the depthless organic rhythm of the temporal cycle, from germination to maturation to death: the coming musk-rose is "child" of the "seasonable month," its cup full of fertilizing winy moisture, while the violets are already dying.

The hero has moved from psychic conflict with his environment, that sick city where all phenomena meant death, and from conflict between estranged, fragmented parts of himself—his brain, his senses, and instincts—to a phase that might be called "composition of the self from below." Later, in the seventh stanza, there will be a kind of "composition from above," from the human level, but now he is at the stage where all spiritual organization has to start—that is, with the body in direct relationship to the earth. The stanza describing the plants in the glade acts as a sanctioning and legitimization of life at the most primitive level, where the primary subject-object nexus is established and where recognition is accorded to the great impersonal "otherness" that both defines and sustains the person. The fable of Antaeus, who had to touch the earth with some part of his body, in order to keep his strength, is a parable of what the hero of Keats's ode has to do in order to begin to find who and what he is. And in all its naturalism, the stanza is a reenactment, through a modern sensibility, of the timeless meaning contained in such fertility rituals as that recorded in *The Flower and the Leaf* (the anonymous fifteenth-century poem that lies in the provenience of Keats's ode), where a company of folk seeks life-renewal and insurance by a May-day rite around a sacred tree in another forest glade where a nightingale sings; or, to move back deeper into ancient parallels of the same instinctive observance, the hero repeats here, in his own way, the requirement made of the Orphic initiate, that he enter into the realm of plant-life (like the plant-god himself), so that he might emerge with a sense of race and parentage, as a "child of Earth and of Starry Heaven." These mysteries have not been lost, even though the formidably abstractive tendencies of our education and environment refuse to recognize their continuity—for we spontaneously repeat them whenever we touch the earth again with awakened senses.

The song of the nightingale has not actually been heard since the first stanza. Our inward ear has been aware of that song all along, but the hero's experience of the dark earth-life of the glade has been a silent one of scent and touch. But with the words "Darkling I listen," opening the sixth stanza, the nightingale bursts into ecstatic clamor, an overwhelming flood of sound. The sense of hearing is, of all the senses, most akin to a spiritual organ. Throughout religious tradition— from the first stirring of the Logos, the Word, on the great waters, to the songs of Orpheus, the utterances of the angel of Annunciation, the voices of St. Joan—gods and spirits have communicated with man through the ear. These voices can be heard only through a peculiar heightening of spiritual attentiveness, of inner "listening," for they come from within, since that is the only way spirit can work on spirit. Our dreams in which voices sound are rare, but they always carry an extraordinary conviction of significance, as if the powers that dream our sleeping life had suddenly recognized a crisis in which communication through the usual visual images were insufficient and had to be transcended by the more specialized human instrument of the voice. The language spoken out of the dream may be a strange one, perhaps a foreign language with fantastic alterations, for the unconscious naturally uses a "magic" language for its powerful purposes and not the devitalized one of grammarians—yet the message deeply insists that we decipher it. The song of the nightingale is one of those magic languages, and it is in a "darkling" state of profound spiritual receptivity that the hero of the ode listens. But because his own powers of perception have been changing, the song that he now hears is subtly different from what it was in the beginning. Earlier, the nightingale had been "singing of summer in full-throated ease"—singing the burgeoning Eros of the springtime forest, in a song sensed as sheer joyousness of the natural creature. But now that the hero has reached the dark interior of the glade, the nature-sound that floods out from the darkness is a song not only of life but of death. The nightingale seems to be pouring forth its soul, its whole creature-vitality, into the night—and the phrase carries an inescapable common association with death, for to pour forth the soul is a metaphor of death.* The responsive impulse that is awakened in the hero as he listens is the impulse of death, a desire to "pour forth" his own soul, effacing the restrictions of individuality and merging with the anonymous dark.

> Darkling I listen; and for many a time
>   I have been half in love with easeful Death,
> Call'd him soft names in many a mused rhyme,
>   To take into the air my quiet breath;
> Now more than ever seems it rich to die,
>   To cease upon the midnight with no pain,
>   While thou art pouring forth thy soul abroad
>   In such an ecstasy!
>   Still wouldst thou sing, and I have ears in vain—
>   To thy high requiem become a sod.

This stanza seems inevitably to awaken anxious scruples, of an ethical kind, in Keats's critics, who almost uniformly deplore the death wish and the escapist tendency shown here. The terms are pseudo-psychological clichés, with pejorative implication, that serve merely to becloud what the stanza is as a dramatic unit, and what its function is within the larger

---

* Aside from the common meaning of the image, Keats has used an image of dying as a pouring forth of the soul in music before, in *Endymion*, where it is Apollo's death that is described:
> When the great deity, for earth too ripe,
> Let his divinity o'erflowing die
> In music, through the vales of Thessaly. . . .
though it was not Apollo, but Orpheus who died this way.

purposive action of the poem. To interpret it by the labels "death wish" and "escapism" is to take it disjunctively, as a random mood appearing by some accidental association in the middle of the poem, hooked onto the next stanza in the same accidental way. The term "death wish" is particularly confusing. Standard criticism seems to assume here a serious suicidal impulse on Keats's part (with a vague Freudian penumbra, never defined). Yet most people "want to die" dozens of times in a lifetime, in accesses of either dejection or ecstasy. As for full-formed fantasies of personal death, a sensibility of any liveliness and profundity enacts such fantasies from childhood throughout maturity, but nothing either pathological or morally reprehensible is to be inferred from this, for the event of personal death carries tremendous emotional charges that insist on being realized, and to imagine it is a way the psyche has of teaching itself, by feeling out the shape and direction of its own mystery.

But the episode cannot be judged by itself, in disjunction from the preceding and succeeding action. If we read the poem as a sustained and consistent psychic drama, projected in a certain direction—to find life, which has been the hero's motive from the start—an action whose beginning, middle, and end are related not by random association but by dramatic probability, then the "death"-stanza is necessary, for life-renewal requires death. All great ritual myth and tragedy (whose purpose, too, is "to find life") have contained this moment; and if these traditional patterns mean anything to us but academic data, they must mean that the "death"-moment is a psychic reality inherent in the quest for life—as apt to occur within the slight frame of a lyric as in larger structures of symbolic action. Indeed, our own dreams and fantasies, when they arise from the deepest, most serious need of spiritual reintegration, involve this moment when the "I" succumbs to an imaged death—and not only once, but perhaps many times, over and over, for the process is never completed (as if one could "find life" once and for all, and keep it under glass). The "death"-stanza holds the same relative position in the poem as the tragic moment or Passion in ritual myth and tragedy.

Let us reconsider the circumstances of this "death." It is so different from death in the sick city, where everybody was dying, that clearly the two kinds of death have nothing in common at all; the difference is not just between "real" and imaginary (with correspondingly unpleasant and pleasant circumstances), for, as we have noted before, conditions in the sick city presume no more factual reality than do those of the hero's "death" in the forest: both are fantasies and can be judged only as symbolic of psychic events. But the psychic events are totally different in kind. The one kind of death is represented as mechanical degeneration of the body, ugly, painful, chaotic, suffered with bitter unwillingness and in full consciousness of despair. The other is a wholly voluntary withdrawal of consciousness, an obliteration of separate ego-awareness in a "darkness" that has no parts or places or boundaries, no within or without; this eclipse of the self is directly associated with the natural processes of creation, in a seed-place of the earth where plant-life flourishes, in the springtime of the year; and it is associated with the ecstasy of the nightingale's song, as both the hero and the instinctive creature of the woods "pour forth their souls." The fantasy touches deeply and distinctly on the primitive impulse for absolute unity with all life, with the pure energy of life itself.

It is a moment of great peril; for to break down differentiating limits, between the self and the rest of life, is to "die." The story of the death of Merlin expresses that peril and temptation with profound nostalgia. In a glade like that of the ode, in the forest of Broceliande, sweet with the perfume of flowering white-thorn trees, Merlin, the supreme "knower," willingly allowed the enchantress Niniane to weave her death-spell about him and bind him, forever invisible, in the plant-life of the forest. In other major stories of the Arthurian cycle, where the hero goes alone into the wilderness to confront the unknown powers of life and of death, there is recognition of the temptation *not* to return to the human order, the danger of extinction of specifically human purpose and of the hero's being swallowed up altogether in the dimensionless dark. The peril at this point of crisis is felt disturbingly in the sixth stanza of Keats's ode; but it cannot be disposed of summarily as a death wish and thus made innocuous (an assumed death wish on the part of the poet would, of course, have nothing to do with *our* normal experience); for the unconscious knows nothing about death wishes and is incapable of wishing its own extinction—although it can "wish" to overwhelm and submerge the conscious mind, which is an event of a quite different character, and a universal risk of the deepening of psychic life. It is only in that region of darkness and danger that one can find the vitalities which redeem consciousness from poverty. The fantasy in the sixth stanza of the ode is particularly disturbing because, using no fictive or allegorical apparatus which would allow us to intellectualize it and thus short-circuit its significance, it is a personal enactment that has all the simplicity and directness of raw experience.

In ritual myth and tragedy, the moment of the Passion is the turning-point or peripety of an action whose purpose is to transform a sterile situation, inimical to life, into a fertile, life-nourishing one. The rhythm is the same, whether it is the land that is threatened with sterility, as in myths of the death of the plant-god, or the community whose welfare is menaced by the commission of some crime which nature and the gods abhor, as in the tragic drama of the theater of Dionysos—or the individual whose "identity" is threatened by the estrangement of instinct, as in Keats's poem. The plant-god returns in living form with the renewal of vegetation. The sickness of the ancient city is healed and the community restored to the order of nature. In Arthurian legend, the heroes who survive the dangers and temptations of the wilderness return to the Round Table, symbol of assemblage and common enterprise. In Keats's ode, the "death"-stanza is followed by a totally new perception of the continuities of human experience.

The heroes of myth and legend almost always need to have extraordinary skill and luck, or else the protection of some interested divine being, to escape the perils that beset them. The hero of the ode is helped by two analogous agencies. One

is "Poesy," a gift of a kind of "skill" which he has received
from the unconscious, and which makes available to him the
whole instinctive redemptive pattern the action of the poem
follows, as myth and ritual made it available to ancient man.
The other is the primordial bird, messenger of the uncon-
scious, whose song first attracted him irresistibly into the night
forest, lured him almost to his death, and now, at the moment
of greatest peril, provides a new apprehension or psychic grasp
of his relationship with the rest of life.

The seventh stanza opens with an exultant intuition:

> Thou wast not born for death, immortal Bird!
>   No hungry generations tread thee down;
> The voice I hear this passing night was heard
>   In ancient days by emperor and clown:
>   Perhaps the self-same song that found a path
>   Through the sad heart of Ruth, when, sick for home,
>   She stood in tears amid the alien corn;
>   The same that oft-times hath
>   Charm'd magic casements, opening on the foam
>   Of perilous seas, in faery lands forlorn.

Keats's critics have worried considerably about the ascription
of immortality to the bird, but have generally agreed, follow-
ing Garrod, that it is the species that is meant and not the
individual. But it seems doubtful that the hero should become
emotionally moved, at this point, by the biological perpetuity
of an ornithological species; furthermore, the bird's species is
no more immortal than any other—than man's, for instance;
as many "hungry generations" tread nightingales down as
tread human beings down. Clearly, there is no simple dis-
tinction here between mortal hero and immortal bird. The
stanza goes on to say that it is the song that is self-same
throughout the ages. The movements of the poem have been
inflected by the hero's changing responses to the bird's song,
a gradually more sensitized listening; indeed, the nightingale
has existed only as its song—the creature itself has remained
invisible among the leaves, in the darkness. Earlier, the song
was spoken of as its "soul," or the vehicle of its soul ("while

thou art pouring forth thy soul abroad"). The revelation in the seventh stanza does not lie in a barren fact of perpetuity—the sheer accumulation of time, with its indiscriminate load of lives and events, during which the song of the nightingale has remained the same; for the song is a spiritual thing—in the literal sense that it is known only through its spiritual effect on the hero. The wonder of it lies in its associations with *symbolic* times and *symbolic* lives. Symbolism occurs only in human apprehension, and the song of the nightingale is something that happens inside, not outside the hero. Coleridge said of himself that he seemed always to be seeking in natural objects "a symbolic language for something within me that already and forever exists." This is what the nightingale's song provides, discovering to the hero what "already and forever exists" within himself: first, the vital energies and rhythms that are of the earth, which he shares with all other instinctive creatures; now—in a dramatic leap of perception generated by his "death" in the forest—the great formative images of his human heritage, dense of substance, borne by the collective memory out of the most ancient past into the living present of individual apprehension, creating that apprehension and forming its character. The song of the immortal bird is the ancestral dimension of his own mind. So far as a few lines of a poem can do so, the seventh stanza makes that total instantaneous resumption of racial history—Biblical, Celtic, Hellenic—in the symbolic forms by which alone it is heritable.

The image of Ruth in Boaz's field implicitly resumes the ancient agricultural life of the Biblical community, the organization of the family, marriage customs, problems of loyalty and survival, the pathos of exile, the meaning of "home." The miraculous little scene is all built of enduring Anglo-Saxon words that have to do with the trodden way, the natural abiding place, the unity of memory, the continuity of "the heart's affections"—except for the Latinic word "alien," which asserts its own alien quality in this context. Actually, Ruth's situation is a simpler, generic form of the exiled situation of the hero—or one might be said to be a harmonic of the other;

the Biblical scene is not merely a legendary moment suffered by a girl in an Asiatic cornfield three thousand years ago, but a portion of his own experience.

The other great image of the stanza—of the magic casements opening on perilous seas in faery lands—resumes the Celtic pagan world of the Arthurian legends and of lays and ballads of enchantment, of Merlin and Morgan le Faye, Niniane and the Lady of the Fountain, Tristan taking a ship without sails on that perilous sea that brought him to Ireland and the magic casements from which Iseult looked out and saw him, Owain and Gawain who went on quests like that of the hero of the ode and encountered similar danger and received a similar revelation of the bonds by which the individual is related to all life. Walter Jackson Bate, commenting on these lines in his critical biography of Keats, says that "Those impossible lands are 'forlorn' because they are not at all for man." What are they for, then? If they are not for man, why have story-tellers and poets and anthropologists and psychologists and literary scholars and critics written so much about them over hundreds of years? Professor Bate feels that the significance of this part of the poem is that Keats is sorry ("forlorn") because he cannot live in those faery lands, which is to attribute to him an attitude that a six-year-old would repudiate. Men may not live in faery lands but faery lands live in men. Merlin and Archimago, Niniane and La Belle Dame sans Merci, the Lady of the Fountain and the Lady of the Lake, magic weapons and magic potions and magic beasts, the Black Knight and the Green Knight, the nameless knight in black armor—under inexhaustibly inventive enchantments and disguises, these have existed in men's dreams for fathomless ages. They are the numinous forms that connect us to ourselves and tell us who we are and what we are doing. And they are indeed "forlorn" (AS *forlorn*, lost utterly) for we no longer understand them, but, as the hero does in the last stanza, dismiss them as deceptions of darkness or vagaries of fancy. The world which the hero of the ode left when he entered the forest, and to which he returns at the end, is one of discontinuities, the "sole self" discontinuous with everything around it and discontinuous even within itself. The immemorial bird, whose song comes from the most profound depths of human experience, has acted as the unifying symbol which brings together the "severed particle"—the hero—and "the rest."

The final stanza recognizes the terrible difficulty of keeping that sense of organic membership in the mysterious fullness of life. The rites of the ancient nature cults and mystery religions had to be reenacted constantly (as the Mass is constantly reenacted) in order to *create again* that vital continuum, which is not automatically guaranteed by existence any more than food is guaranteed. But in the modern world, the shattering of natural unity begins almost at birth and is carried on—with the formidable hubris of rational "truth"—by standard education and everything we are taught about ourselves and our environment. Any individual effort to achieve a unifying grasp of life, that is not merely doctrinaire or a complacent intellectualization, is monumental and agonizing, for we have lost all symbolic orientation. Although the great collective images, like those about which the central action of the ode is constructed, represent the healing and formative wisdom of the race, we have fallen into the delusion that we have invented those images ourselves and that they therefore can have nothing to do with objective truth. The last stanza of the poem is a realistic expression of this predicament.

> Forlorn! the very word is like a bell
> > To toll me back from thee to my sole self!
> Adieu! the fancy cannot cheat so well
> > As she is fam'd to do, deceiving elf.
> Adieu! adieu! thy plaintive anthem fades
> > Past the near meadows, over the still stream,
> > > Up the hill-side; and now 'tis buried deep
> > > > In the next valley-glades:
> > Was it a vision, or a waking dream?
> > Fled is that music:—Do I wake or sleep?

But the aloneness and deathliness of this return to the "sole self" and skeptical rationality implicitly evaluate the kind of "truth" with which the hero is left, for he has lost his substance and is as spectral as the phthisic youths of the diseased city, or as the pale knight of the ballad, loitering forlornly in a place where no birds sing.

If the poem is read "historically" or biographically, as a succession of temporal events (changes of mood) experienced by the poet (and it is consistently read this way in Keatsian criticism), one would have to say that the psychic process set in motion by the nightingale had not worked, that the purpose of the action had not been fulfilled, that this was a "night journey" that failed. From this point of view, the last stanza is a simple negation of all that has preceded it. But the poem is obviously not just an historical account of Keats's moods and attitudes; it cannot be "just" this, for the elements of which it is composed derive from collective experience and have symbolic dimensions that extend infinitely beyond the individual. That collective experience and the symbolism it has evolved are manifestly impossible to negate, for they exist, they are "there" in the human psyche like the breath in the lungs and the protein in the cells. In other words, what happened to the hero in the forest was real—or perhaps we should say is real, for it happens every time we read the poem—and not a cheat and deception of fancy as the hero (like Keats's critics) decides at the end. Whether in a vision or a waking dream, the mind has bent again over its own mysterious depths and, listening in the darkness, has had revealed to it there the greater reality to which it belongs. By such moments of grace, life is constantly renewed.

Reference Notes

CHAPTER I

1. Stanley Edgar Hyman, "The Ritual View of Myth and the Mythos," *Journal of American Folklore*, 68 (1955), p. 464.
2. F. M. Cornford, *From Religion to Philosophy* (New York: 1957), p. 124.
3. Joseph Campbell, *The Hero with a Thousand Faces* (Cleveland: 1956), pp. 30-31.

CHAPTER II

1. Apuleius, *The Golden Ass*, trans. William Adlington, 1566, quoted in Robert Graves, *The White Goddess* (New York: 1958), pp. 62-63.
2. Campbell, p. 81.
3. Northrop Frye, *The Anatomy of Criticism* (Princeton: 1957), p. 205.
4. Edmund Spenser, *The Faerie Queene*, Book III, Canto VI, Stanzas 46-71, in *The Works of Edmund Spenser*, vol. III (Baltimore: 1934).
5. John Winckelmann, *The History of Ancient Art*, II, trans. G. Henry Lodge (London: 1881), pp. 247-48.
6. Stephen A. Larrabee, *English Bards and Grecian Marbles* (New York: 1943), p. 215.
7. William Hazlitt, "On the Elgin Marbles," in *The Complete Works of William Hazlitt*, ed. P. P. Howe, XVIII (London: 1933), p. 146.
8. Ibid., p. 156.
9. Denis de Rougemont, *Love in the Western World*, trans. Montgomery Belgion (Garden City: 1956), p. 52.
10. Rougemont, p. 8.
11. Campbell, p. 122.

CHAPTER III

1. Jacques Maritain, *Creative Intuition in Art and Poetry*, Bollingen XXXV (New York: 1953), p. 229.
2. Heinrich Zimmer, *The King and the Corpse*, ed. Joseph Campbell, Bollingen XI, 1948 (New York: 1948), pp. 82-84.

CHAPTER IV

1. Campbell, *The Hero with a Thousand Faces*, p. 30.
2. Ibid., p. 173.
3. Kenneth Burke, *A Grammar of Motives* (Berkeley: 1969), p. 456.
4. Campbell, pp. 245-46.
5. Robert Graves, *The White Goddess*, p. 232.
6. Erich Neumann, *The Great Mother*, trans. Ralph Manheim Bollingen Series, XLVII (Princeton: 1972), p. 233.
7. Jessie L. Weston, *From Ritual to Romance* (Garden City: 1957), pp. 30-31.
8. Neumann, p. 203.
9. Quoted in Graves, *The White Goddess*, p. 479.
10. Ibid., p. 431.
11. Ernst Cassirer, *The Philosophy of Symbolic Forms*, trans. Ralph Manheim, II (New Haven: 1955), p. 5.
12. Denis de Rougemont, p. 134.
13. Hyder Rollins, *The Keats Circle*, II (Cambridge, Mass.: 1948), p. 293.

CHAPTER V

1. George Thomson, *Studies in Ancient Greek Society* (New York: 1961), p. 442.
2. Ibid., p. 443.

CHAPTER VI

1. Jane Ellen Harrison, *Epilegomena to the Study of Greek Religion and Themis* (New York: 1962), pp. 453-54.
2. Ibid., p. 454.
3. Ibid., p. 458.
4. Ibid., p. 246.
5. Ibid., p. 248.
6. Jane Ellen Harrison, *Prolegomena to the Study of Greek Religion* (Cambridge: 1903), p. 495.
7. Winckelmann, I, pp. 318, 325.
8. Larrabee, p. 217.
9. Hazlitt, XVIII, p. 113.

CHAPTER VII

1. Weston, pp. 158-59.
2. Joseph Campbell, *The Hero with a Thousand Faces*, p. 173.
3. Ibid., p. 43.
4. Ibid., pp. 91-92.
5. Harrison, *Prolegomena*, p. 498.
6. Neumann, p. 166.
7. Theodore Reik, "The Three Women in a Man's Life," *Art and Psychoanalysis*, ed. William Phillips (Cleveland: 1963), p. 161.
8. Campbell, *The Hero with a Thousand Faces*, p. 193.

Index

Library of Congress Cataloging in Publication Data

Van Ghent, Dorothy Bendon, 1907-
  Keats, the myth of the hero.

  Bibliography: p.
  Includes index.
  1. Keats, John, 1795-1821—Criticism and interpreta-
tion.   2. Keats, John, 1795-1821—Knowledge—Folklore,
mythology.   3. Heroes in literature.   4. Myth in
literature.   I. Robinson, Jeffrey Cane, 1943-   .
II. Title.   PR4838.H4V36   1983   821'.7   82-61391
ISBN 0-691-06569-1